D1492197

HOUSE of NIGHT

LEGACY

P. C. CAST

KRISTIN CAST

KENT DALIAN

JOËLLE JONES

WITH

KARL KERSCHL

JOSHUA COVEY

DANIEL KRALL

JONATHAN CASE

ERIC CANETE

JENNY FRISON

STEVE MORRIS

DARK HORSE BOOKS

WOW! THE MAKING OF A GRAPHIC NOVEL is a complex, crazy, creative, and absolutely satisfying experience! I've long been a fan of the comic-book genre—I grew up immersed in the worlds of Superman, Swamp Thing, Batman, the Fantastic Four, etc. Long before Dark Horse and I found each other, I had a great affection and respect for comics. I just didn't have a clue about the process it took to create them. I have to tell ya, working with the Dark Horse team has been dreamy! (I can hear my daughter's editorial voice right now telling me that I'd better be more specific and say it has been a dreamy-good, not a dreamy-nightmare, kind of experience. See, she "edits" me even when she's not editing me!) Scott Allie, Sierra Hahn, and Jim Gibbons were specific and smart and super easy to understand. They were supportive when I asked to bring in my own adapter, my screenwriter friend Kent Dalian, even though Kent had the same amount of experience in the genre as me—none. Dark Horse was patient and encouraging. Add that good writing karma to a team of talented artists, with Joëlle Jones headlining as our modern-day House of Night illustrator, and what we produced is absolute magick.

House of Night fans—I believe you'll have the same reaction to this first collection as did Kent and I. While the comics were being sketched and then inked and colored, Kent and I were like preteen girls at a boy-band concert! We were squealing and breathless. And then we had the actual comics in our hands! Seeing Zoey, Stevie Rae, Damien, Aphrodite, and the twins come to life, along with the school and even the secondary players (Nala! Dragon Lankford! Persephone!) had Kent and me tearing up with emotion, especially as we saw the different and exquisite artistic interpretations of the Goddess of Night herself, Nyx. IT'S JUST SO DAMN COOL!

So, as the creatress of House of Night, I want to officially voice my profound appreciation for my Dark Horse family, their artists, and Kent Dalian. I tend to manifest in my life what I foresee, and I foresee lots of happy *HoN* fans and a long and fulfilling relationship with Dark Horse.

Wishing all of my readers, whether new to my world or longtime fans, to eternally blessed be . . .

P. C. Cast

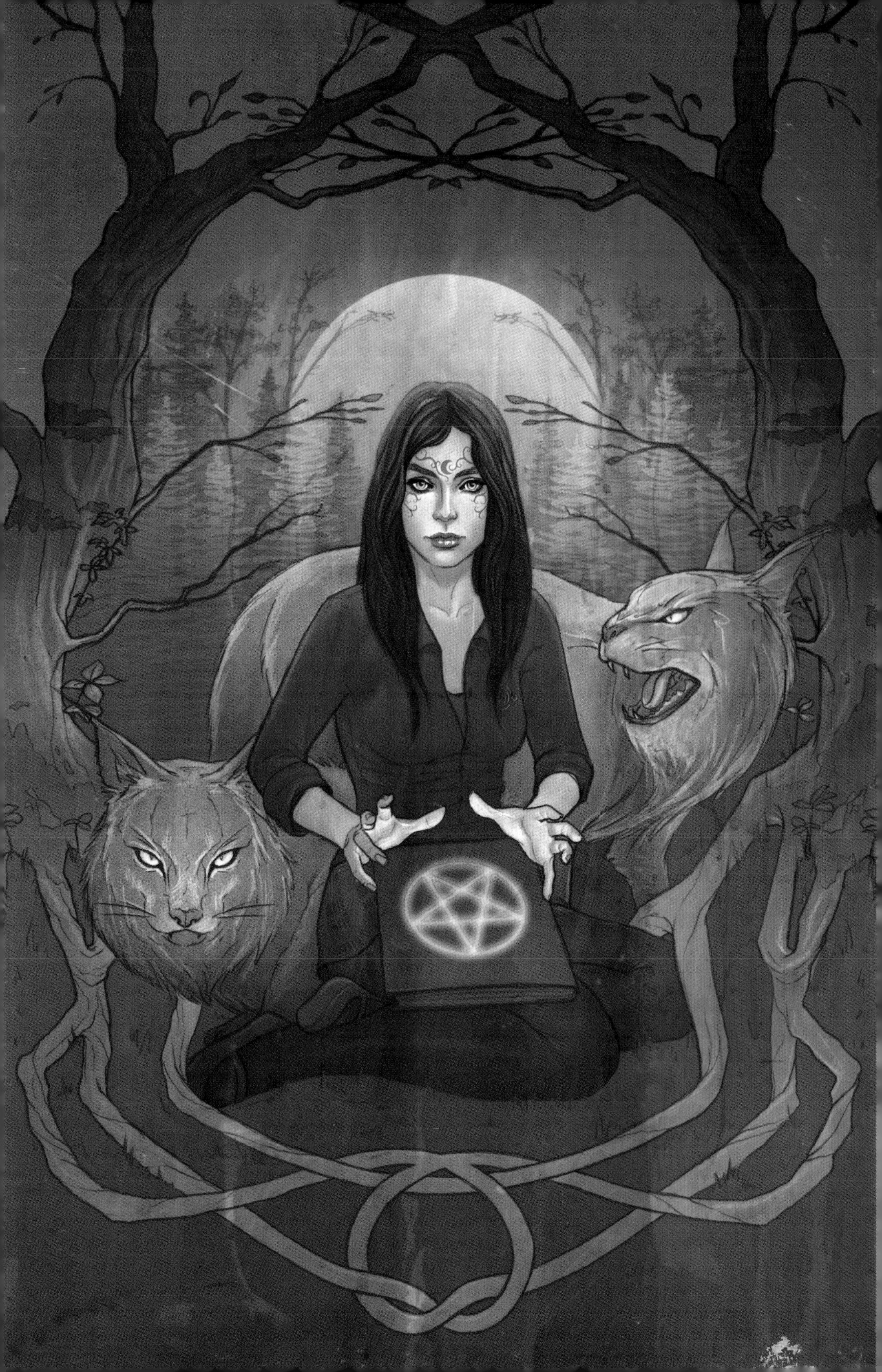

EARTH

Story by
P. C. CAST
and **KRISTIN CAST**

Script by
KENT DALIAN

Art by
JOËLLE JONES
and **KARL KERSCHL**

Colors by
RYAN HILL
and **TYSON HESSE**

Letters by
NATE PIEKOS of **BLAMBOT®**

Chapter Illustration by
JENNY FRISON

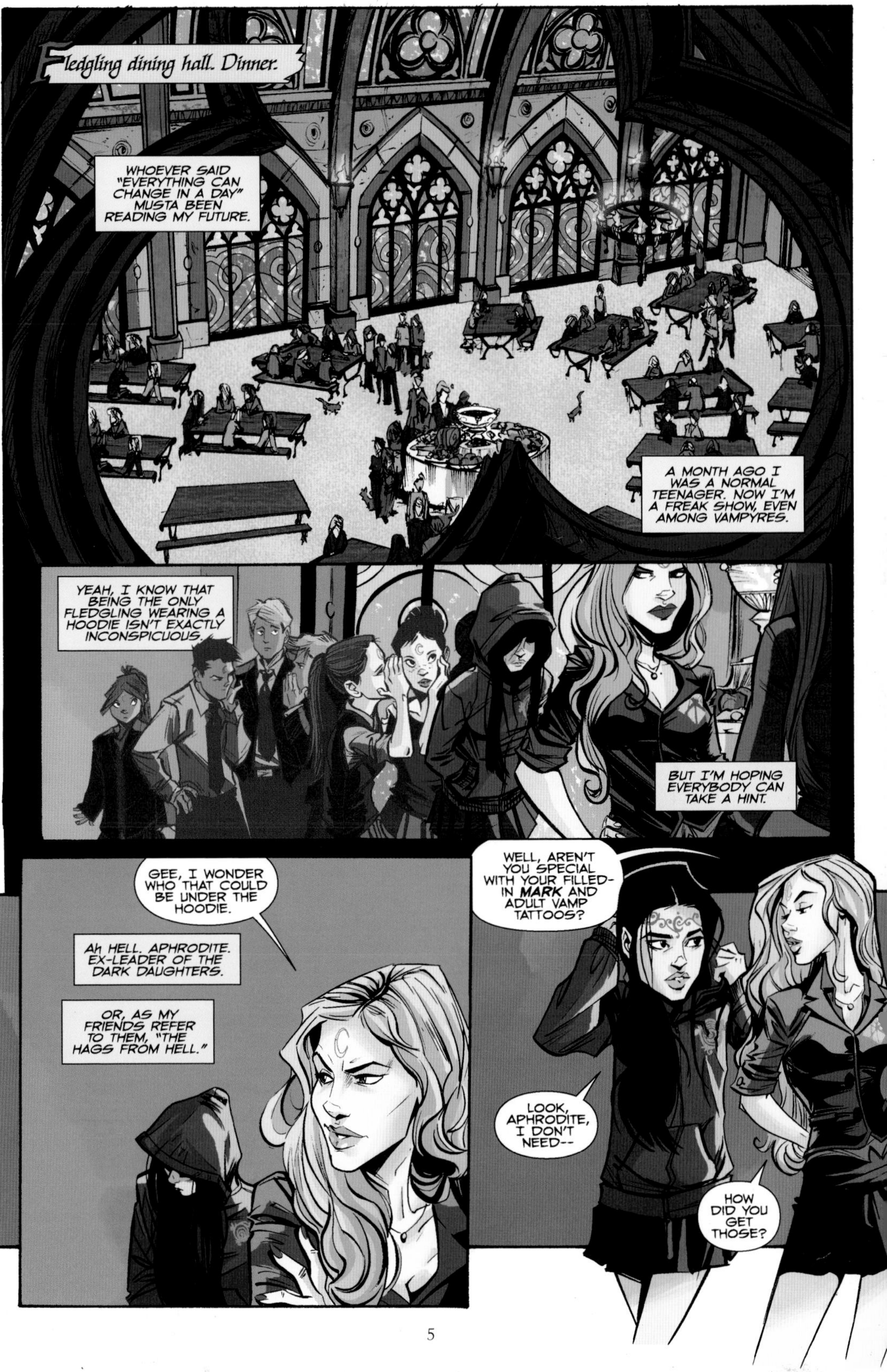
Fledgling dining hall. Dinner.
WHOEVER SAID "EVERYTHING CAN CHANGE IN A DAY" MUSTA BEEN READING MY FUTURE.
A MONTH AGO I WAS A NORMAL TEENAGER. NOW I'M A FREAK SHOW, EVEN AMONG VAMPYRES.
YEAH, I KNOW THAT BEING THE ONLY FLEDGLING WEARING A HOODIE ISN'T EXACTLY INCONSPICUOUS.
BUT I'M HOPING EVERYBODY CAN TAKE A HINT.
GEE, I WONDER WHO THAT COULD BE UNDER THE HOODIE.
Ah HELL. APHRODITE. EX-LEADER OF THE DARK DAUGHTERS.
OR, AS MY FRIENDS REFER TO THEM, "THE HAGS FROM HELL."
WELL, AREN'T YOU SPECIAL WITH YOUR FILLED-IN MARK AND ADULT VAMP TATTOOS?
LOOK, APHRODITE, I DON'T NEED--
HOW DID YOU GET THOSE?

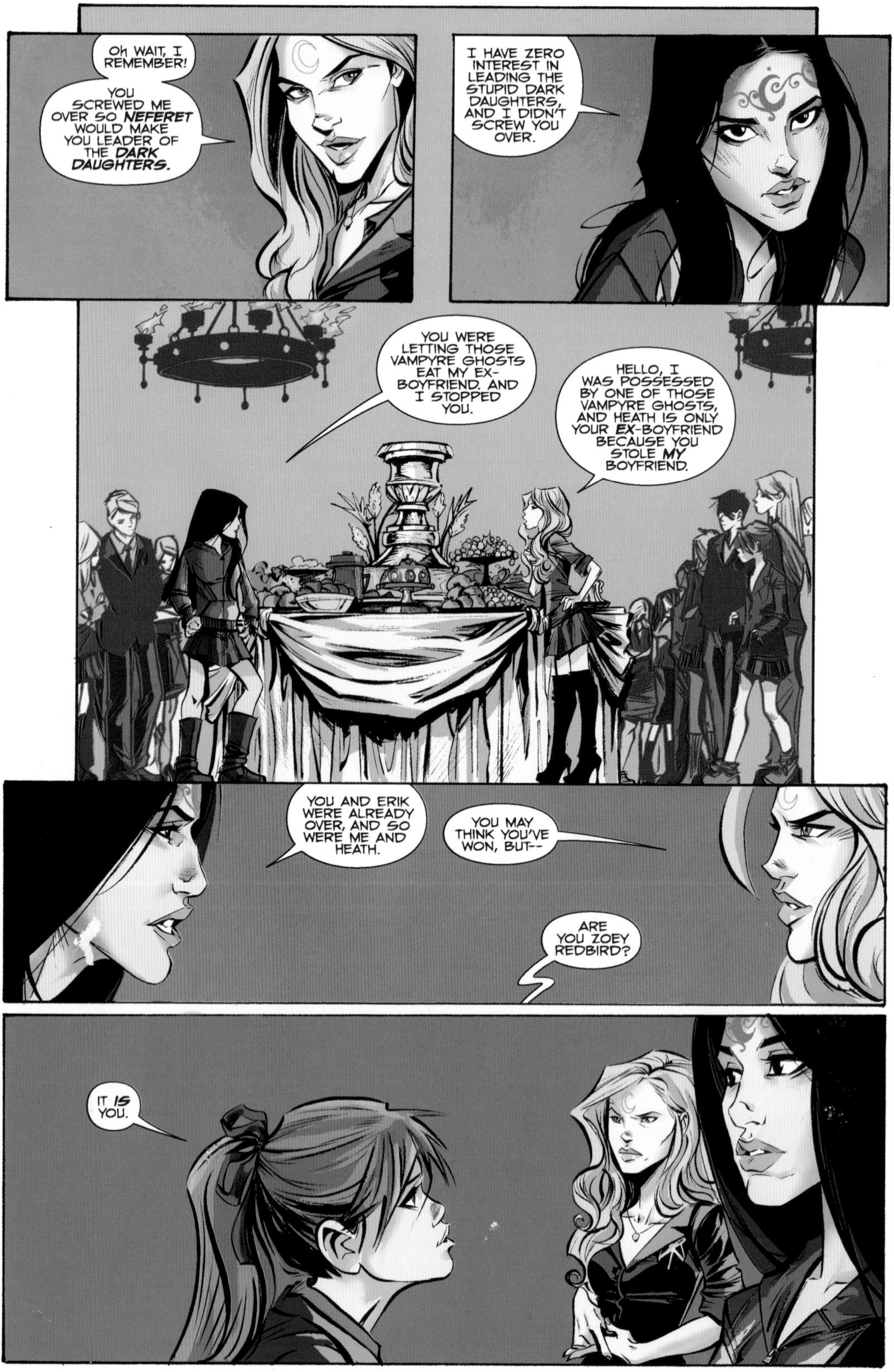
Oh WAIT, I REMEMBER!
YOU SCREWED ME OVER SO NEFERET WOULD MAKE YOU LEADER OF THE DARK DAUGHTERS.
I HAVE ZERO INTEREST IN LEADING THE STUPID DARK DAUGHTERS, AND I DIDN'T SCREW YOU OVER.
YOU WERE LETTING THOSE VAMPYRE GHOSTS EAT MY EX-BOYFRIEND. AND I STOPPED YOU.
HELLO, I WAS POSSESSED BY ONE OF THOSE VAMPYRE GHOSTS, AND HEATH IS ONLY YOUR EX-BOYFRIEND BECAUSE YOU STOLE MY BOYFRIEND.
YOU AND ERIK WERE ALREADY OVER, AND SO WERE ME AND HEATH.
YOU MAY THINK YOU'VE WON, BUT--
ARE YOU ZOEY REDBIRD?
IT IS YOU.

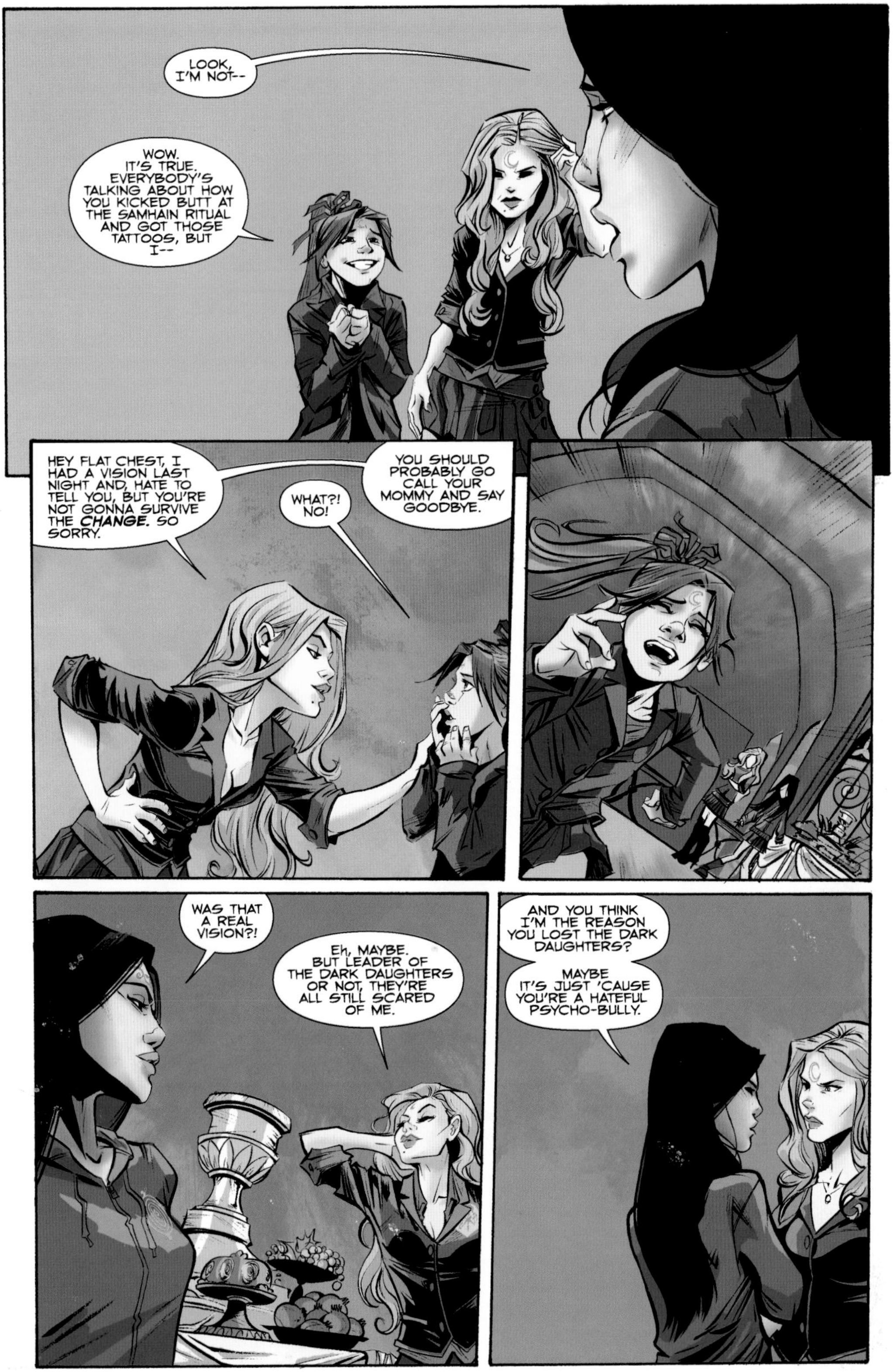
LOOK, I'M NOT--
WOW. IT'S TRUE. EVERYBODY'S TALKING ABOUT HOW YOU KICKED BUTT AT THE SAMHAIN RITUAL AND GOT THOSE TATTOOS, BUT I--
HEY FLAT CHEST, I HAD A VISION LAST NIGHT AND, HATE TO TELL YOU, BUT YOU'RE NOT GONNA SURVIVE THE **CHANGE.** SO SORRY.
WHAT?! NO!
YOU SHOULD PROBABLY GO CALL YOUR MOMMY AND SAY GOODBYE.
WAS THAT A REAL VISION?!
Eh, MAYBE. BUT LEADER OF THE DARK DAUGHTERS OR NOT, THEY'RE ALL STILL SCARED OF ME.
AND YOU THINK I'M THE REASON YOU LOST THE DARK DAUGHTERS?
MAYBE IT'S JUST 'CAUSE YOU'RE A HATEFUL PSYCHO-BULLY.

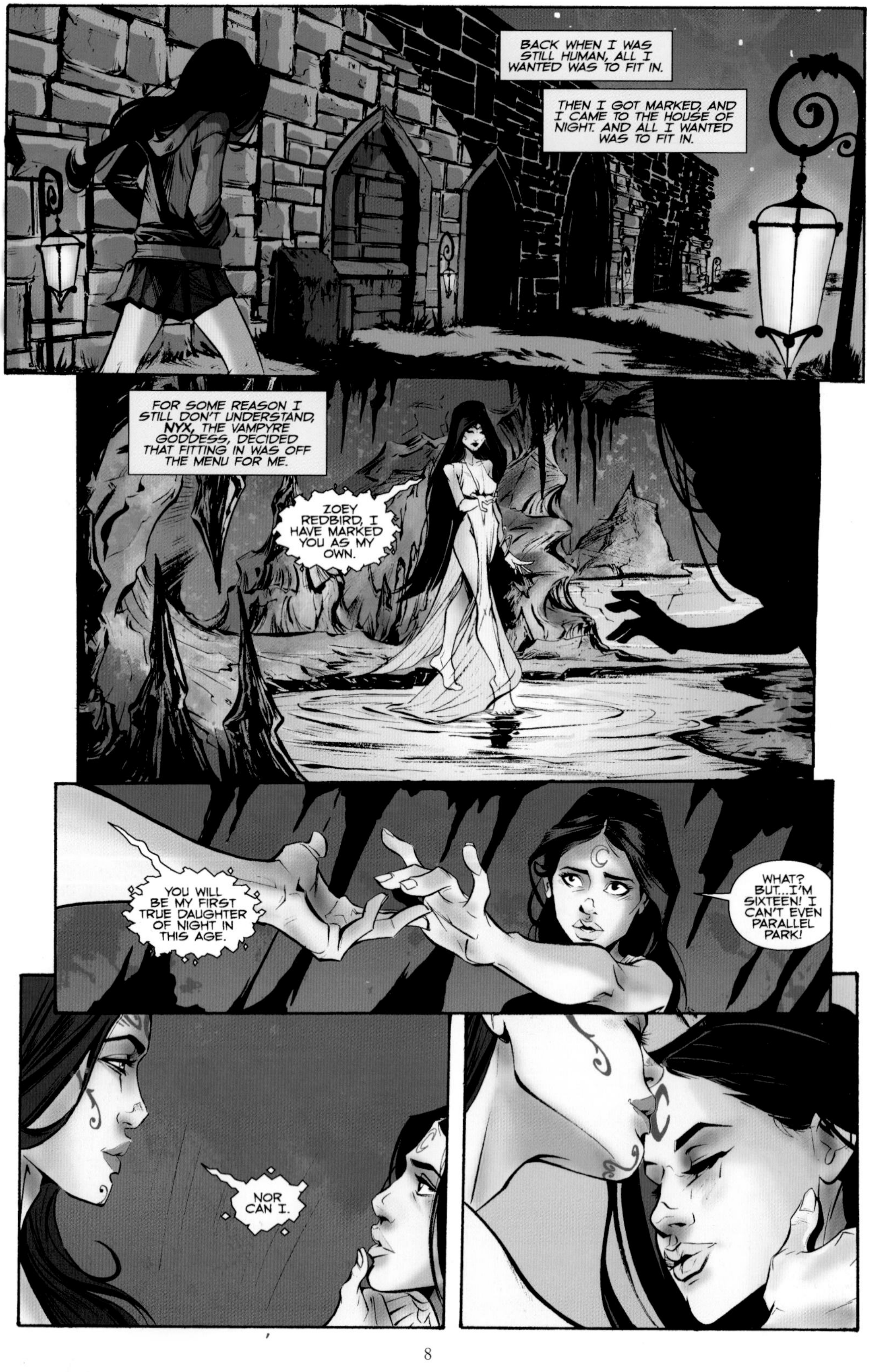
BACK WHEN I WAS STILL HUMAN, ALL I WANTED WAS TO FIT IN.
THEN I GOT MARKED, AND I CAME TO THE HOUSE OF NIGHT. AND ALL I WANTED WAS TO FIT IN.
FOR SOME REASON I STILL DON'T UNDERSTAND, NYX, THE VAMPYRE GODDESS, DECIDED THAT FITTING IN WAS OFF THE MENU FOR ME.
ZOEY REDBIRD, I HAVE MARKED YOU AS MY OWN.
YOU WILL BE MY FIRST TRUE DAUGHTER OF NIGHT IN THIS AGE.
WHAT? BUT...I'M SIXTEEN! I CAN'T EVEN PARALLEL PARK!
NOR CAN I.

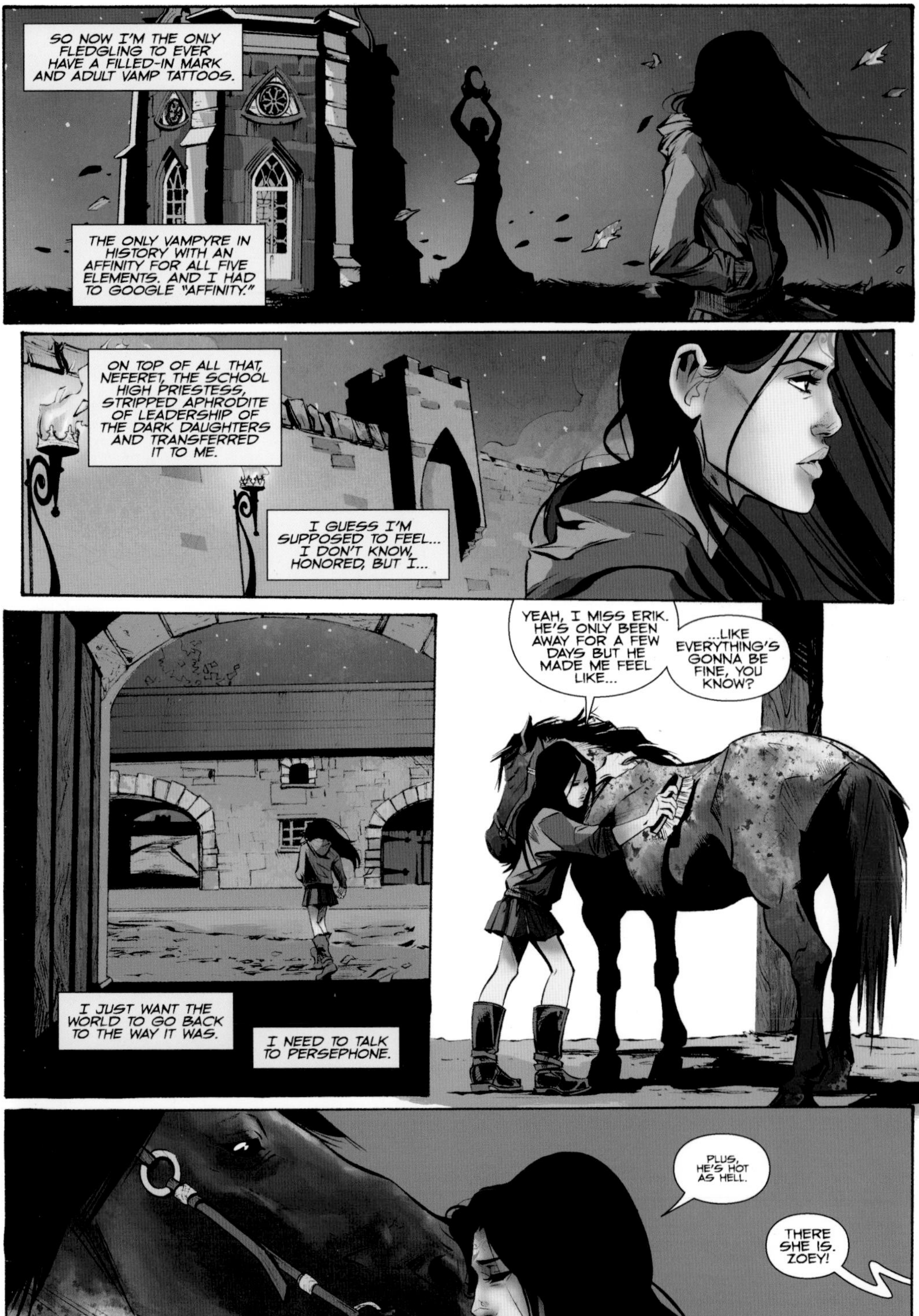
SO NOW I'M THE ONLY FLEDGLING TO EVER HAVE A FILLED-IN MARK AND ADULT VAMP TATTOOS.
THE ONLY VAMPYRE IN HISTORY WITH AN AFFINITY FOR ALL FIVE ELEMENTS. AND I HAD TO GOOGLE "AFFINITY."
ON TOP OF ALL THAT, NEFERET, THE SCHOOL HIGH PRIESTESS, STRIPPED APHRODITE OF LEADERSHIP OF THE DARK DAUGHTERS AND TRANSFERRED IT TO ME.
I GUESS I'M SUPPOSED TO FEEL... I DON'T KNOW, HONORED, BUT I...
I JUST WANT THE WORLD TO GO BACK TO THE WAY IT WAS.
I NEED TO TALK TO PERSEPHONE.
YEAH, I MISS ERIK. HE'S ONLY BEEN AWAY FOR A FEW DAYS BUT HE MADE ME FEEL LIKE...
...LIKE EVERYTHING'S GONNA BE FINE, YOU KNOW?
PLUS, HE'S HOT AS HELL.
THERE SHE IS. ZOEY!

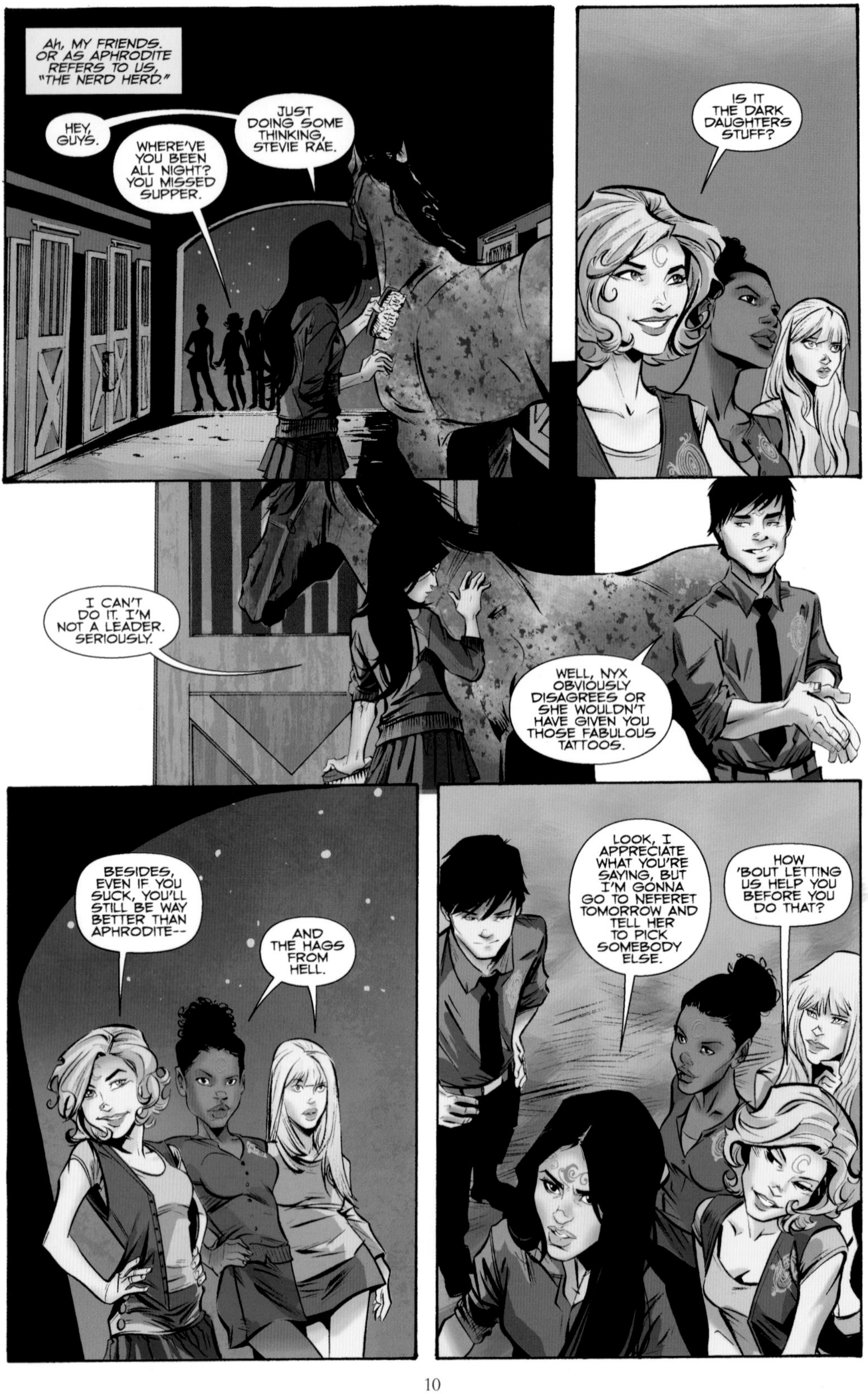

Ah, MY FRIENDS. OR AS APHRODITE REFERS TO US, "THE NERD HERD."
HEY, GUYS.
JUST DOING SOME THINKING, STEVIE RAE.
WHERE'VE YOU BEEN ALL NIGHT? YOU MISSED SUPPER.
IS IT THE DARK DAUGHTERS STUFF?
I CAN'T DO IT. I'M NOT A LEADER. SERIOUSLY.
WELL, NYX OBVIOUSLY DISAGREES OR SHE WOULDN'T HAVE GIVEN YOU THOSE FABULOUS TATTOOS.
BESIDES, EVEN IF YOU SUCK, YOU'LL STILL BE WAY BETTER THAN APHRODITE--
AND THE HAGS FROM HELL.
LOOK, I APPRECIATE WHAT YOU'RE SAYING, BUT I'M GONNA GO TO NEFERET TOMORROW AND TELL HER TO PICK SOMEBODY ELSE.
HOW 'BOUT LETTING US HELP YOU BEFORE YOU DO THAT?

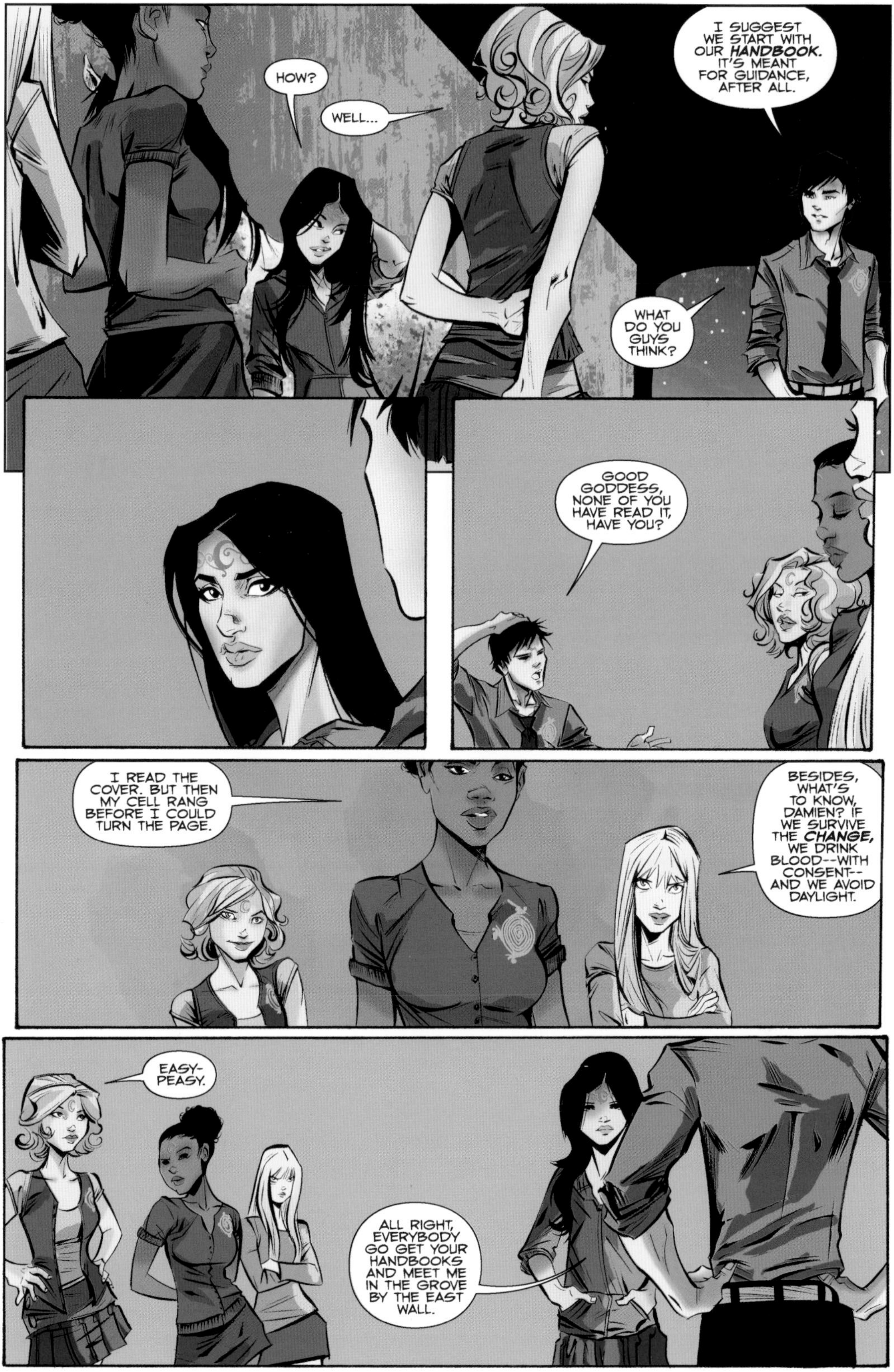
HOW?
WELL...
I SUGGEST WE START WITH OUR HANDBOOK. IT'S MEANT FOR GUIDANCE, AFTER ALL.
WHAT DO YOU GUYS THINK?
GOOD GODDESS, NONE OF YOU HAVE READ IT, HAVE YOU?
I READ THE COVER. BUT THEN MY CELL RANG BEFORE I COULD TURN THE PAGE.
BESIDES, WHAT'S TO KNOW, DAMIEN? IF WE SURVIVE THE CHANGE, WE DRINK BLOOD--WITH CONSENT-- --AND WE AVOID DAYLIGHT.
EASY-PEASY.
ALL RIGHT, EVERYBODY GO GET YOUR HANDBOOKS AND MEET ME IN THE GROVE BY THE EAST WALL.

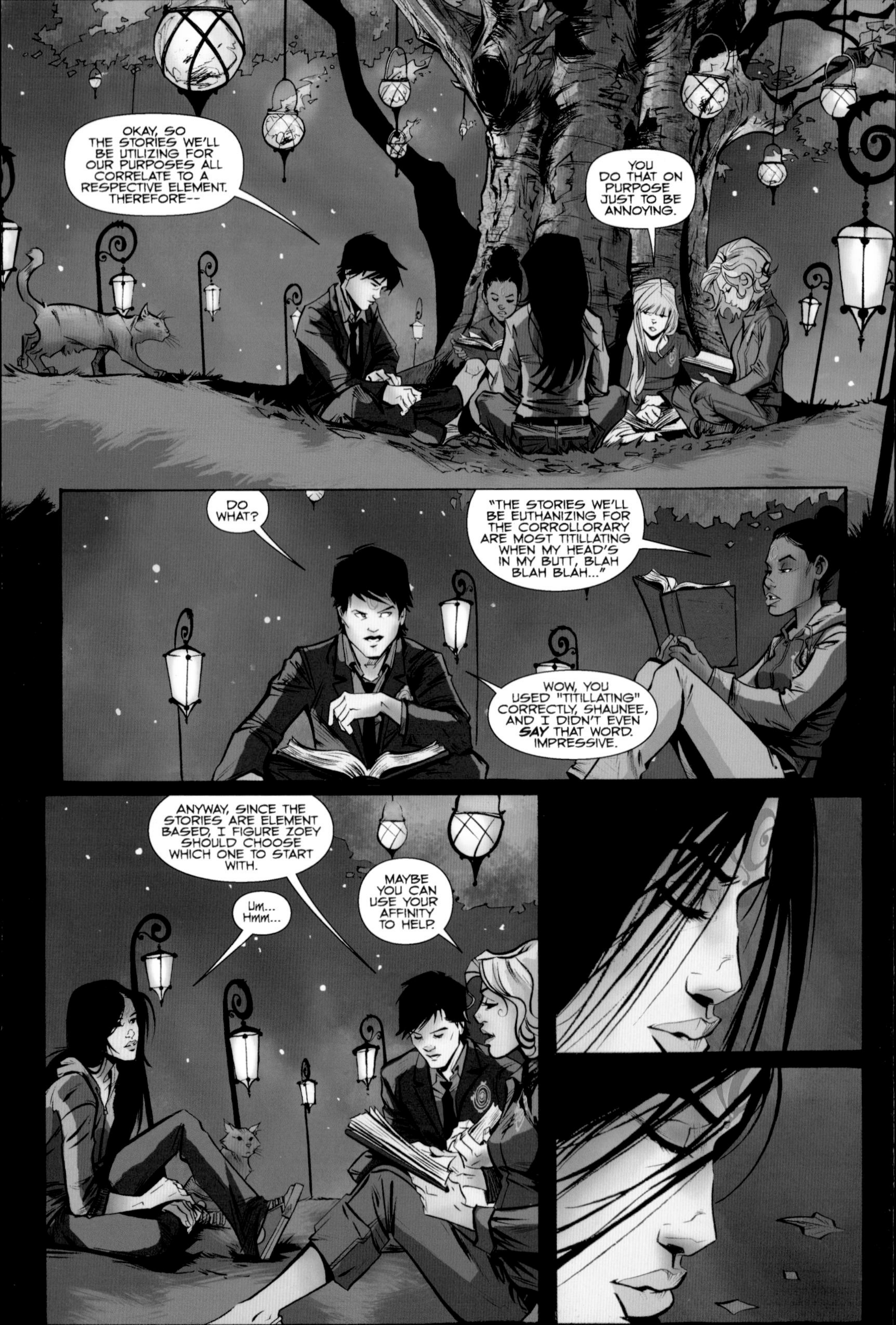
OKAY, SO THE STORIES WE'LL BE UTILIZING FOR OUR PURPOSES ALL CORRELATE TO A RESPECTIVE ELEMENT. THEREFORE--
YOU DO THAT ON PURPOSE JUST TO BE ANNOYING.
DO WHAT?
"THE STORIES WE'LL BE EUTHANIZING FOR THE CORROLLORARY ARE MOST TITILLATING WHEN MY HEAD'S IN MY BUTT, BLAH BLAH BLAH..."
WOW, YOU USED "TITILLATING" CORRECTLY, SHAUNEE, AND I DIDN'T EVEN SAY THAT WORD. IMPRESSIVE.
ANYWAY, SINCE THE STORIES ARE ELEMENT BASED, I FIGURE ZOEY SHOULD CHOOSE WHICH ONE TO START WITH.
Um... Hmm...
MAYBE YOU CAN USE YOUR AFFINITY TO HELP.

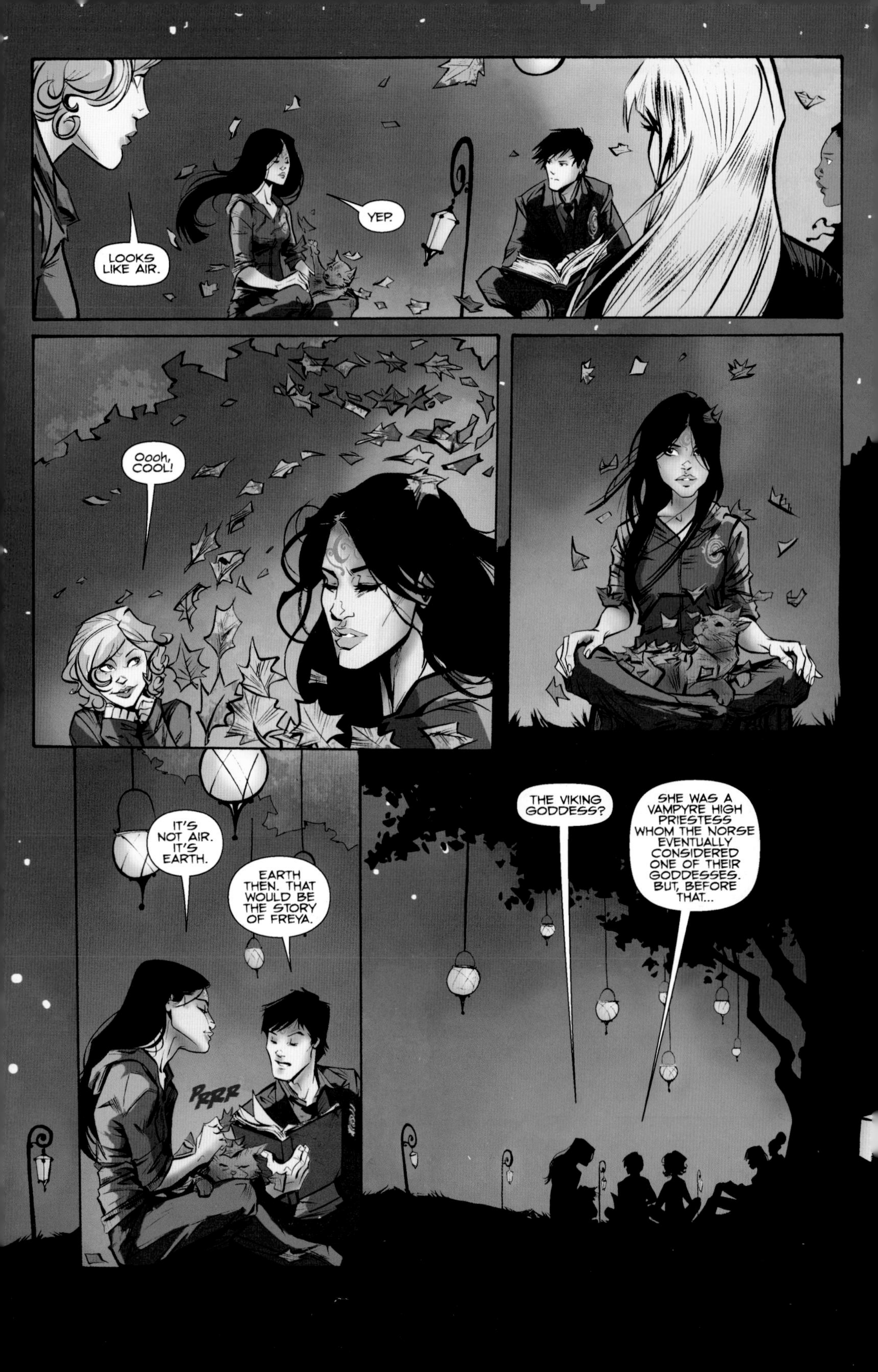
LOOKS LIKE AIR.
YEP.
Oooh, COOL!
IT'S NOT AIR. IT'S EARTH.
EARTH THEN. THAT WOULD BE THE STORY OF FREYA.
RRRR
THE VIKING GODDESS?
SHE WAS A VAMPYRE HIGH PRIESTESS WHOM THE NORSE EVENTUALLY CONSIDERED ONE OF THEIR GODDESSES. BUT, BEFORE THAT...

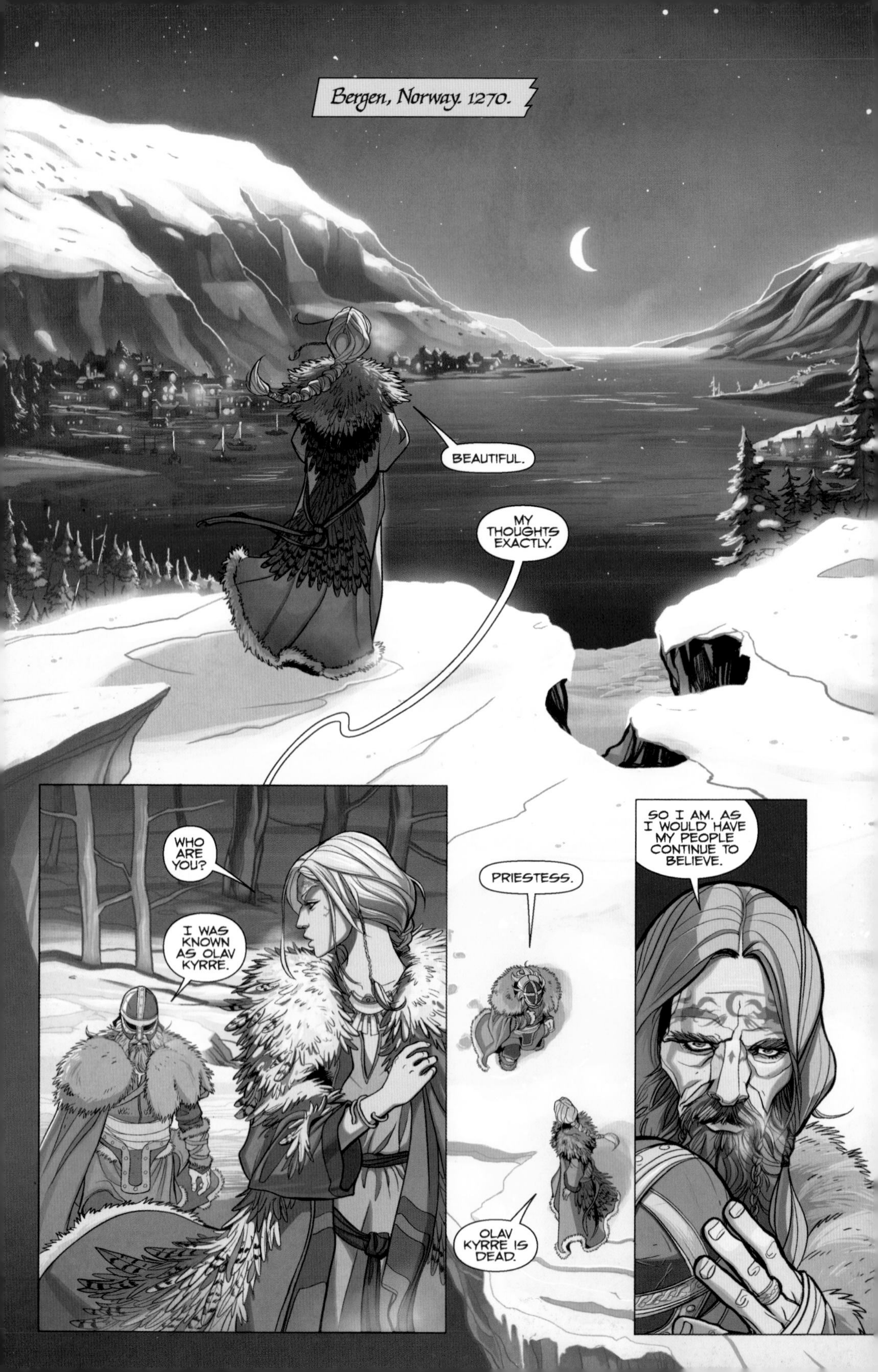
Bergen, Norway. 1270.
BEAUTIFUL.
MY THOUGHTS EXACTLY.
WHO ARE YOU?
I WAS KNOWN AS OLAV KYRRE.
PRIESTESS.
OLAV KYRRE IS DEAD.
SO I AM. AS I WOULD HAVE MY PEOPLE CONTINUE TO BELIEVE.

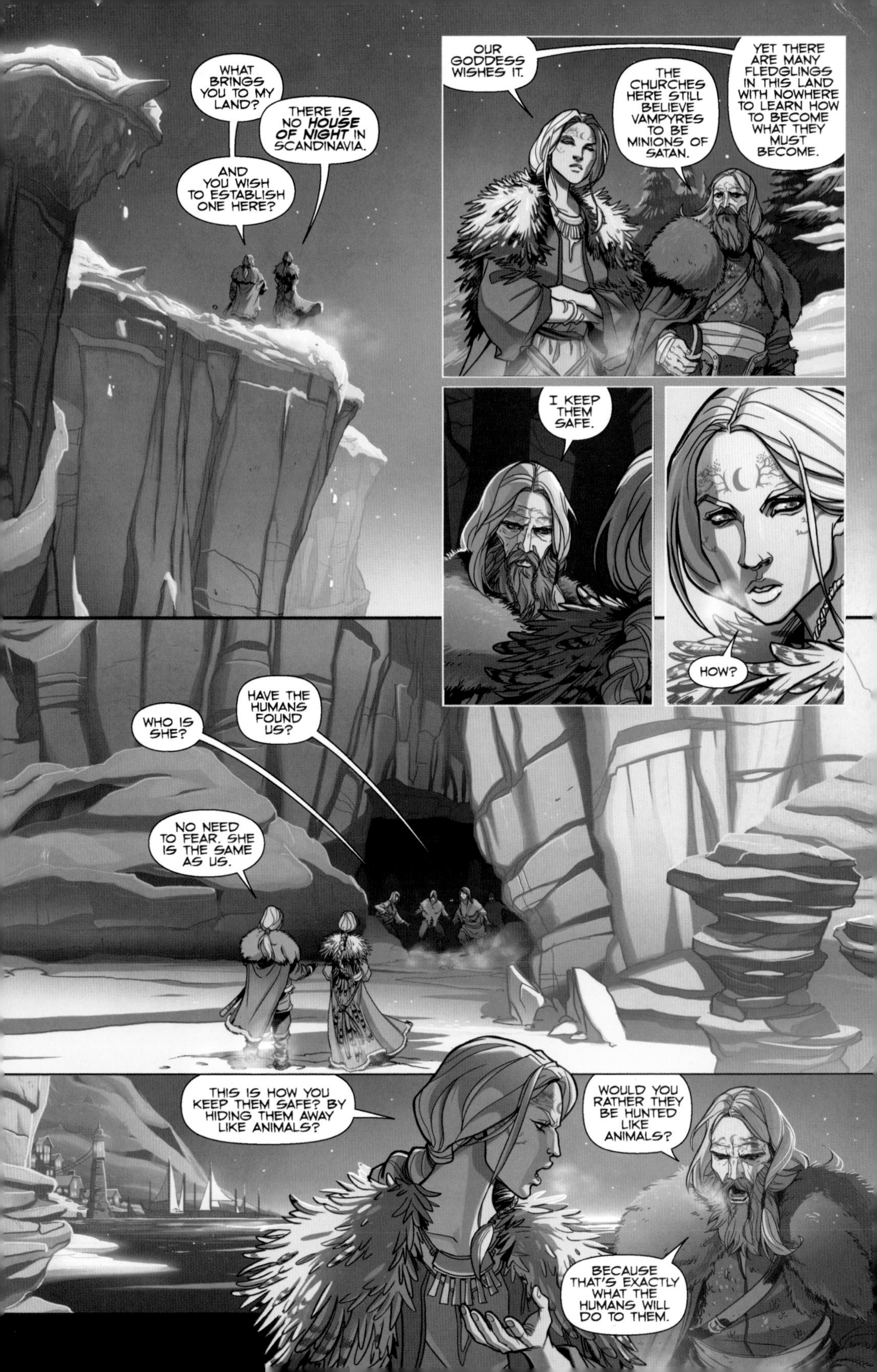
WHAT BRINGS YOU TO MY LAND?
THERE IS NO HOUSE OF NIGHT IN SCANDINAVIA.
AND YOU WISH TO ESTABLISH ONE HERE?
OUR GODDESS WISHES IT.
THE CHURCHES HERE STILL BELIEVE VAMPYRES TO BE MINIONS OF SATAN.
YET THERE ARE MANY FLEDGLINGS IN THIS LAND WITH NOWHERE TO LEARN HOW TO BECOME WHAT THEY MUST BECOME.
I KEEP THEM SAFE.
HOW?
WHO IS SHE?
HAVE THE HUMANS FOUND US?
NO NEED TO FEAR. SHE IS THE SAME AS US.
THIS IS HOW YOU KEEP THEM SAFE? BY HIDING THEM AWAY LIKE ANIMALS?
WOULD YOU RATHER THEY BE HUNTED LIKE ANIMALS?
BECAUSE THAT'S EXACTLY WHAT THE HUMANS WILL DO TO THEM.

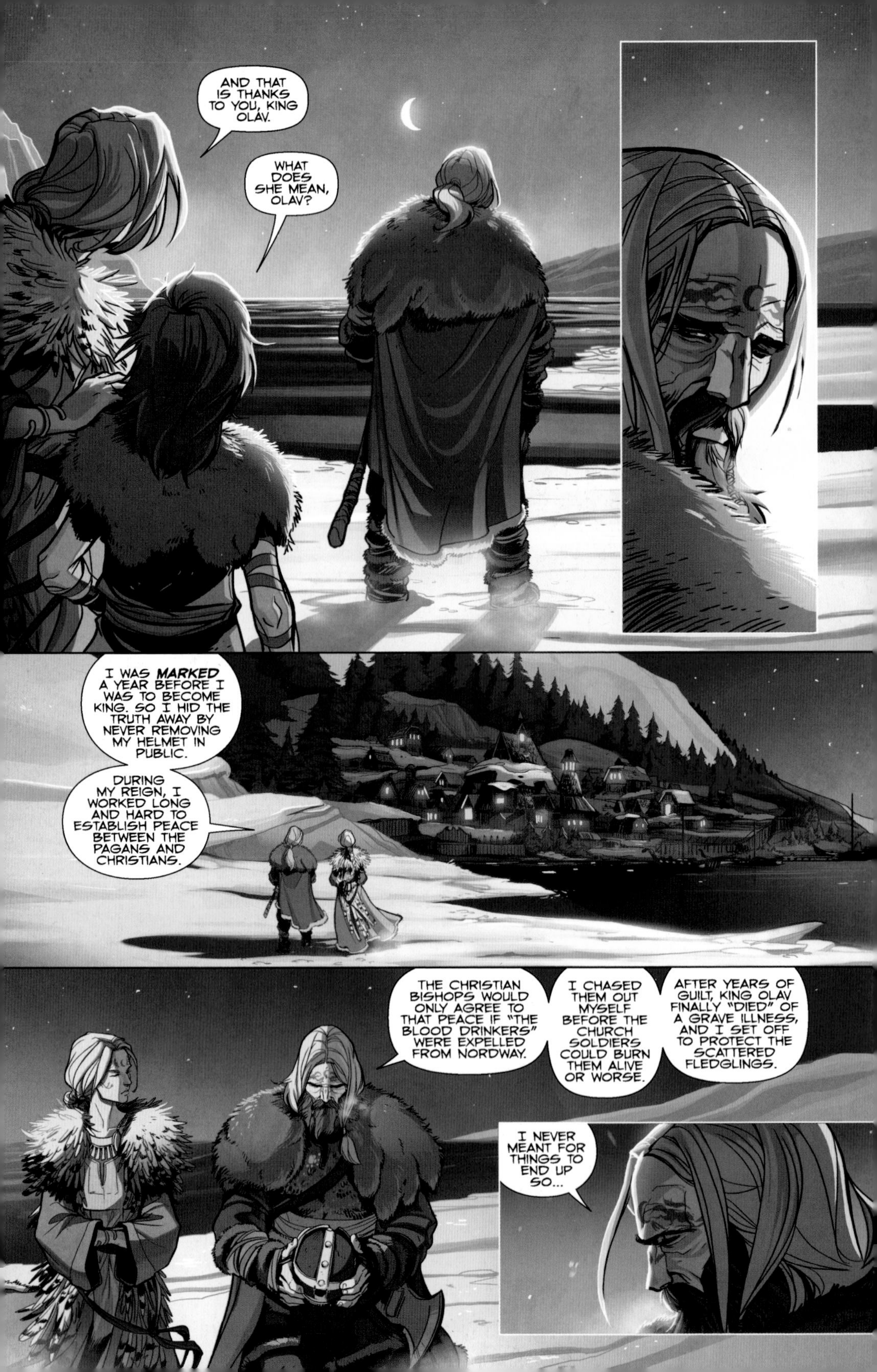
AND THAT IS THANKS TO YOU, KING OLAV.
WHAT DOES SHE MEAN, OLAV?
I WAS MARKED A YEAR BEFORE I WAS TO BECOME KING. SO I HID THE TRUTH AWAY BY NEVER REMOVING MY HELMET IN PUBLIC.
DURING MY REIGN, I WORKED LONG AND HARD TO ESTABLISH PEACE BETWEEN THE PAGANS AND CHRISTIANS.
THE CHRISTIAN BISHOPS WOULD ONLY AGREE TO THAT PEACE IF "THE BLOOD DRINKERS" WERE EXPELLED FROM NORDWAY.
I CHASED THEM OUT MYSELF BEFORE THE CHURCH SOLDIERS COULD BURN THEM ALIVE OR WORSE.
AFTER YEARS OF GUILT, KING OLAV FINALLY "DIED" OF A GRAVE ILLNESS, AND I SET OFF TO PROTECT THE SCATTERED FLEDGLINGS.
I NEVER MEANT FOR THINGS TO END UP SO...

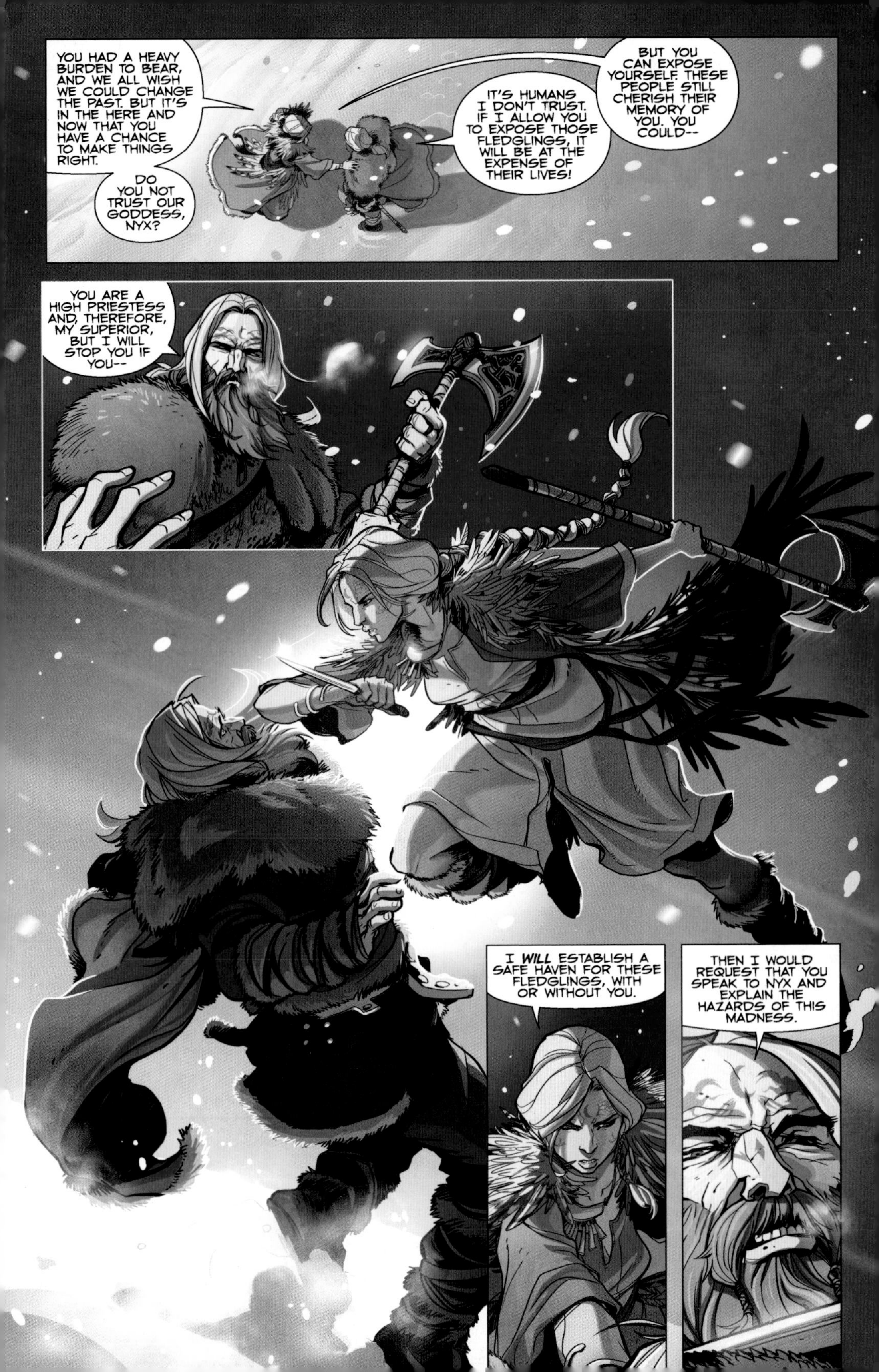
YOU HAD A HEAVY BURDEN TO BEAR, AND WE ALL WISH WE COULD CHANGE THE PAST. BUT IT'S IN THE HERE AND NOW THAT YOU HAVE A CHANCE TO MAKE THINGS RIGHT.
DO YOU NOT TRUST OUR GODDESS, NYX?
IT'S HUMANS I DON'T TRUST. IF I ALLOW YOU TO EXPOSE THOSE FLEDGLINGS, IT WILL BE AT THE EXPENSE OF THEIR LIVES!
BUT YOU CAN EXPOSE YOURSELF. THESE PEOPLE STILL CHERISH THEIR MEMORY OF YOU. YOU COULD--
YOU ARE A HIGH PRIESTESS AND, THEREFORE, MY SUPERIOR, BUT I WILL STOP YOU IF YOU--
I ***WILL*** ESTABLISH A SAFE HAVEN FOR THESE FLEDGLINGS, WITH OR WITHOUT YOU.
THEN I WOULD REQUEST THAT YOU SPEAK TO NYX AND EXPLAIN THE HAZARDS OF THIS MADNESS.

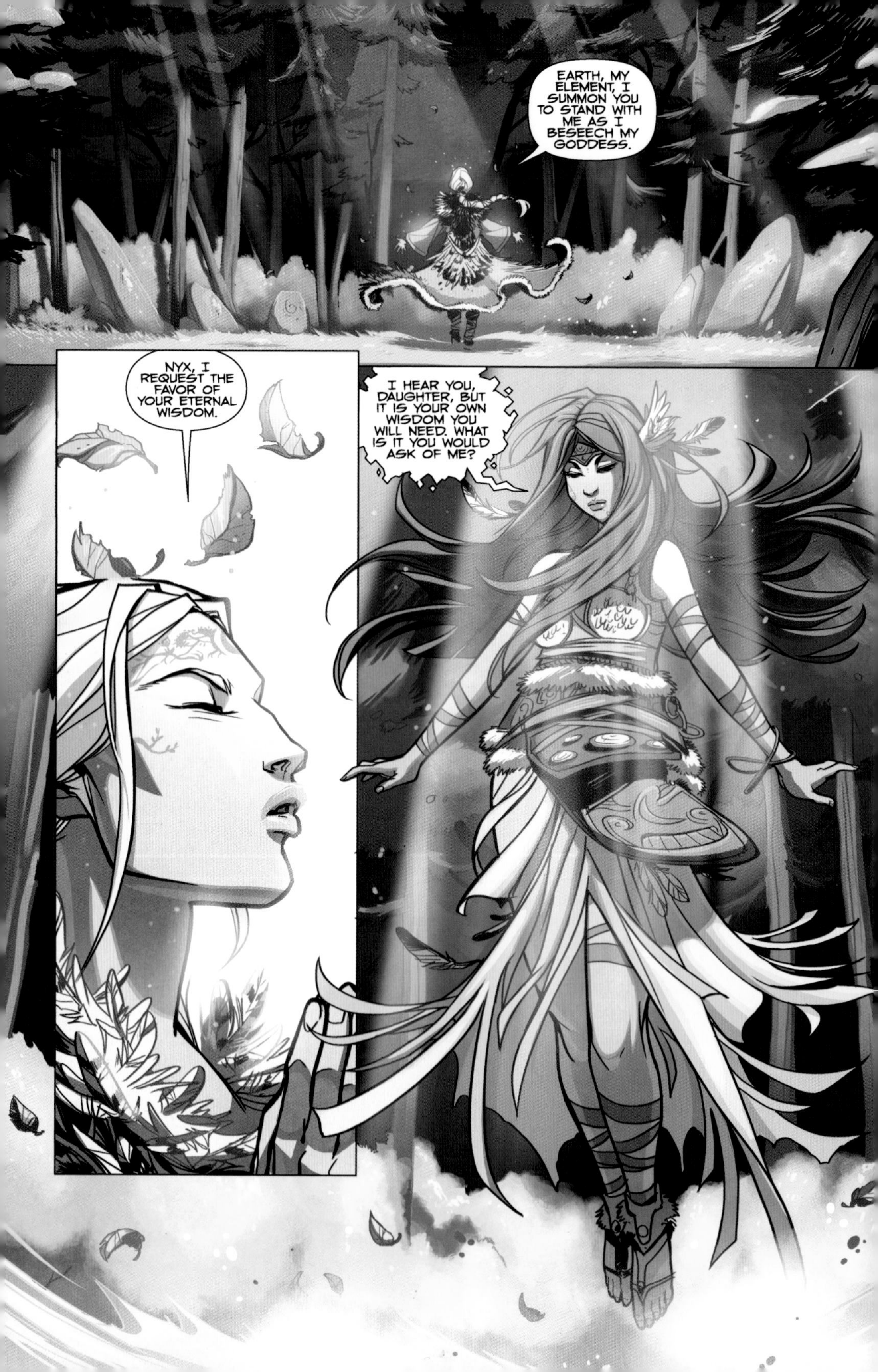
EARTH, MY ELEMENT, I SUMMON YOU TO STAND WITH ME AS I BESEECH MY GODDESS.
NYX, I REQUEST THE FAVOR OF YOUR ETERNAL WISDOM.
I HEAR YOU, DAUGHTER, BUT IT IS YOUR OWN WISDOM YOU WILL NEED. WHAT IS IT YOU WOULD ASK OF ME?

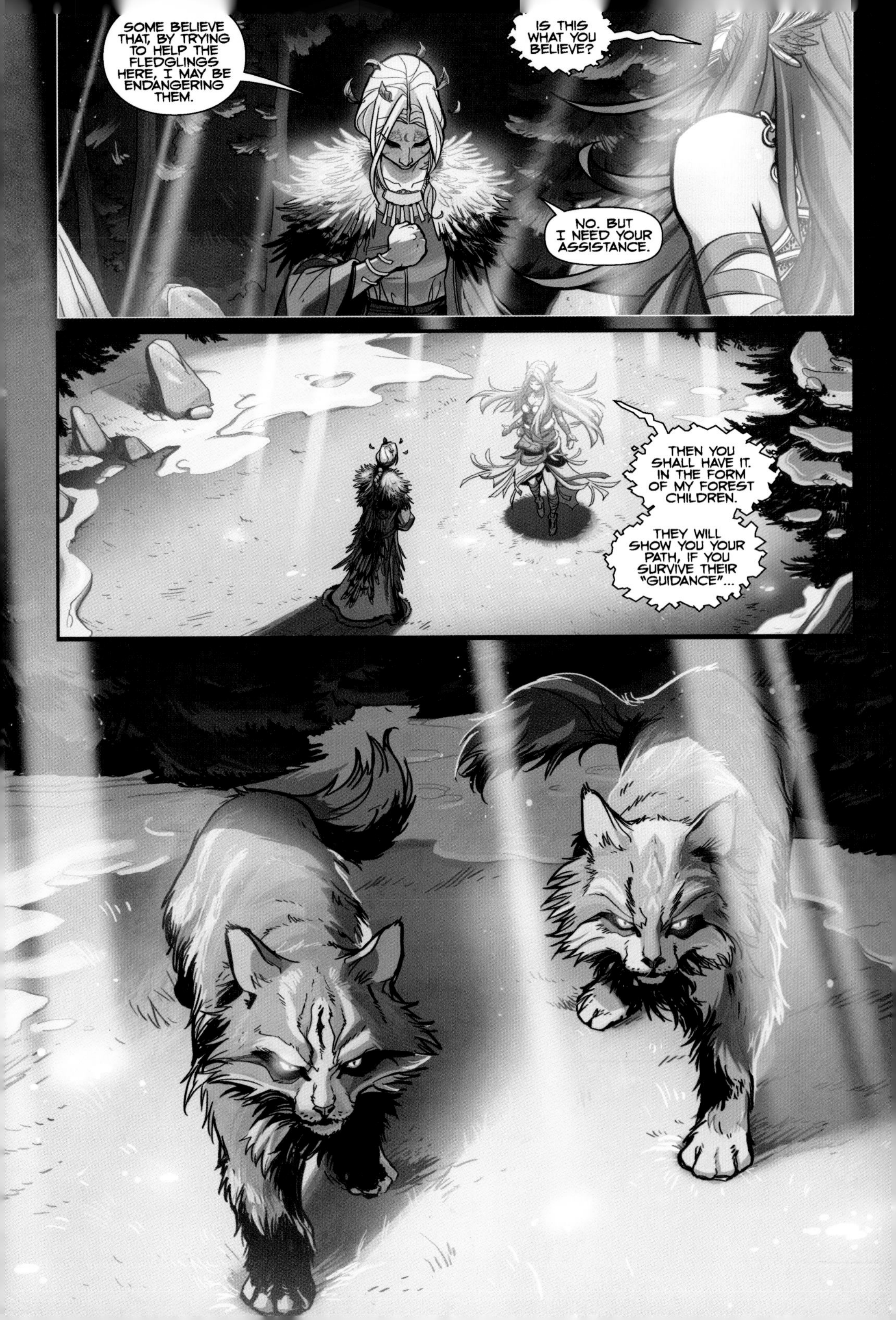
SOME BELIEVE THAT, BY TRYING TO HELP THE FLEDGLINGS HERE, I MAY BE ENDANGERING THEM.
IS THIS WHAT YOU BELIEVE?
NO. BUT I NEED YOUR ASSISTANCE.
THEN YOU SHALL HAVE IT. IN THE FORM OF MY FOREST CHILDREN.
THEY WILL SHOW YOU YOUR PATH, IF YOU SURVIVE THEIR "GUIDANCE"...

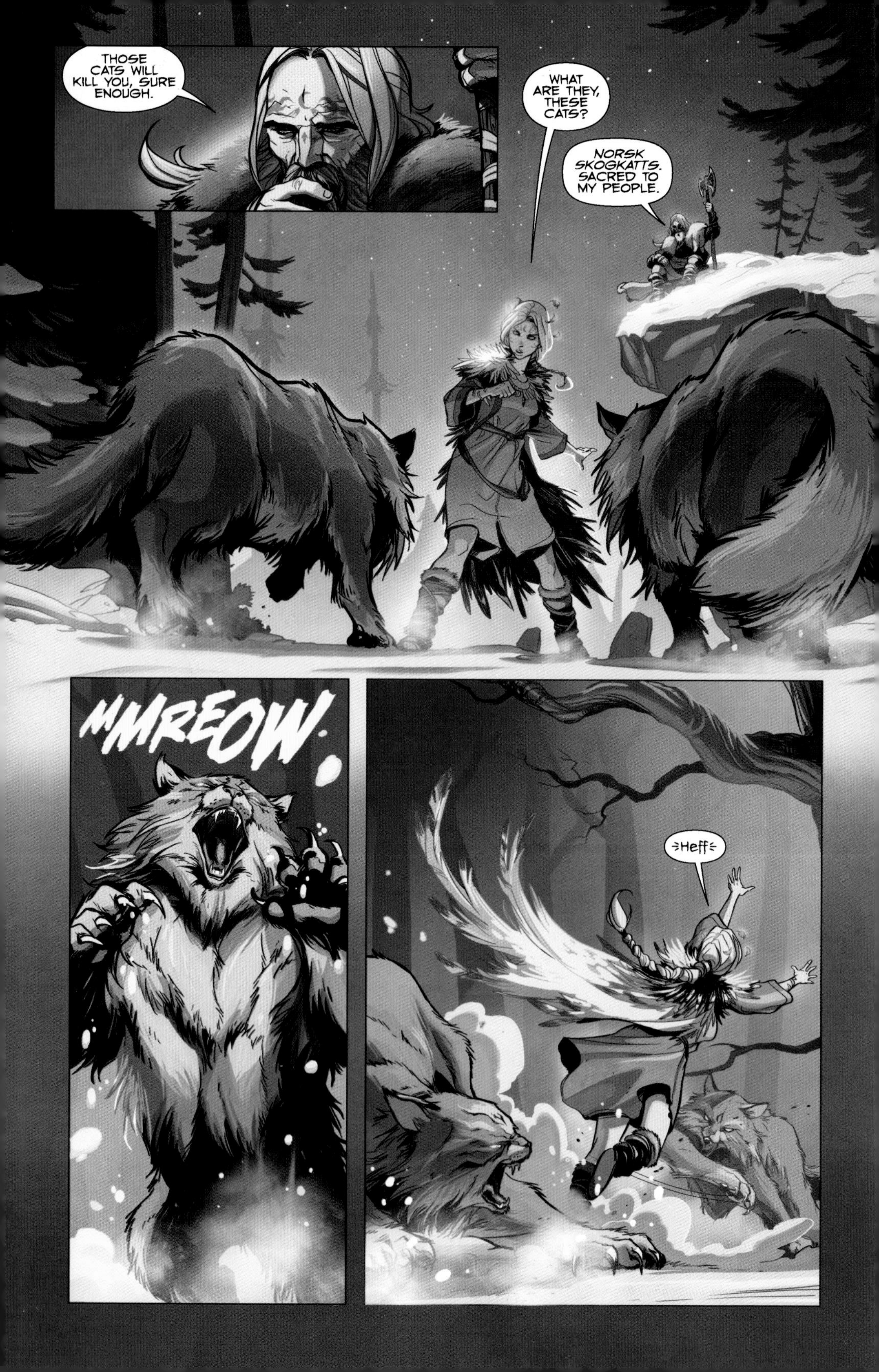
THOSE CATS WILL KILL YOU, SURE ENOUGH.
WHAT ARE THEY, THESE CATS?
NORSK SKOGKATTS. SACRED TO MY PEOPLE.
MMREOW
Heff

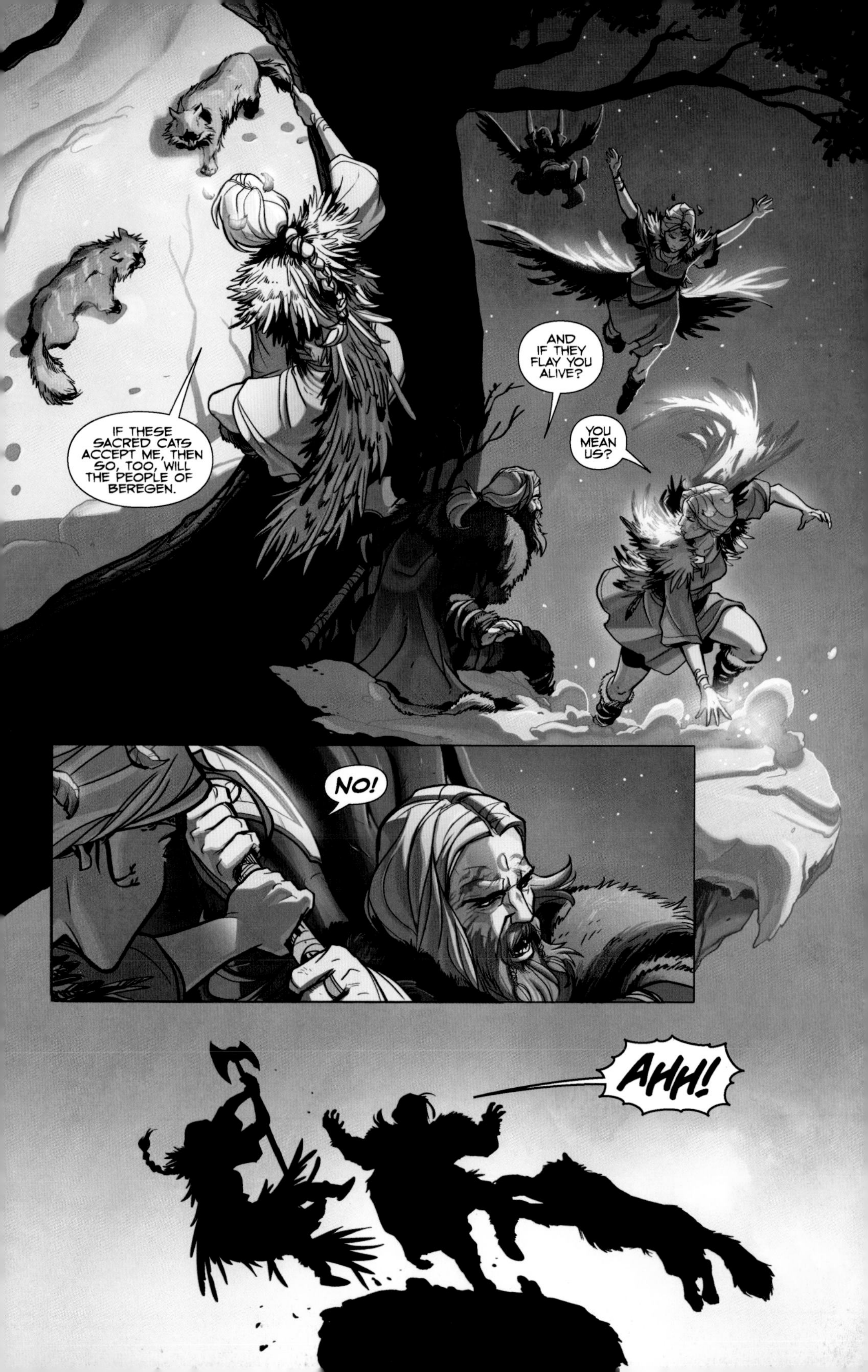
IF THESE SACRED CATS ACCEPT ME, THEN SO, TOO, WILL THE PEOPLE OF BEREGEN.
AND IF THEY FLAY YOU ALIVE?
YOU MEAN US?
NO!
AHH!

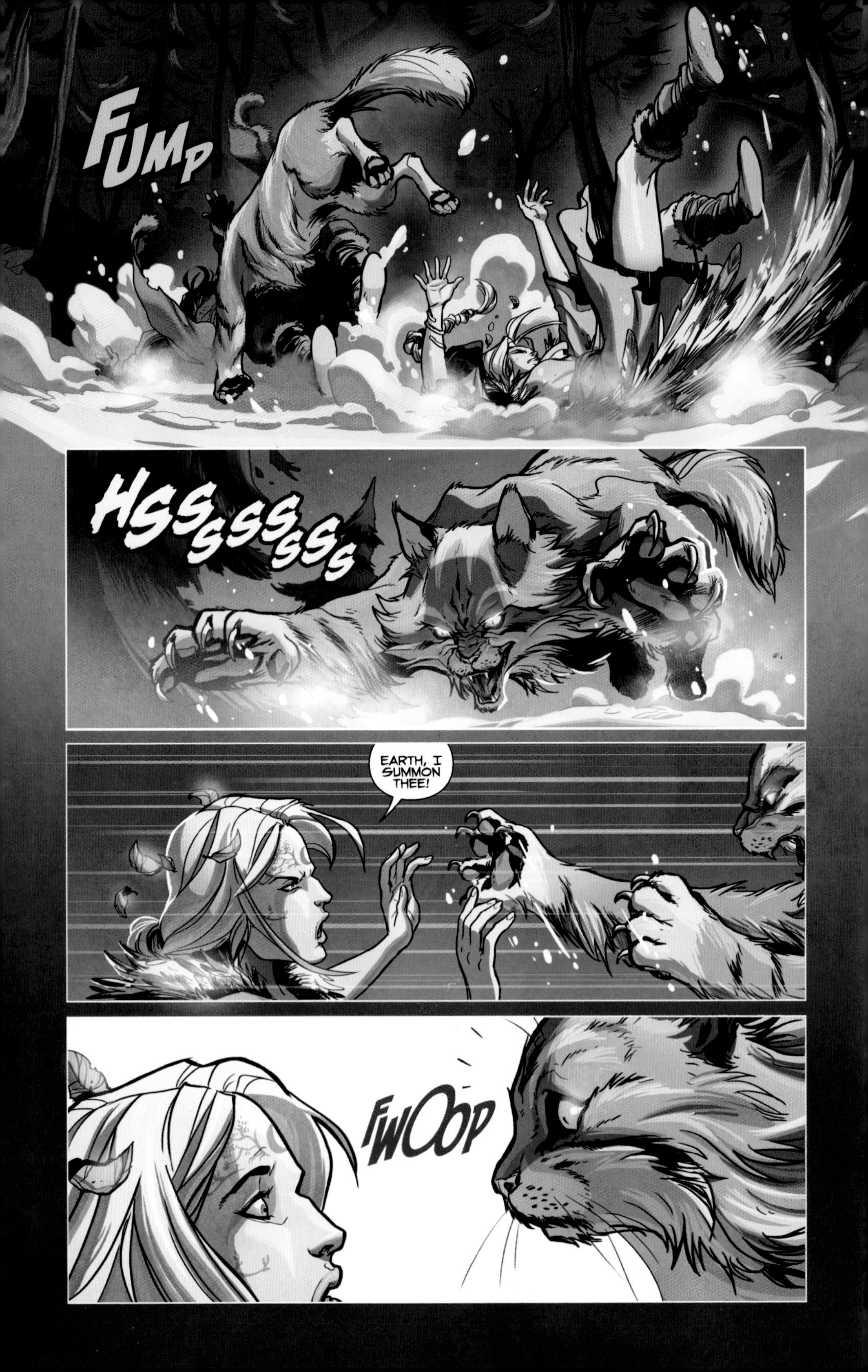
FUMP
HSSSSSSSSS
EARTH, I SUMMON THEE!
FWOOP

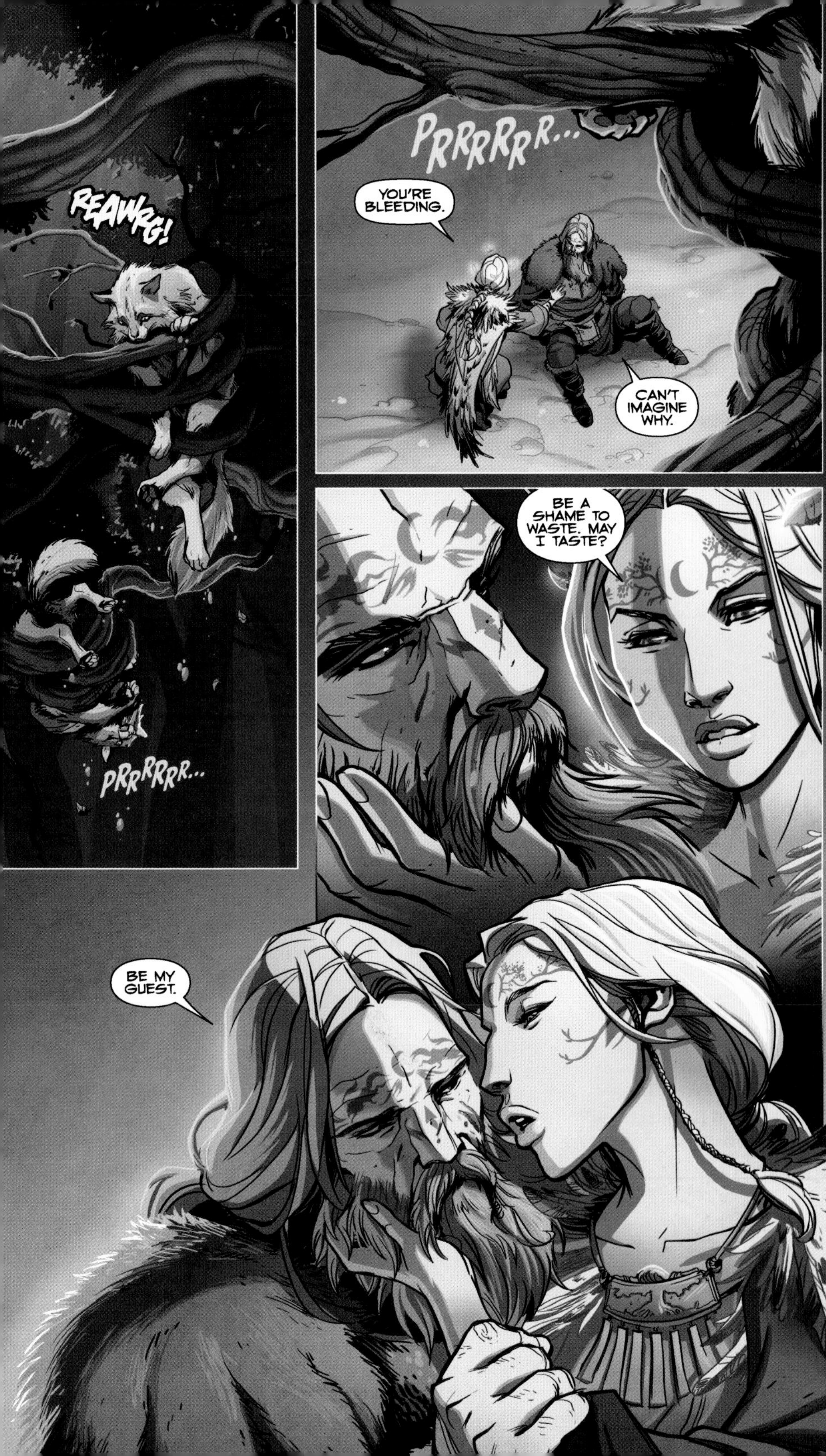
REAWRG!
PRRRRR...
PRRRRRR...
YOU'RE BLEEDING.
CAN'T IMAGINE WHY.
BE A SHAME TO WASTE. MAY I TASTE?
BE MY GUEST.

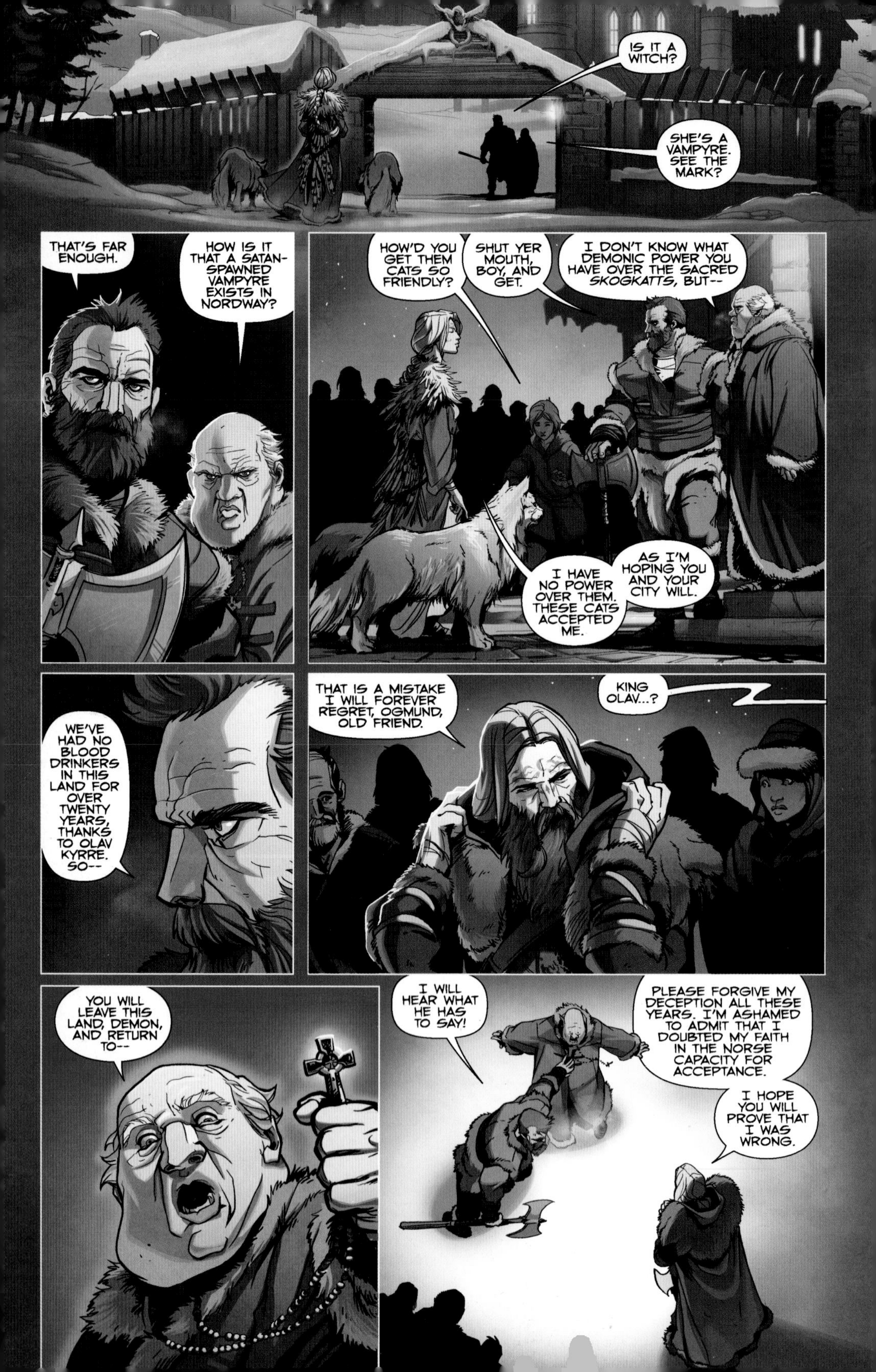
IS IT A WITCH?
SHE'S A VAMPYRE. SEE THE MARK?
THAT'S FAR ENOUGH.
HOW IS IT THAT A SATAN-SPAWNED VAMPYRE EXISTS IN NORDWAY?
HOW'D YOU GET THEM CATS SO FRIENDLY?
SHUT YER MOUTH, BOY, AND GET.
I DON'T KNOW WHAT DEMONIC POWER YOU HAVE OVER THE SACRED SKOGKATTS, BUT--
I HAVE NO POWER OVER THEM. THESE CATS ACCEPTED ME.
AS I'M HOPING YOU AND YOUR CITY WILL.
WE'VE HAD NO BLOOD DRINKERS IN THIS LAND FOR OVER TWENTY YEARS, THANKS TO OLAV KYRRE. SO--
THAT IS A MISTAKE I WILL FOREVER REGRET, OGMUND, OLD FRIEND.
KING OLAV...?
YOU WILL LEAVE THIS LAND, DEMON, AND RETURN TO--
I WILL HEAR WHAT HE HAS TO SAY!
PLEASE FORGIVE MY DECEPTION ALL THESE YEARS. I'M ASHAMED TO ADMIT THAT I DOUBTED MY FAITH IN THE NORSE CAPACITY FOR ACCEPTANCE.
I HOPE YOU WILL PROVE THAT I WAS WRONG.

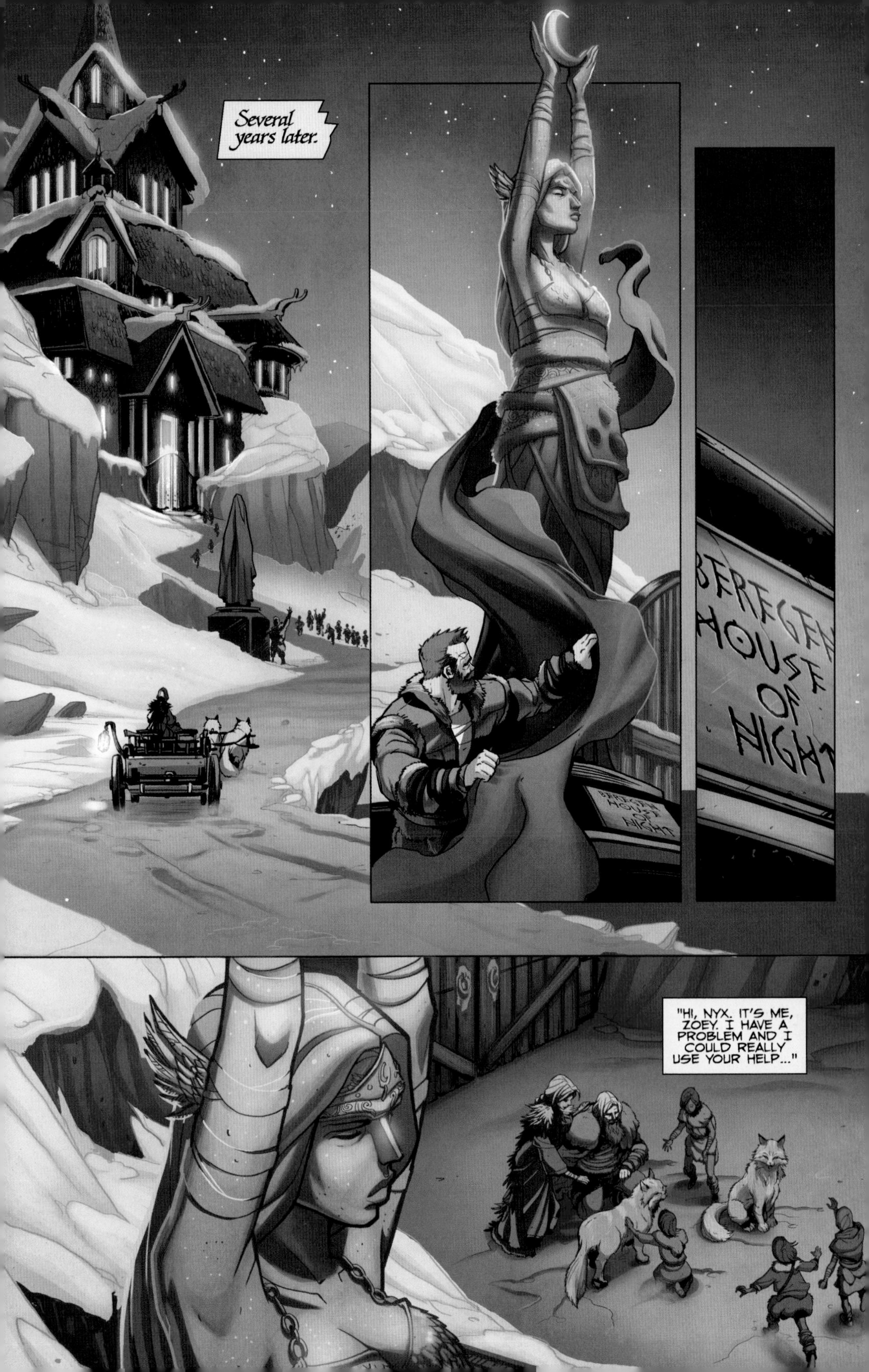
Several years later.
BERGEN HOUSE OF NIGHT
BERGEN HOUSE OF NIGHT
"HI, NYX. IT'S ME, ZOEY. I HAVE A PROBLEM AND I COULD REALLY USE YOUR HELP..."

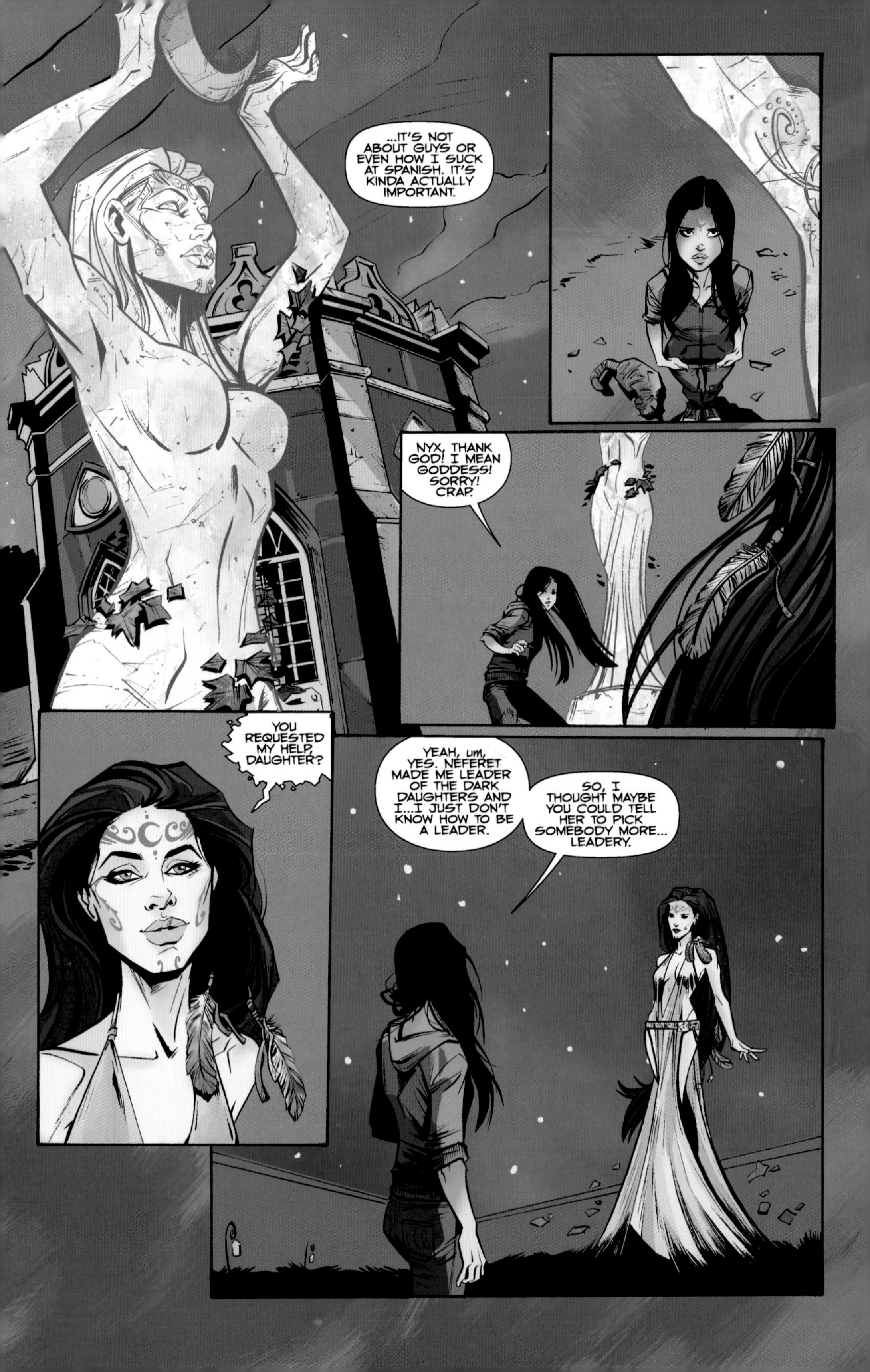
...IT'S NOT ABOUT GUYS OR EVEN HOW I SUCK AT SPANISH. IT'S KINDA ACTUALLY IMPORTANT.
NYX, THANK GOD! I MEAN GODDESS! SORRY! CRAP.
YOU REQUESTED MY HELP, DAUGHTER?
YEAH, um, YES. NEFERET MADE ME LEADER OF THE DARK DAUGHTERS AND I...I JUST DON'T KNOW HOW TO BE A LEADER.
SO, I THOUGHT MAYBE YOU COULD TELL HER TO PICK SOMEBODY MORE... LEADERY.

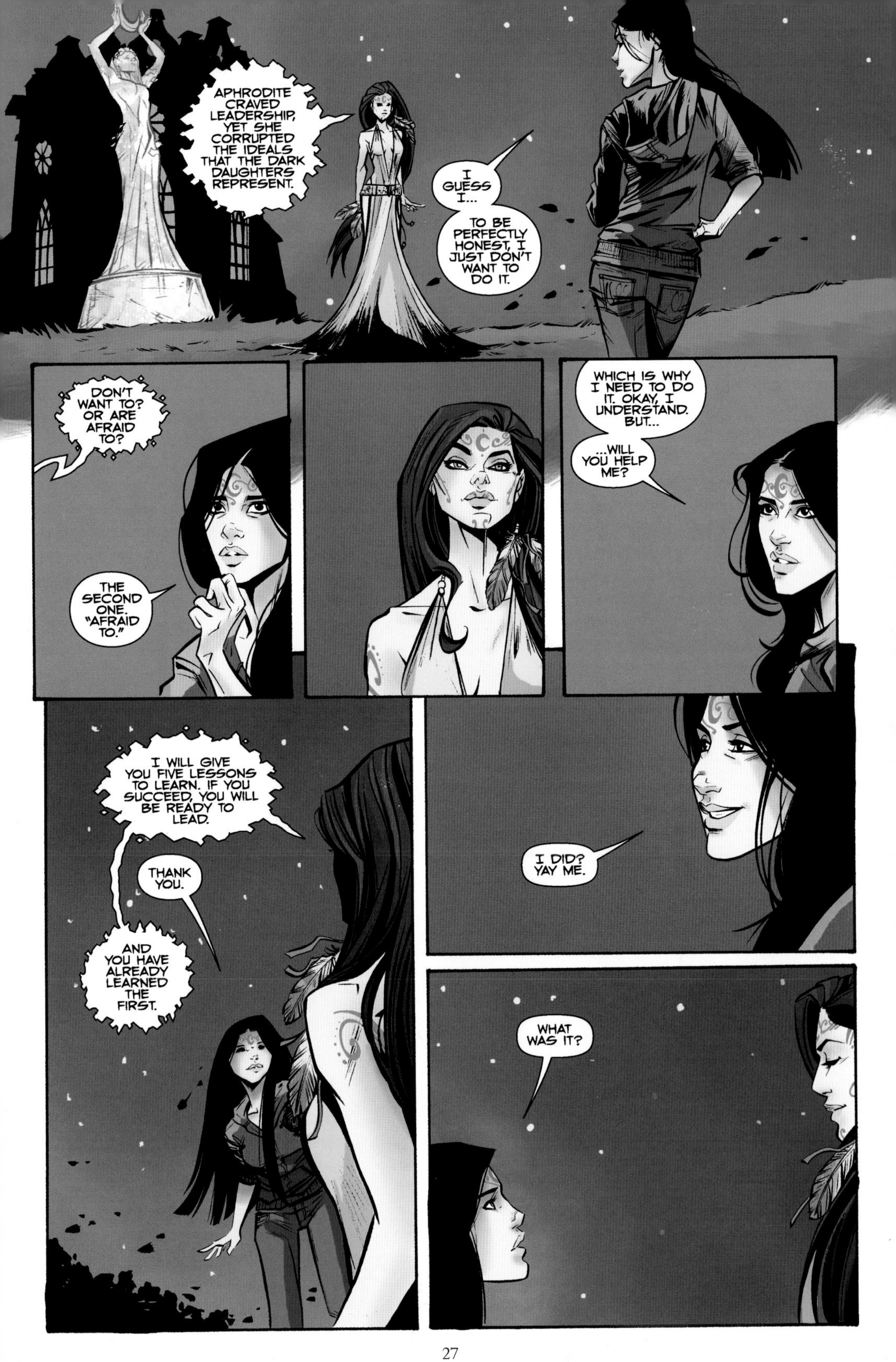
APHRODITE CRAVED LEADERSHIP, YET SHE CORRUPTED THE IDEALS THAT THE DARK DAUGHTERS REPRESENT.
I GUESS I...
TO BE PERFECTLY HONEST, I JUST DON'T WANT TO DO IT.
DON'T WANT TO? OR ARE AFRAID TO?
THE SECOND ONE. "AFRAID TO."
WHICH IS WHY I NEED TO DO IT. OKAY, I UNDERSTAND. BUT...
...WILL YOU HELP ME?
I WILL GIVE YOU FIVE LESSONS TO LEARN. IF YOU SUCCEED, YOU WILL BE READY TO LEAD.
THANK YOU.
AND YOU HAVE ALREADY LEARNED THE FIRST.
I DID? YAY ME.
WHAT WAS IT?

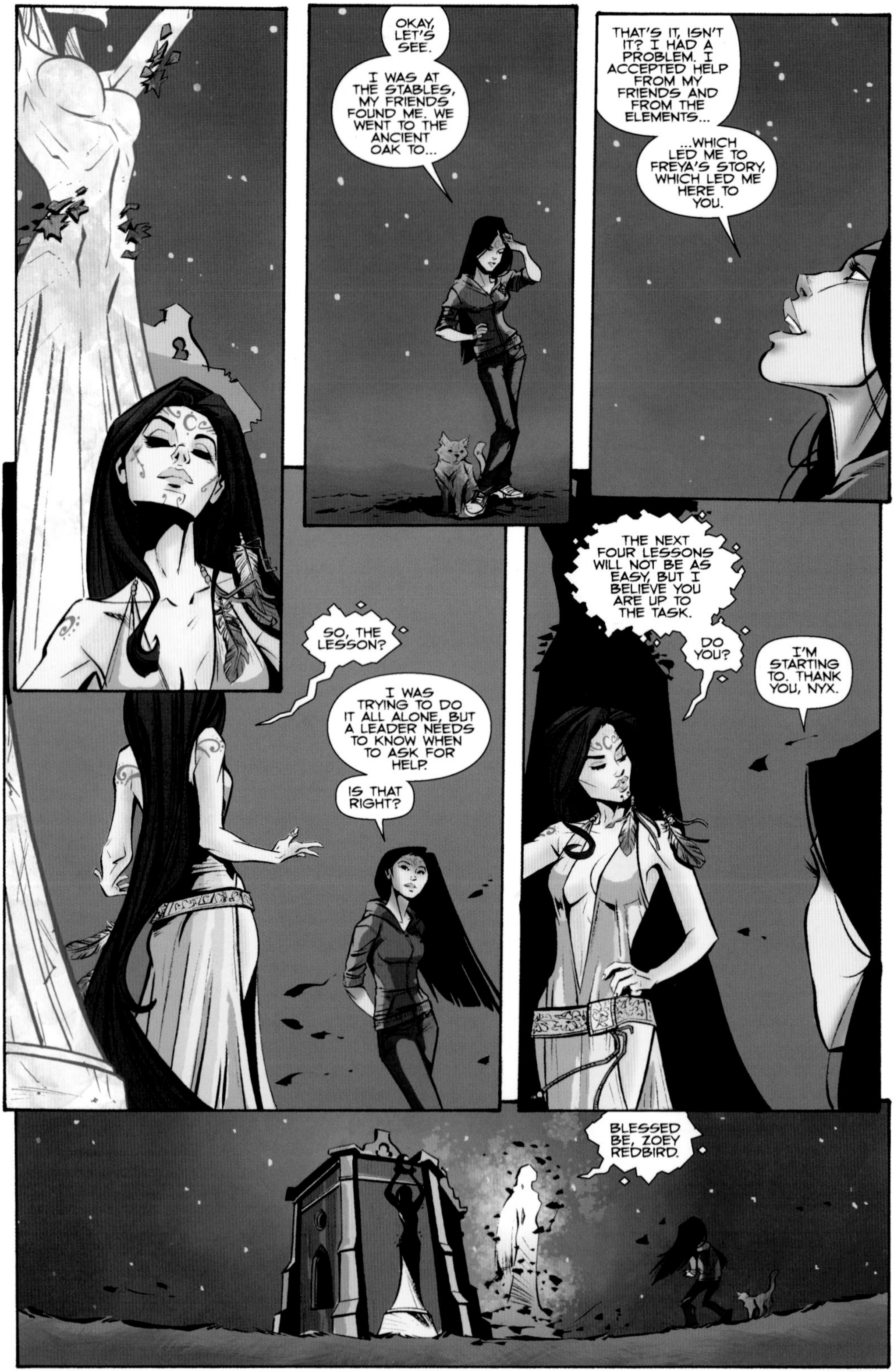

OKAY, LET'S SEE.
I WAS AT THE STABLES, MY FRIENDS FOUND ME. WE WENT TO THE ANCIENT OAK TO...
THAT'S IT, ISN'T IT? I HAD A PROBLEM. I ACCEPTED HELP FROM MY FRIENDS AND FROM THE ELEMENTS...
...WHICH LED ME TO FREYA'S STORY, WHICH LED ME HERE TO YOU.
SO, THE LESSON?
I WAS TRYING TO DO IT ALL ALONE, BUT A LEADER NEEDS TO KNOW WHEN TO ASK FOR HELP.
IS THAT RIGHT?
THE NEXT FOUR LESSONS WILL NOT BE AS EASY, BUT I BELIEVE YOU ARE UP TO THE TASK.
DO YOU?
I'M STARTING TO. THANK YOU, NYX.
BLESSED BE, ZOEY REDBIRD.

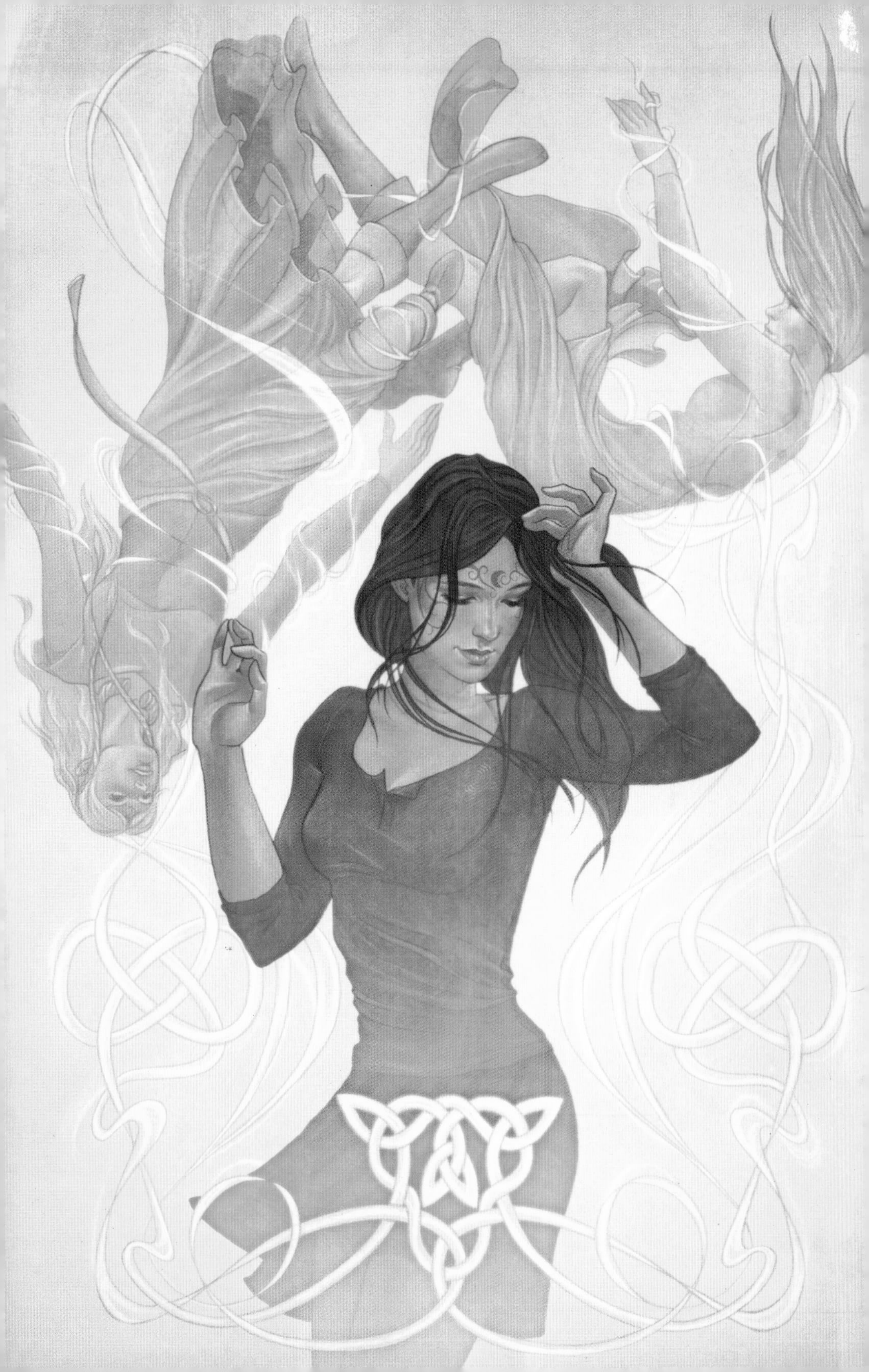

AIR

STORY BY
P. C. CAST
AND KRISTIN CAST

SCRIPT BY
KENT DALIAN

ART BY
JOËLLE JONES
AND JOSHUA COVEY

COLORS BY
RYAN HILL
AND DAN JACKSON

LETTERS BY
NATE PIEKOS OF BLAMBOT®

CHAPTER ILLUSTRATION BY
JENNY FRISON

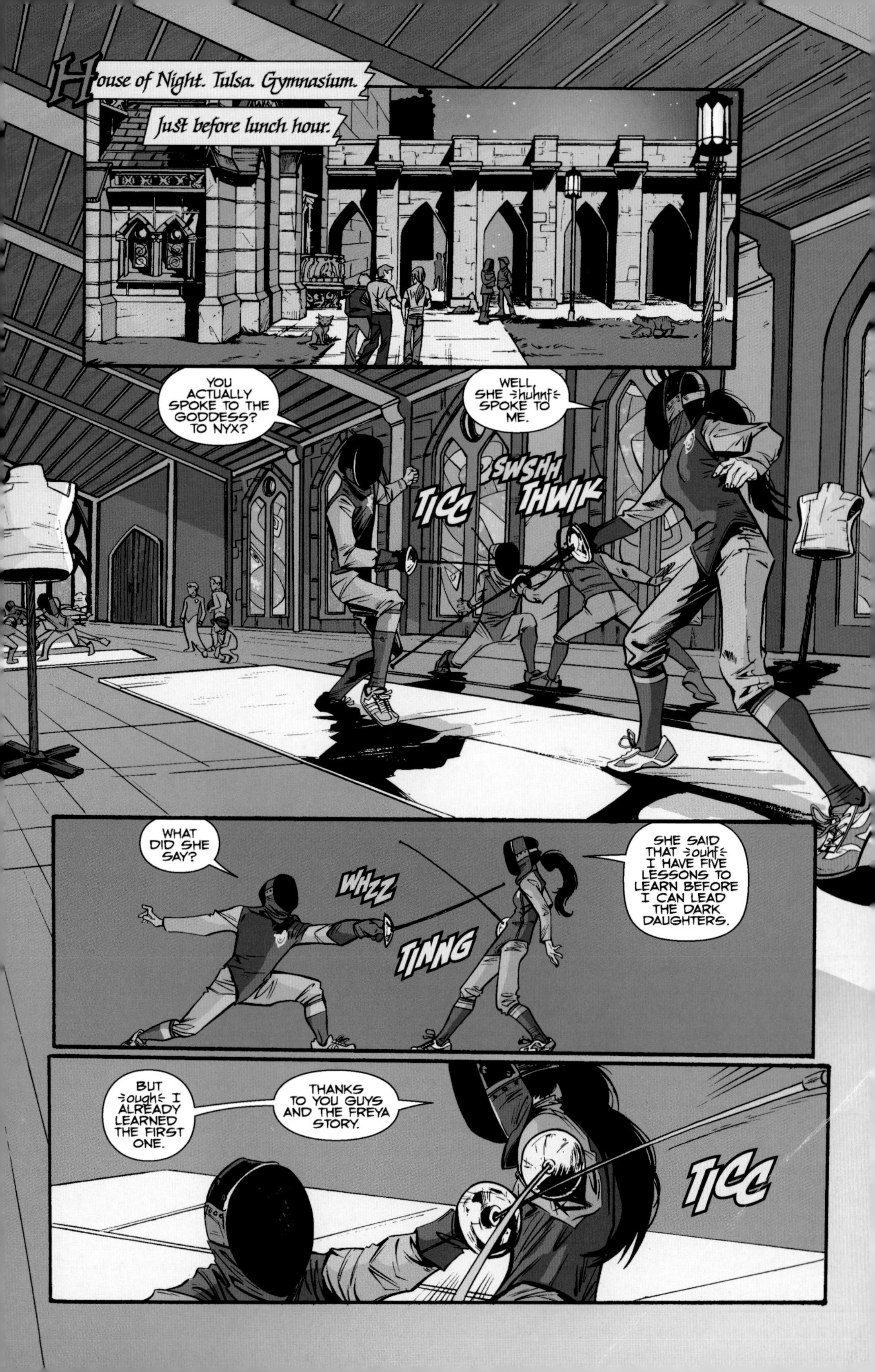
House of Night. Tulsa. Gymnasium.
Just before lunch hour.
YOU ACTUALLY SPOKE TO THE GODDESS? TO NYX?
WELL, SHE ≈huhnf≈ SPOKE TO ME.
SWSHH
TICC
THWIK
WHAT DID SHE SAY?
SHE SAID THAT ≈ouhf≈ I HAVE FIVE LESSONS TO LEARN BEFORE I CAN LEAD THE DARK DAUGHTERS.
WHZZ
TINNG
BUT ≈ough≈ I ALREADY LEARNED THE FIRST ONE.
THANKS TO YOU GUYS AND THE FREYA STORY.
TICC

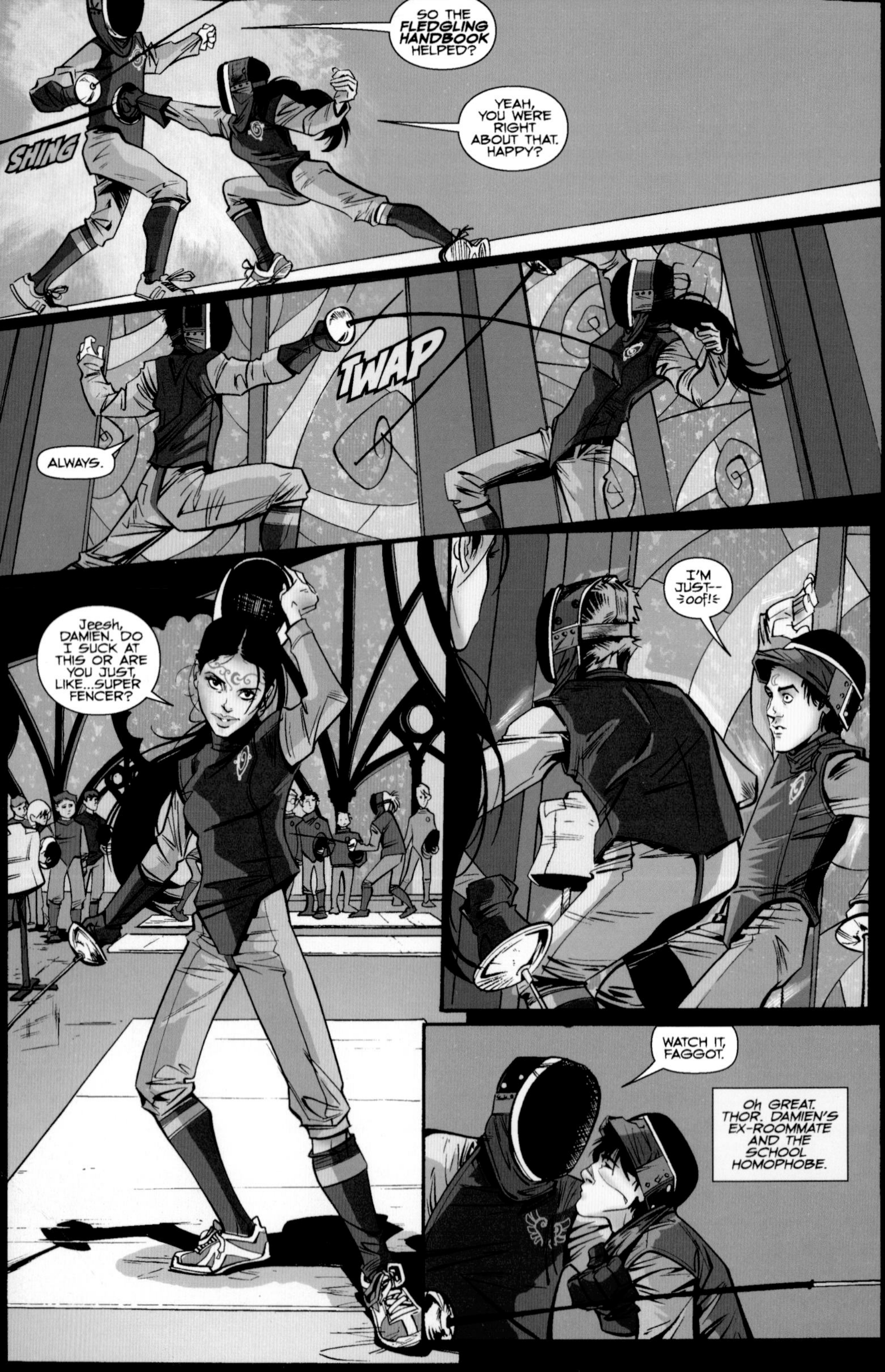

SO THE FLEDGLING HANDBOOK HELPED?
SHING
YEAH, YOU WERE RIGHT ABOUT THAT. HAPPY?
TWAP
ALWAYS.
Jeesh, DAMIEN. DO I SUCK AT THIS OR ARE YOU JUST, LIKE...SUPER FENCER?
I'M JUST-- oof!
WATCH IT, FAGGOT.
Oh GREAT. THOR. DAMIEN'S EX-ROOMMATE AND THE SCHOOL HOMOPHOBE.

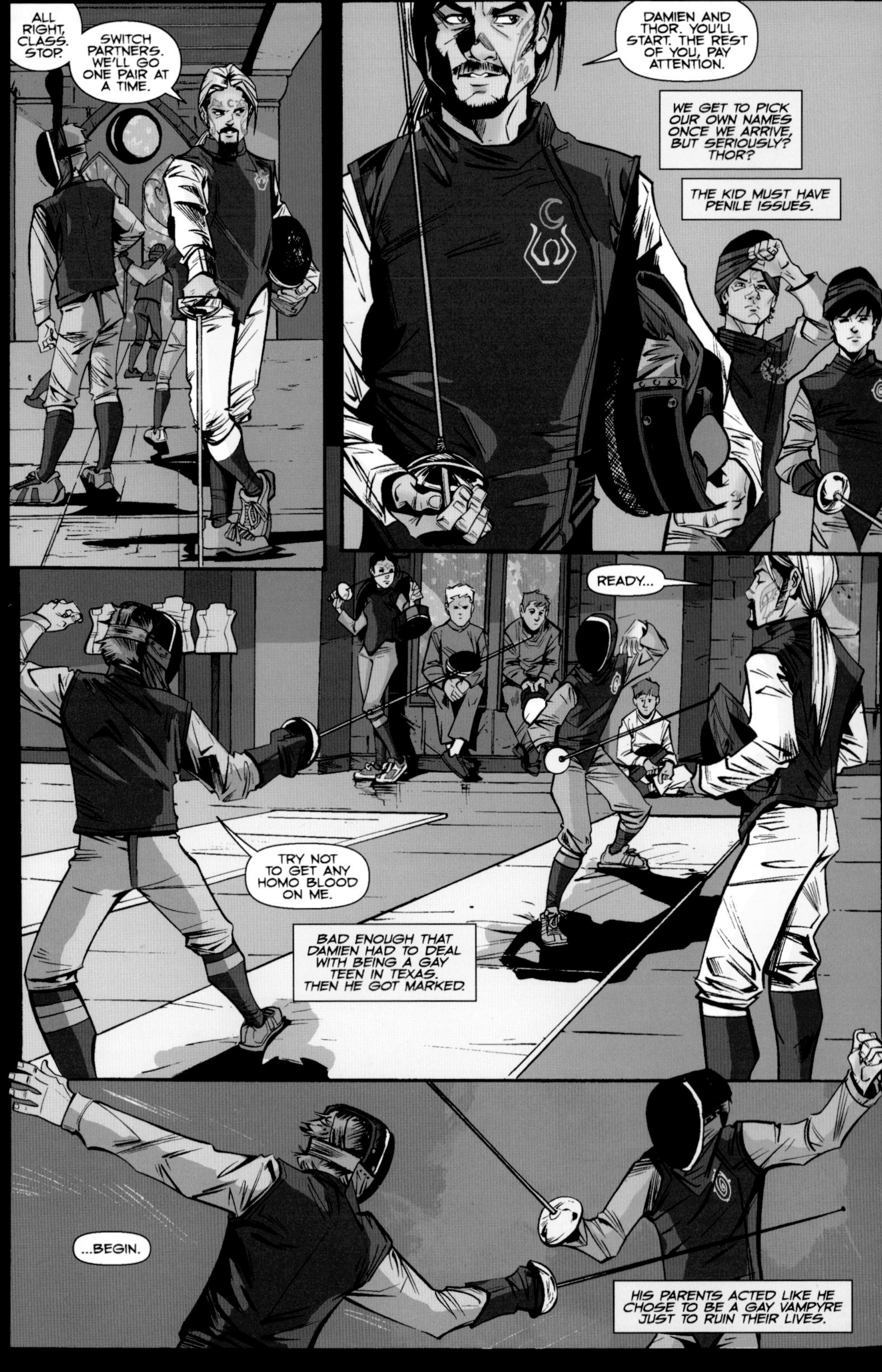
ALL RIGHT, CLASS. STOP.
SWITCH PARTNERS. WE'LL GO ONE PAIR AT A TIME.
DAMIEN AND THOR. YOU'LL START. THE REST OF YOU, PAY ATTENTION.
WE GET TO PICK OUR OWN NAMES ONCE WE ARRIVE, BUT SERIOUSLY? THOR?
THE KID MUST HAVE PENILE ISSUES.
READY...
TRY NOT TO GET ANY HOMO BLOOD ON ME.
BAD ENOUGH THAT DAMIEN HAD TO DEAL WITH BEING A GAY TEEN IN TEXAS. THEN HE GOT MARKED.
...BEGIN.
HIS PARENTS ACTED LIKE HE CHOSE TO BE A GAY VAMPYRE JUST TO RUIN THEIR LIVES.

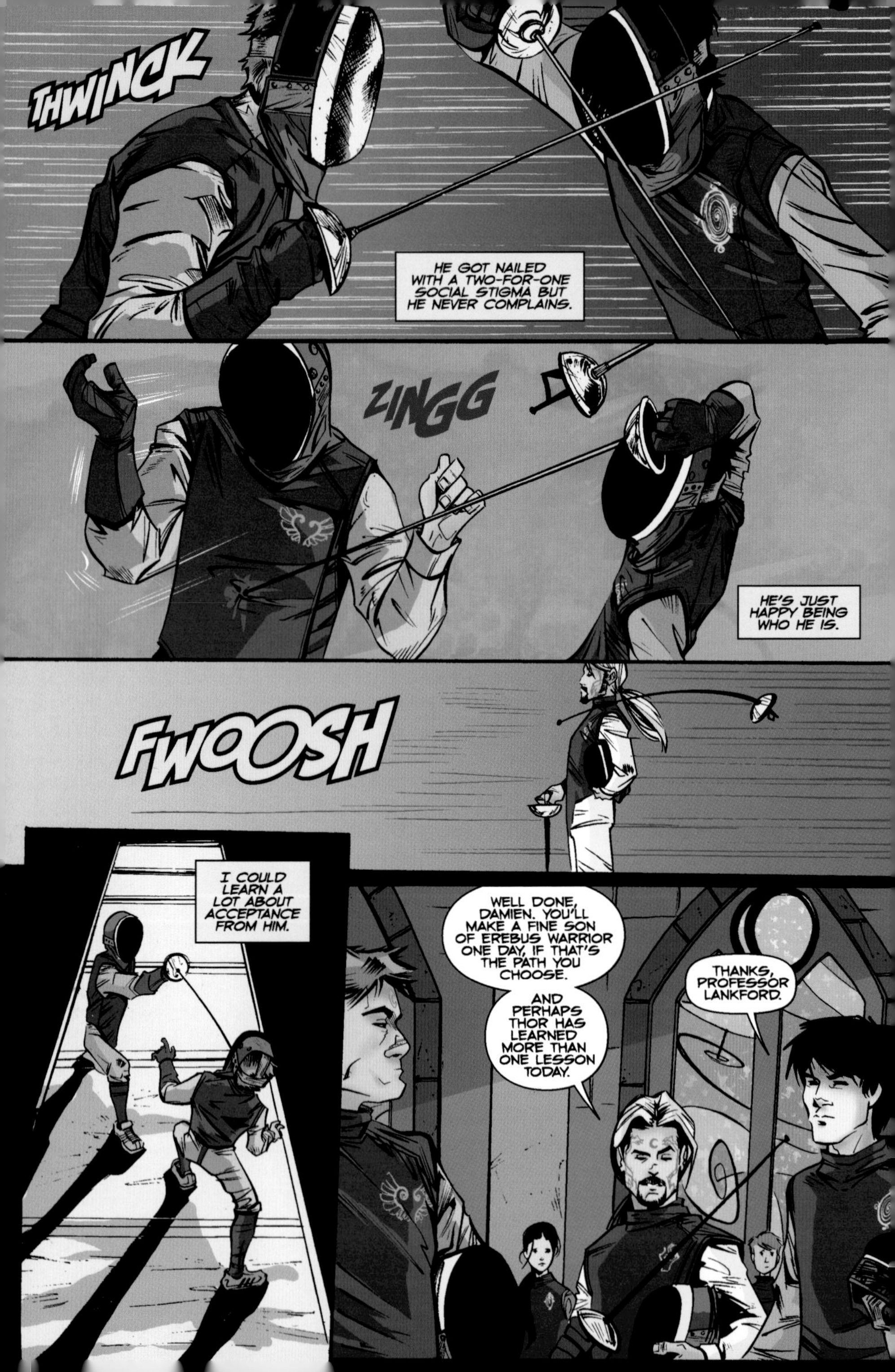
THWINCK
HE GOT NAILED WITH A TWO-FOR-ONE SOCIAL STIGMA BUT HE NEVER COMPLAINS.
ZINGG
HE'S JUST HAPPY BEING WHO HE IS.
FWOOSH
I COULD LEARN A LOT ABOUT ACCEPTANCE FROM HIM.
WELL DONE, DAMIEN. YOU'LL MAKE A FINE SON OF EREBUS WARRIOR ONE DAY, IF THAT'S THE PATH YOU CHOOSE.
AND PERHAPS THOR HAS LEARNED MORE THAN ONE LESSON TODAY.
THANKS, PROFESSOR LANKFORD.

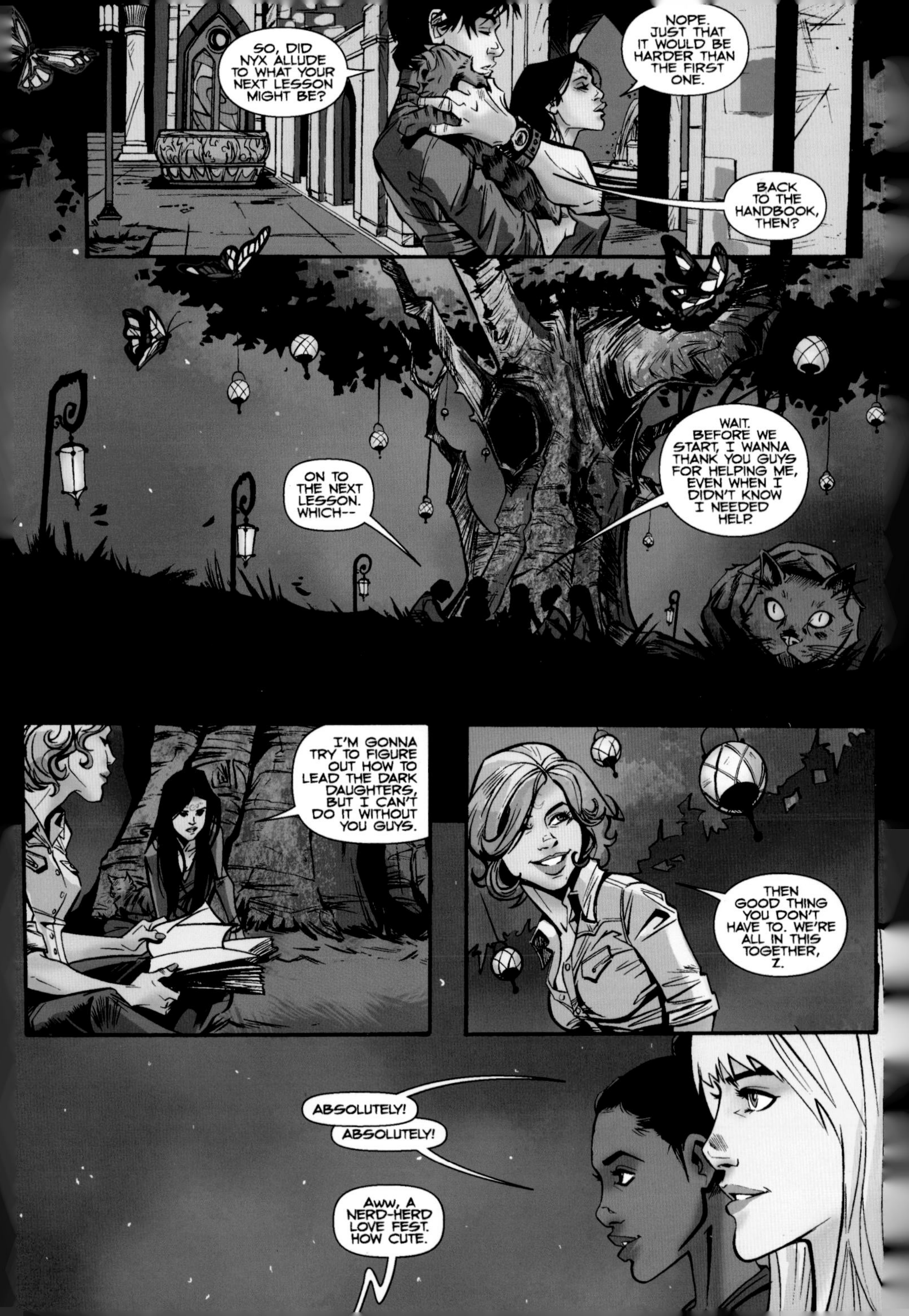
SO, DID NYX ALLUDE TO WHAT YOUR NEXT LESSON MIGHT BE?
NOPE. JUST THAT IT WOULD BE HARDER THAN THE FIRST ONE.
BACK TO THE HANDBOOK, THEN?
ON TO THE NEXT LESSON. WHICH--
WAIT. BEFORE WE START, I WANNA THANK YOU GUYS FOR HELPING ME, EVEN WHEN I DIDN'T KNOW I NEEDED HELP.
I'M GONNA TRY TO FIGURE OUT HOW TO LEAD THE DARK DAUGHTERS, BUT I CAN'T DO IT WITHOUT YOU GUYS.
THEN GOOD THING YOU DON'T HAVE TO. WE'RE ALL IN THIS TOGETHER, Z.
ABSOLUTELY!
ABSOLUTELY!
AWW, A NERD-HERD LOVE FEST. HOW CUTE.

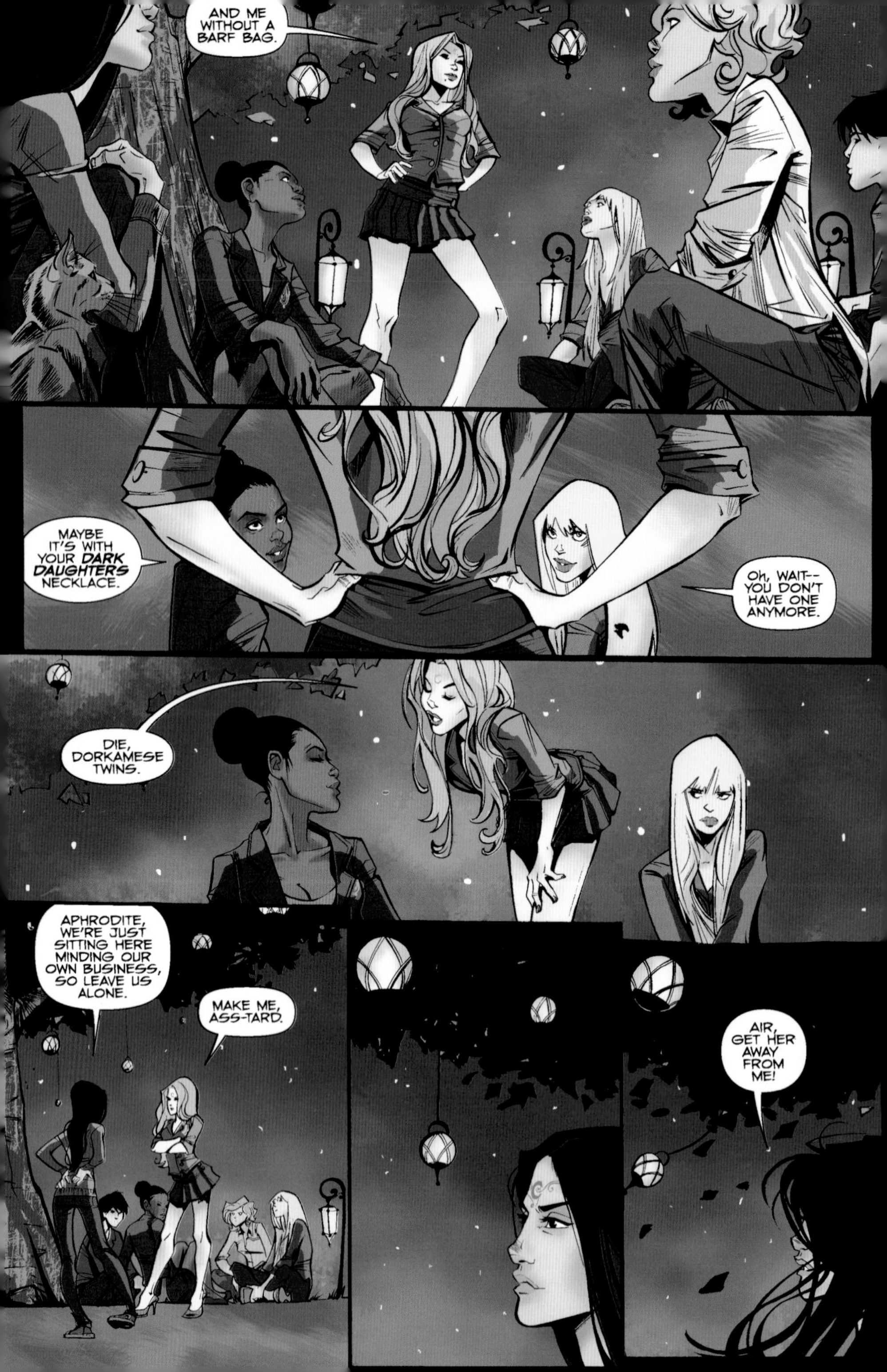
AND ME WITHOUT A BARF BAG.
MAYBE IT'S WITH YOUR **DARK DAUGHTERS** NECKLACE.
Oh, WAIT-- YOU DON'T HAVE ONE ANYMORE.
DIE, DORKAMESE TWINS.
APHRODITE, WE'RE JUST SITTING HERE MINDING OUR OWN BUSINESS, SO LEAVE US ALONE.
MAKE ME, ASS-TARD.
AIR, GET HER AWAY FROM ME!

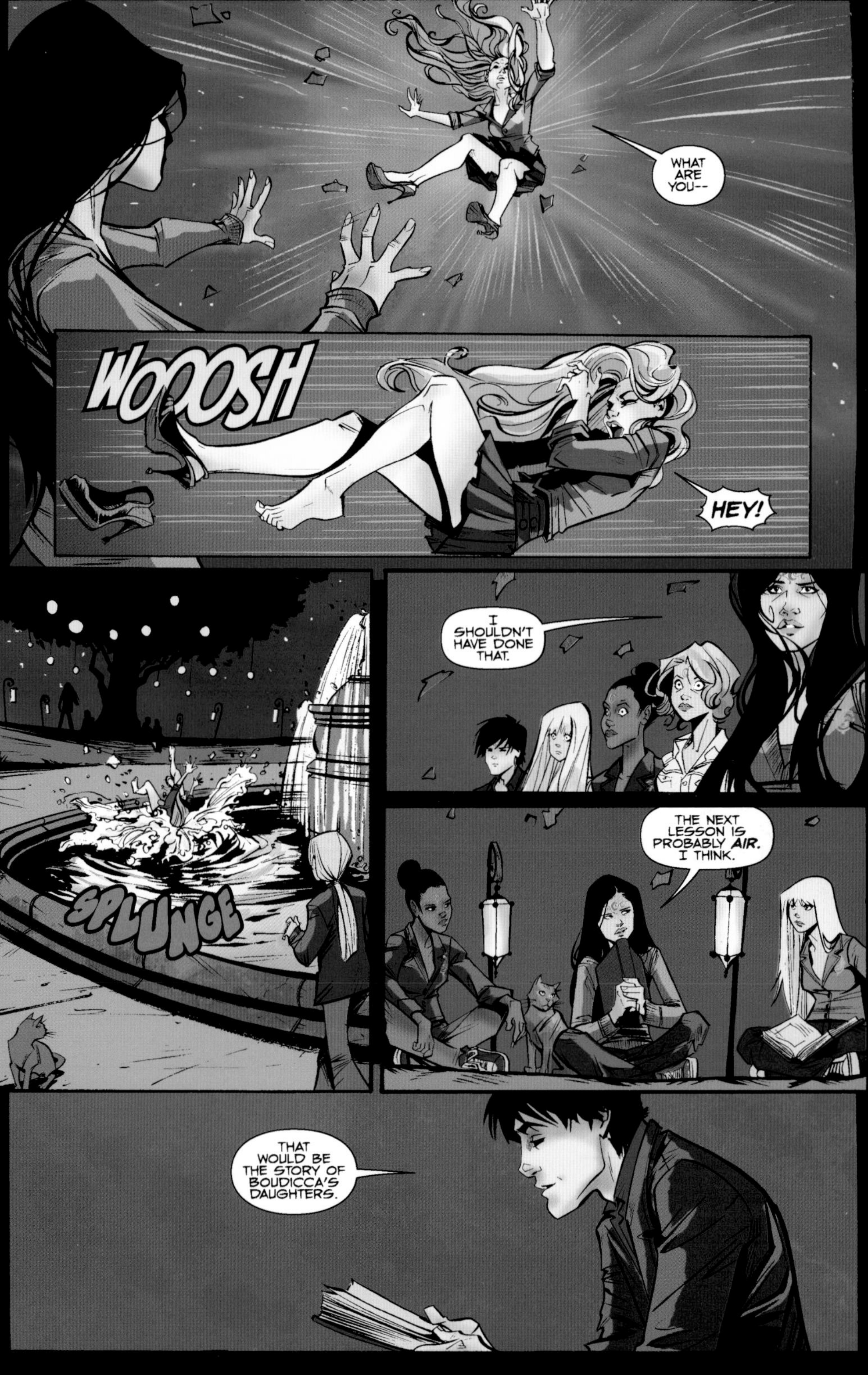
WHAT ARE YOU--
WOOOSH
HEY!
SPLUNGE
I SHOULDN'T HAVE DONE THAT.
THE NEXT LESSON IS PROBABLY AIR. I THINK.
THAT WOULD BE THE STORY OF BOUDICCA'S DAUGHTERS.

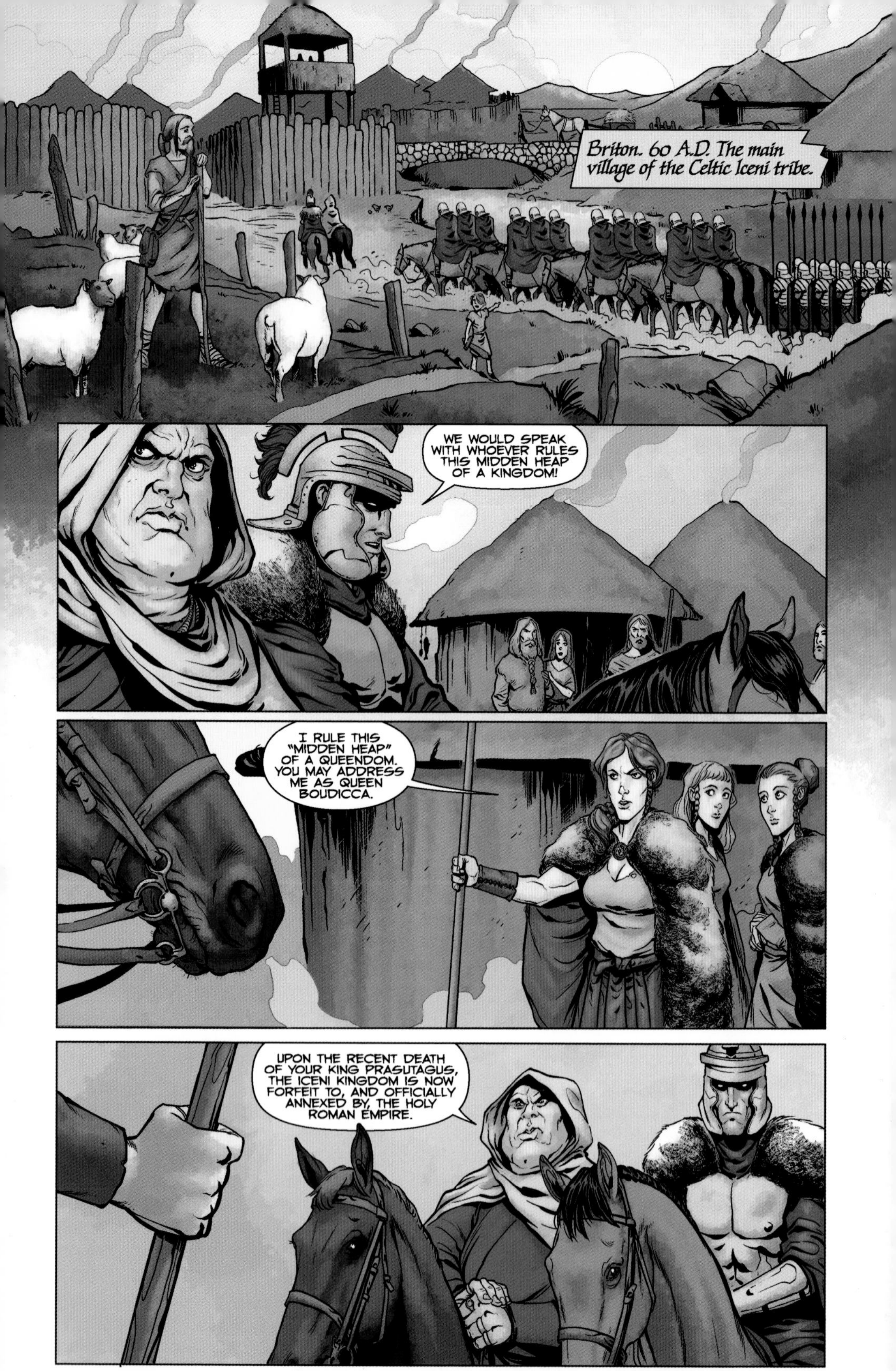

Briton. 60 A.D. The main village of the Celtic Iceni tribe.
WE WOULD SPEAK WITH WHOEVER RULES THIS MIDDEN HEAP OF A KINGDOM!
I RULE THIS "MIDDEN HEAP" OF A QUEENDOM. YOU MAY ADDRESS ME AS QUEEN BOUDICCA.
UPON THE RECENT DEATH OF YOUR KING PRASUTAGUS, THE ICENI KINGDOM IS NOW FORFEIT TO, AND OFFICIALLY ANNEXED BY, THE HOLY ROMAN EMPIRE.

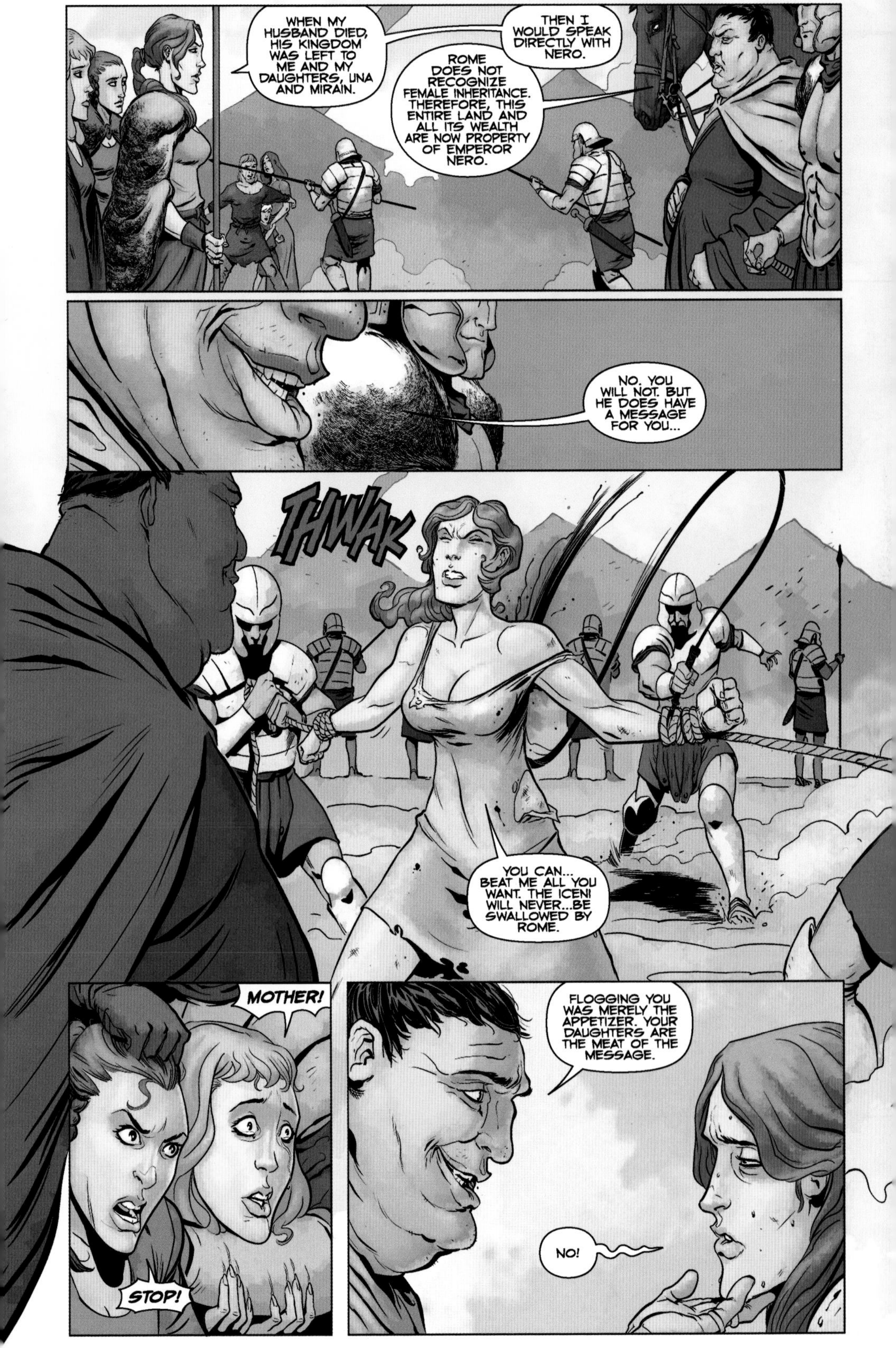
WHEN MY HUSBAND DIED, HIS KINGDOM WAS LEFT TO ME AND MY DAUGHTERS, UNA AND MIRAIN.
ROME DOES NOT RECOGNIZE FEMALE INHERITANCE. THEREFORE, THIS ENTIRE LAND AND ALL ITS WEALTH ARE NOW PROPERTY OF EMPEROR NERO.
THEN I WOULD SPEAK DIRECTLY WITH NERO.
NO. YOU WILL NOT. BUT HE DOES HAVE A MESSAGE FOR YOU...
THWAK
YOU CAN... BEAT ME ALL YOU WANT. THE ICENI WILL NEVER...BE SWALLOWED BY ROME.
MOTHER!
STOP!
FLOGGING YOU WAS MERELY THE APPETIZER. YOUR DAUGHTERS ARE THE MEAT OF THE MESSAGE.
NO!

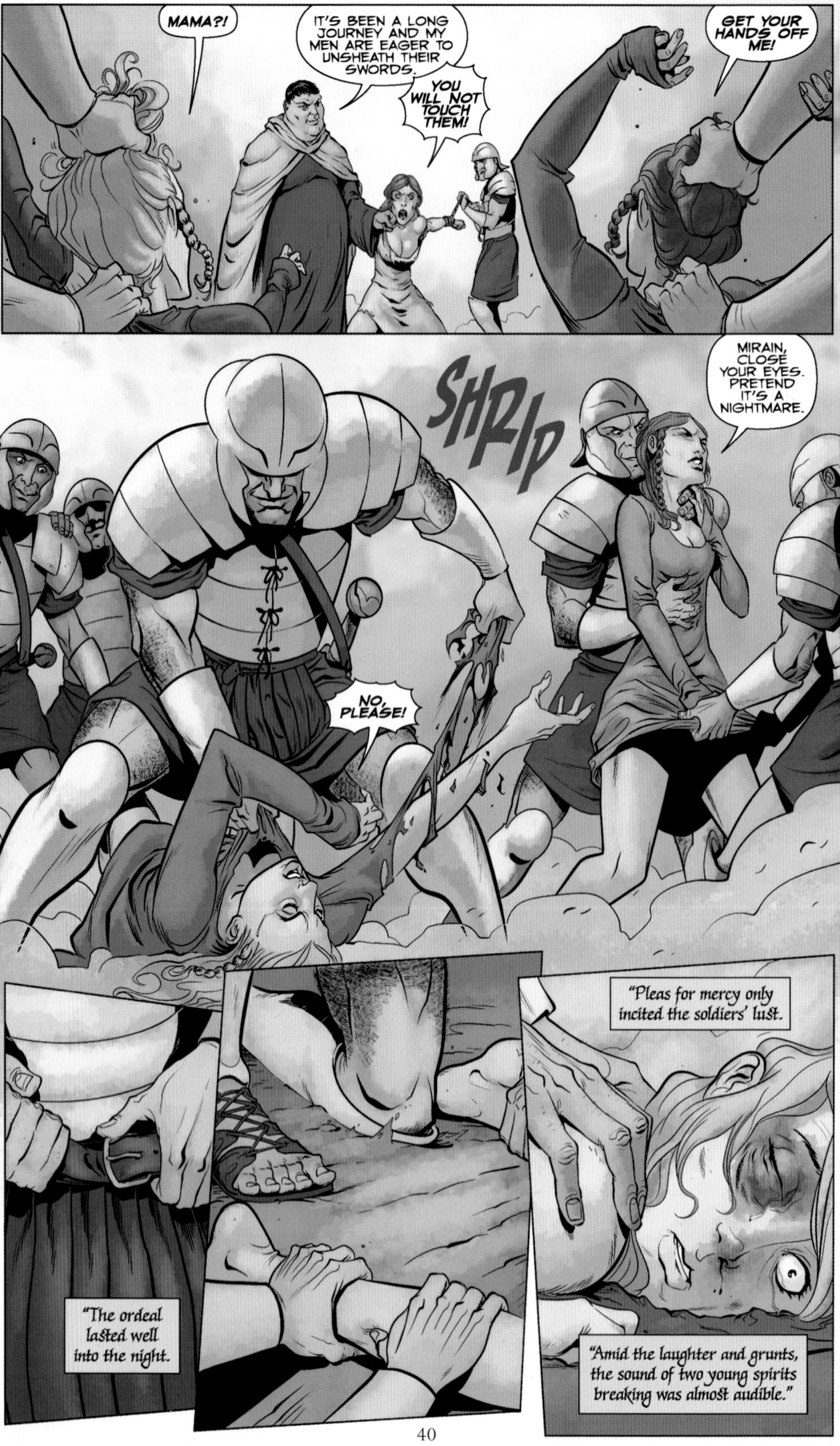
MAMA?!
IT'S BEEN A LONG JOURNEY AND MY MEN ARE EAGER TO UNSHEATH THEIR SWORDS.
YOU WILL NOT TOUCH THEM!
GET YOUR HANDS OFF ME!
SHRIP
MIRAIN, CLOSE YOUR EYES. PRETEND IT'S A NIGHTMARE.
NO, PLEASE!
"The ordeal lasted well into the night.
"Pleas for mercy only incited the soldiers' lust.
"Amid the laughter and grunts, the sound of two young spirits breaking was almost audible."

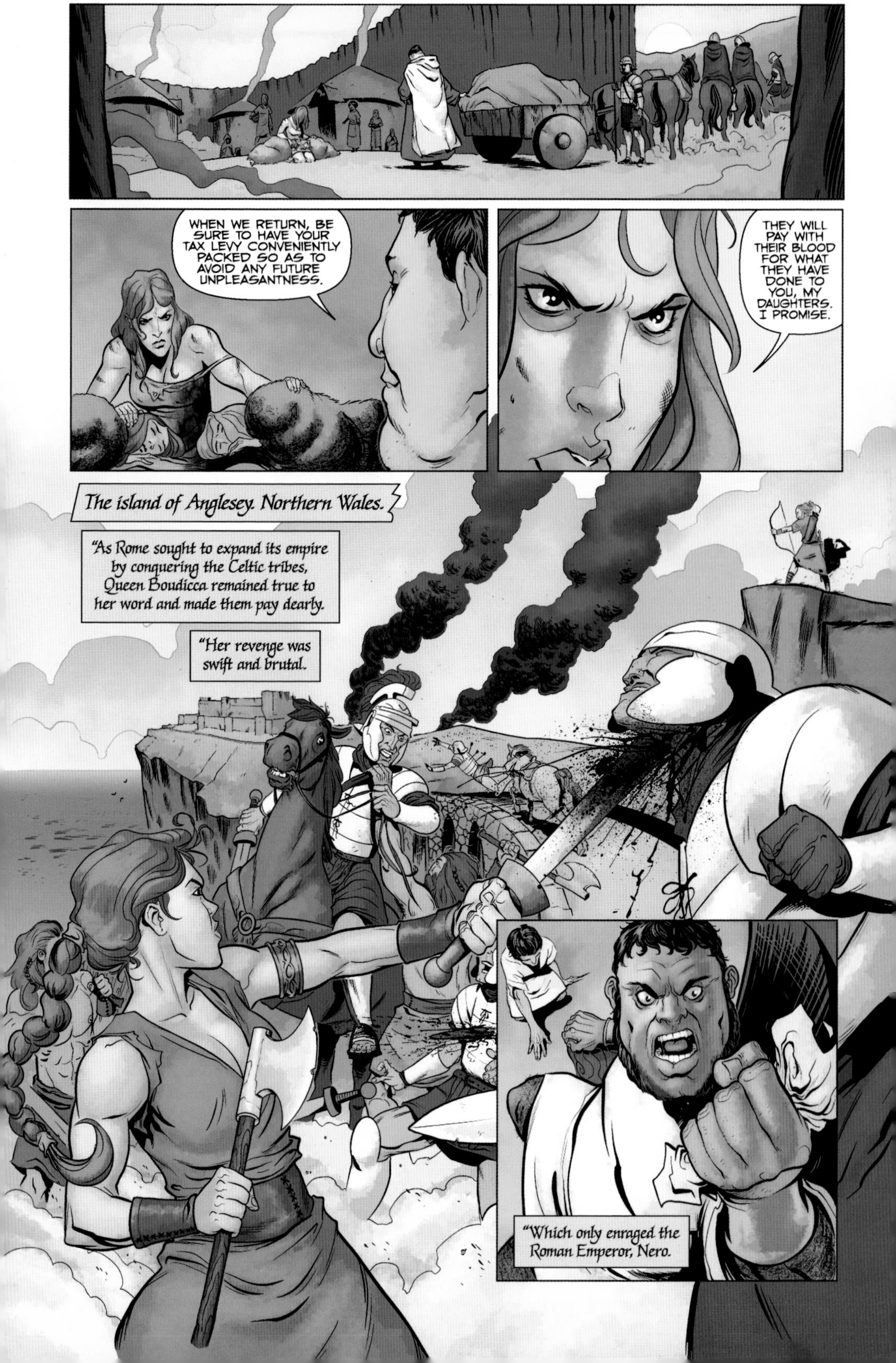
WHEN WE RETURN, BE SURE TO HAVE YOUR TAX LEVY CONVENIENTLY PACKED SO AS TO AVOID ANY FUTURE UNPLEASANTNESS.
THEY WILL PAY WITH THEIR BLOOD FOR WHAT THEY HAVE DONE TO YOU, MY DAUGHTERS. I PROMISE.
The island of Anglesey. Northern Wales.
"As Rome sought to expand its empire by conquering the Celtic tribes, Queen Boudicca remained true to her word and made them pay dearly.
"Her revenge was swift and brutal.
"Which only enraged the Roman Emperor, Nero.

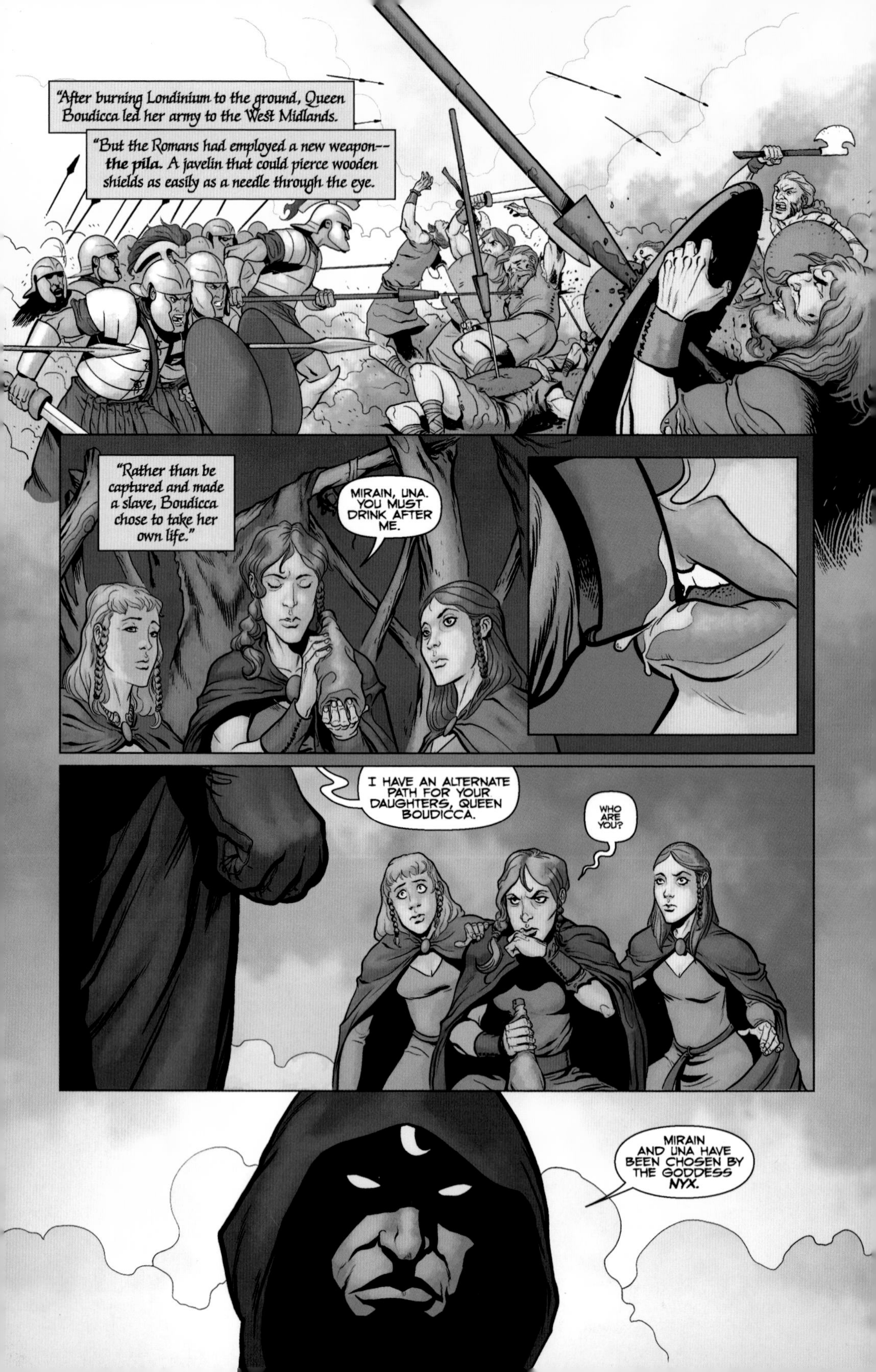
"After burning Londinium to the ground, Queen Boudicca led her army to the West Midlands.
"But the Romans had employed a new weapon-- the pila. A javelin that could pierce wooden shields as easily as a needle through the eye.
"Rather than be captured and made a slave, Boudicca chose to take her own life."
MIRAIN, UNA. YOU MUST DRINK AFTER ME.
I HAVE AN ALTERNATE PATH FOR YOUR DAUGHTERS, QUEEN BOUDICCA.
WHO ARE YOU?
MIRAIN AND UNA HAVE BEEN CHOSEN BY THE GODDESS NYX.

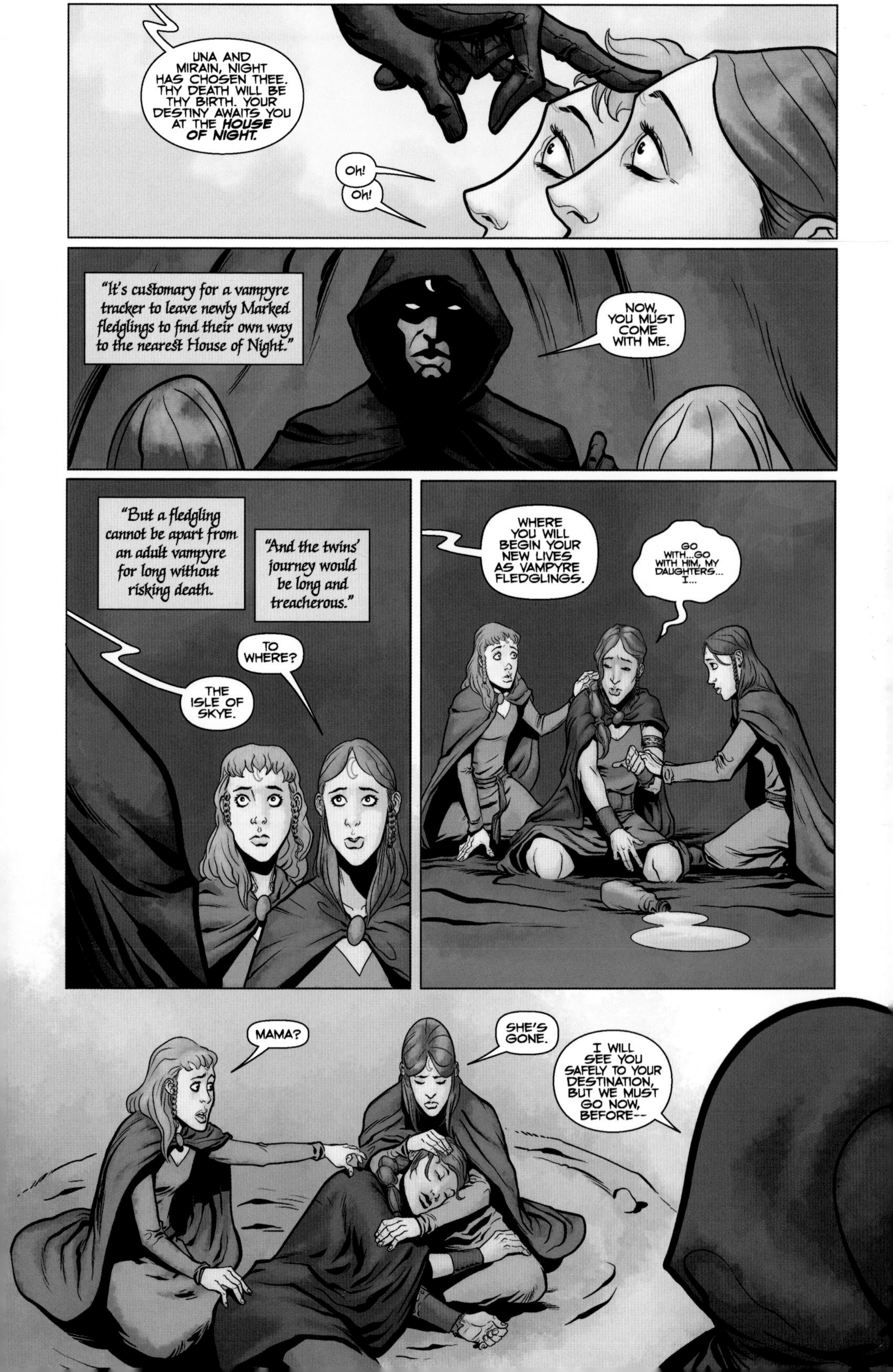
UNA AND MIRAIN, NIGHT HAS CHOSEN THEE. THY DEATH WILL BE THY BIRTH. YOUR DESTINY AWAITS YOU AT THE HOUSE OF NIGHT.
Oh!
Oh!
"It's customary for a vampyre tracker to leave newly Marked fledglings to find their own way to the nearest House of Night."
NOW, YOU MUST COME WITH ME.
"But a fledgling cannot be apart from an adult vampyre for long without risking death.
"And the twins' journey would be long and treacherous."
TO WHERE?
THE ISLE OF SKYE.
WHERE YOU WILL BEGIN YOUR NEW LIVES AS VAMPYRE FLEDGLINGS.
GO WITH...GO WITH HIM, MY DAUGHTERS... I...
MAMA?
SHE'S GONE.
I WILL SEE YOU SAFELY TO YOUR DESTINATION, BUT WE MUST GO NOW, BEFORE--

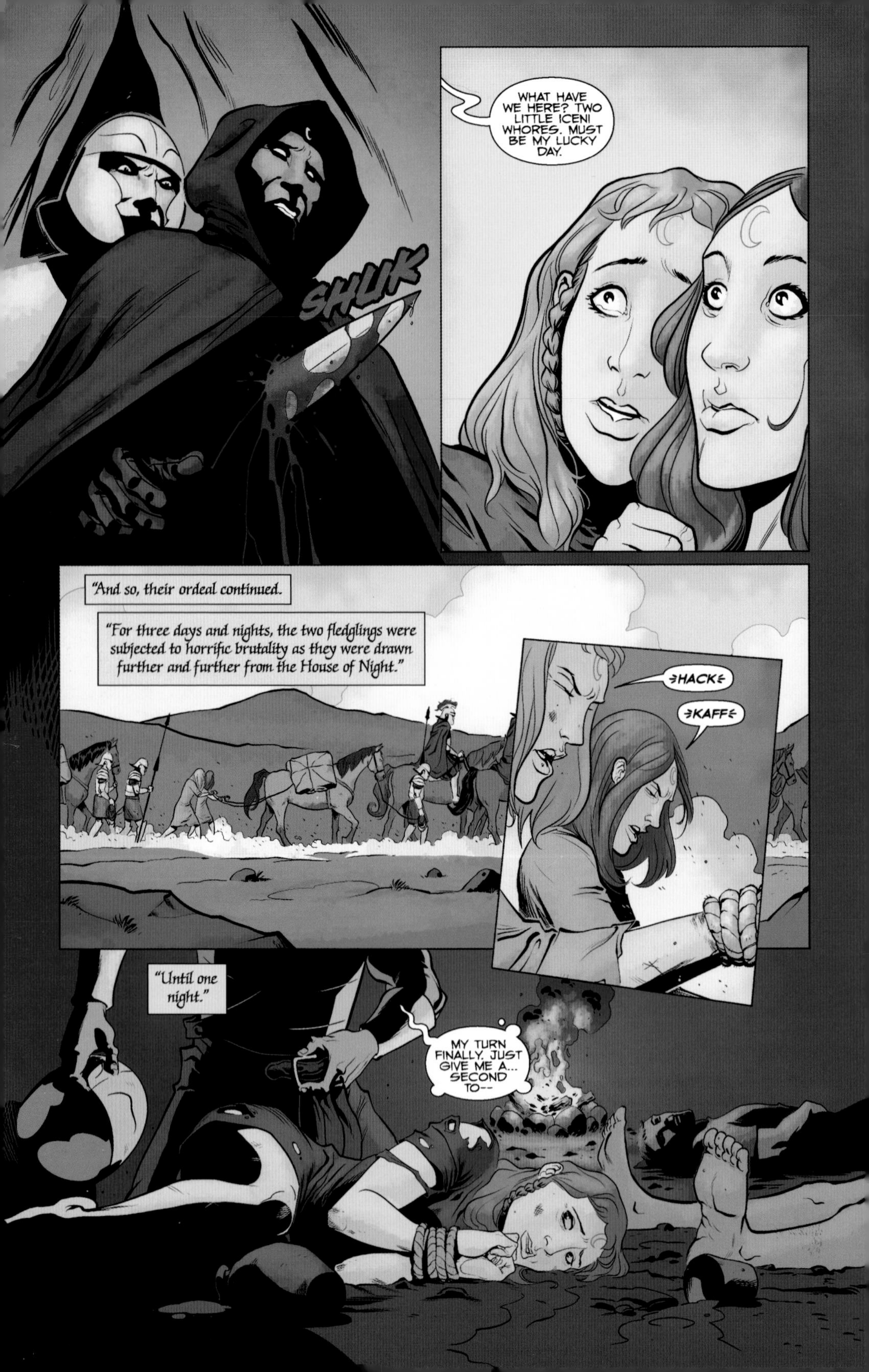
SHUK
WHAT HAVE WE HERE? TWO LITTLE ICENI WHORES. MUST BE MY LUCKY DAY.
"And so, their ordeal continued.
"For three days and nights, the two fledglings were subjected to horrific brutality as they were drawn further and further from the House of Night."
HACK
KAFF
"Until one night."
MY TURN FINALLY. JUST GIVE ME A... SECOND TO--

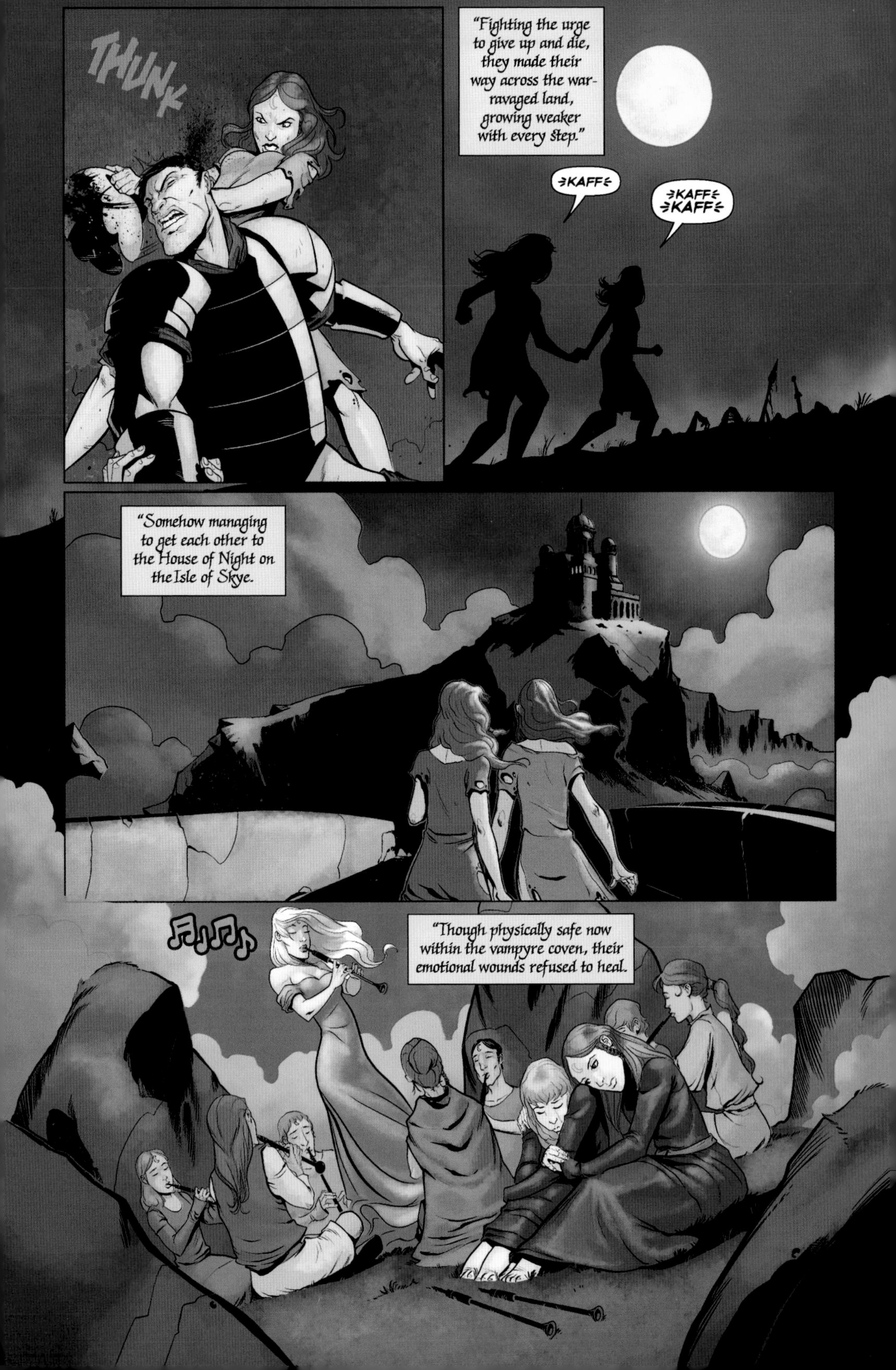
THUNK
"Fighting the urge to give up and die, they made their way across the war-ravaged land, growing weaker with every step."
KAFF
KAFF KAFF
"Somehow managing to get each other to the House of Night on the Isle of Skye.
"Though physically safe now within the vampyre coven, their emotional wounds refused to heal.

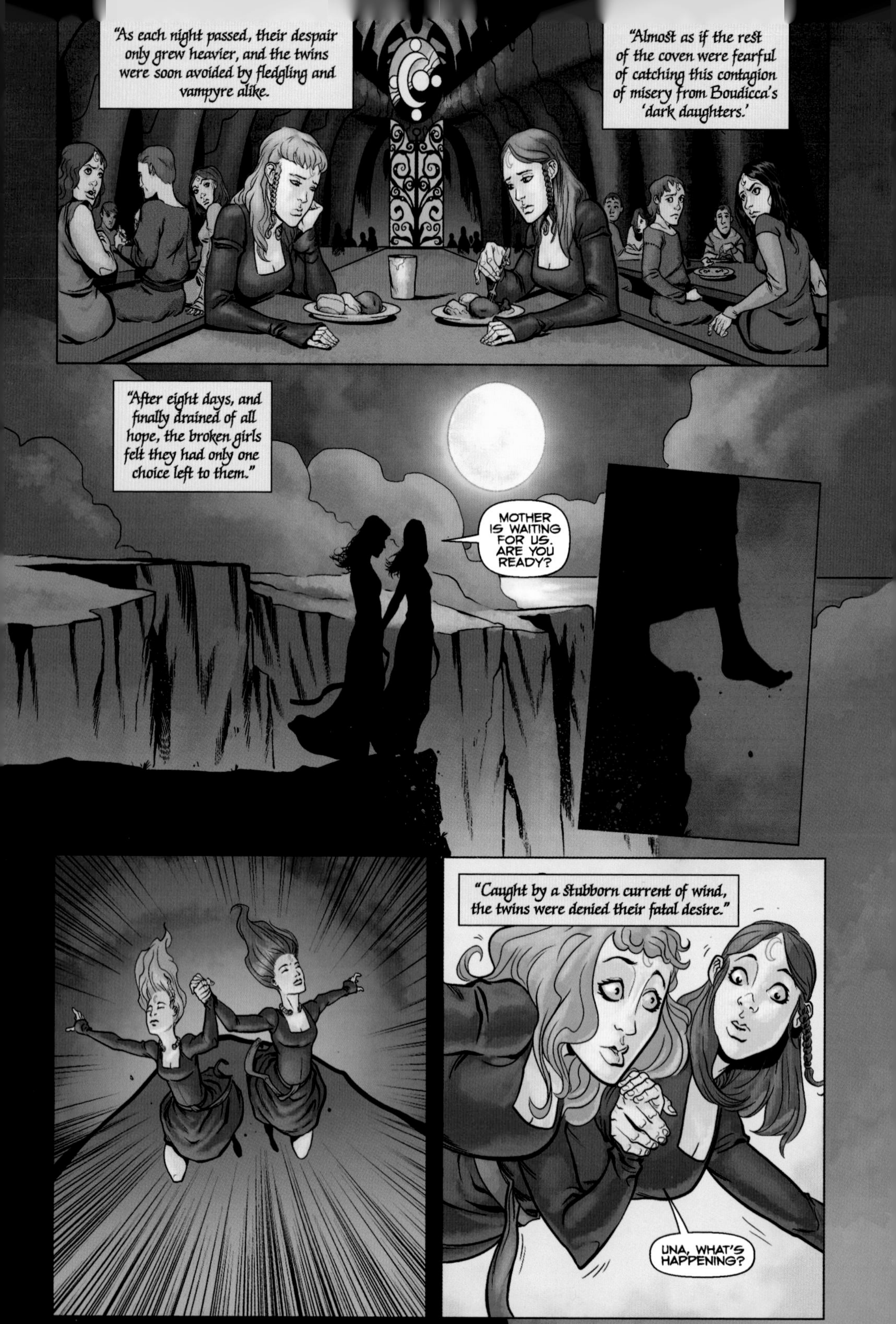
"As each night passed, their despair only grew heavier, and the twins were soon avoided by fledgling and vampyre alike.
"Almost as if the rest of the coven were fearful of catching this contagion of misery from Boudicca's 'dark daughters.'
"After eight days, and finally drained of all hope, the broken girls felt they had only one choice left to them."
MOTHER IS WAITING FOR US. ARE YOU READY?
"Caught by a stubborn current of wind, the twins were denied their fatal desire."
UNA, WHAT'S HAPPENING?

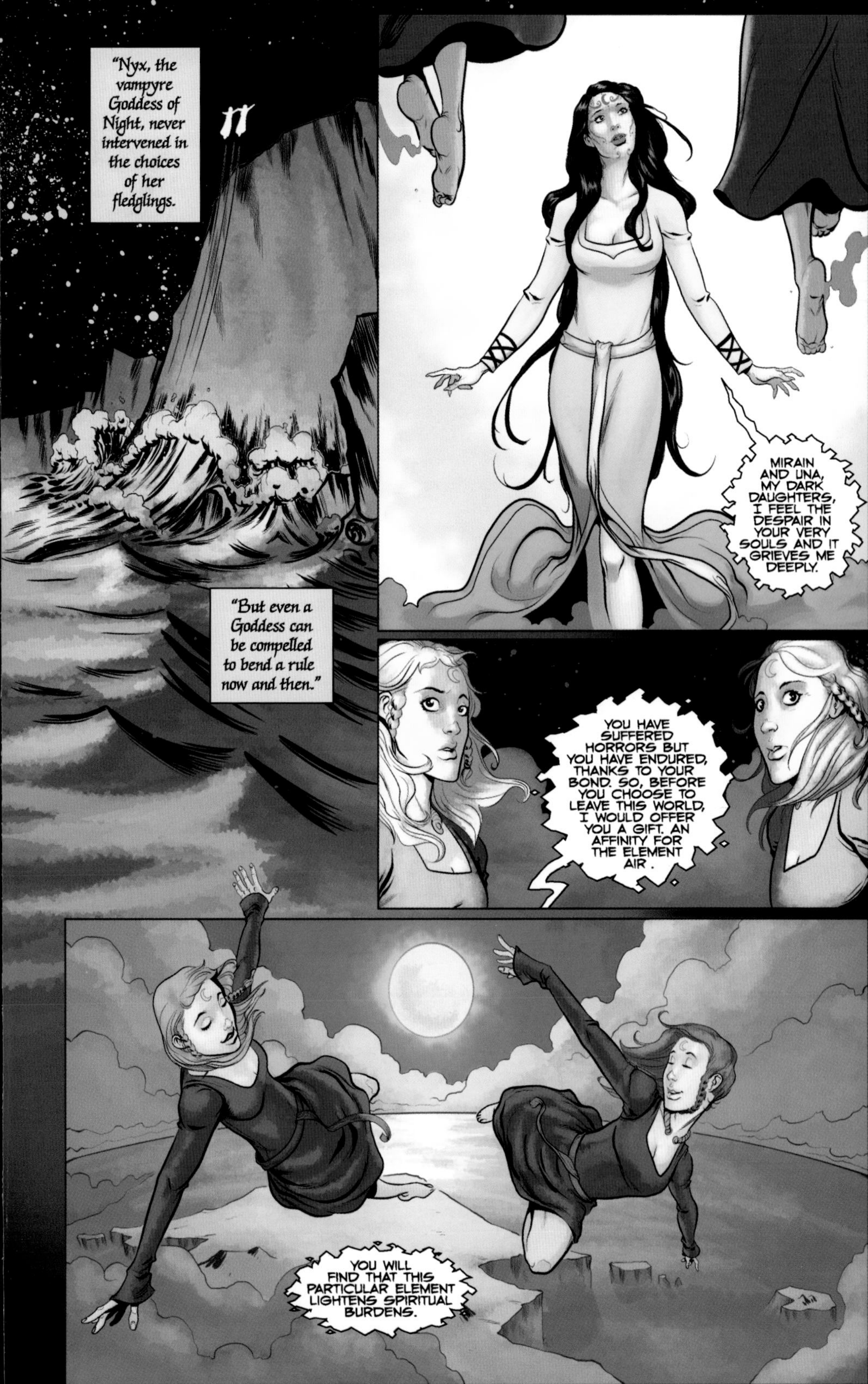
"Nyx, the vampyre Goddess of Night, never intervened in the choices of her fledglings.
"But even a Goddess can be compelled to bend a rule now and then."
MIRAIN AND UNA, MY DARK DAUGHTERS, I FEEL THE DESPAIR IN YOUR VERY SOULS AND IT GRIEVES ME DEEPLY.
YOU HAVE SUFFERED HORRORS BUT YOU HAVE ENDURED, THANKS TO YOUR BOND. SO, BEFORE YOU CHOOSE TO LEAVE THIS WORLD, I WOULD OFFER YOU A GIFT. AN AFFINITY FOR THE ELEMENT AIR.
YOU WILL FIND THAT THIS PARTICULAR ELEMENT LIGHTENS SPIRITUAL BURDENS.

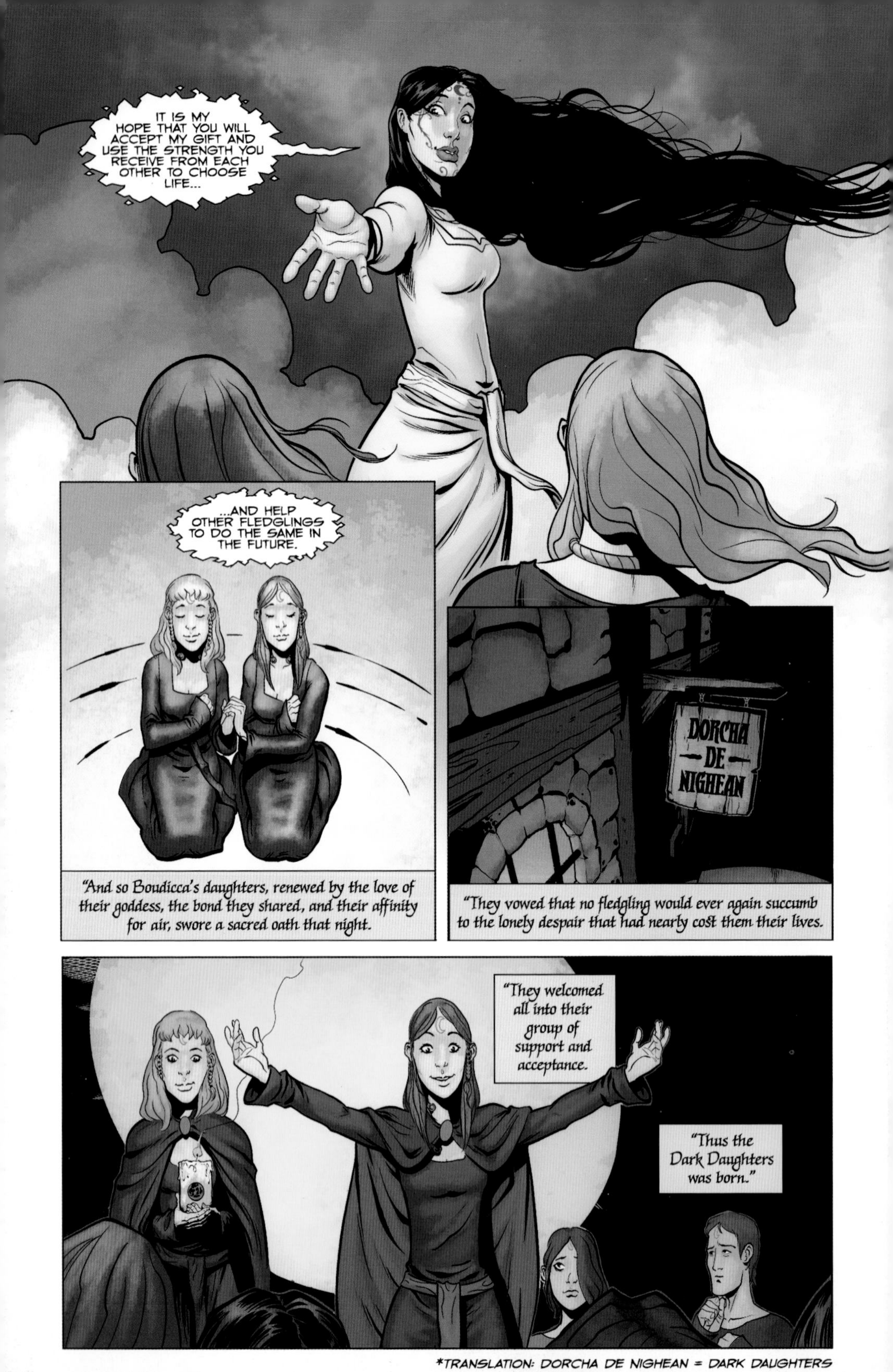
IT IS MY HOPE THAT YOU WILL ACCEPT MY GIFT AND USE THE STRENGTH YOU RECEIVE FROM EACH OTHER TO CHOOSE LIFE...
...AND HELP OTHER FLEDGLINGS TO DO THE SAME IN THE FUTURE.
"And so Boudicca's daughters, renewed by the love of their goddess, the bond they shared, and their affinity for air, swore a sacred oath that night.
DORCHA DE NIGHEAN
"They vowed that no fledgling would ever again succumb to the lonely despair that had nearly cost them their lives.
"They welcomed all into their group of support and acceptance.
"Thus the Dark Daughters was born."

*TRANSLATION: DORCHA DE NIGHEAN = DARK DAUGHTERS

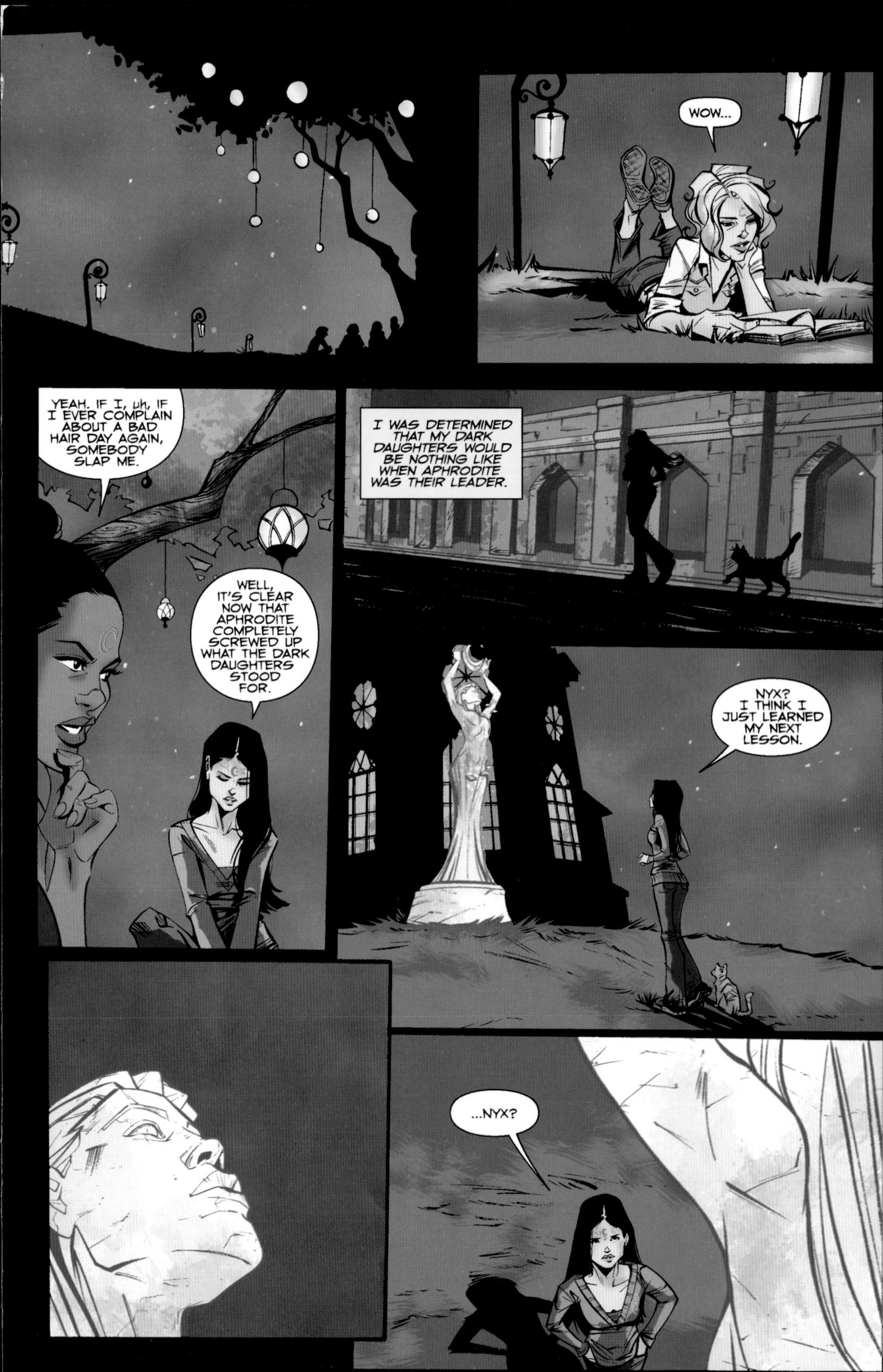
WOW...
YEAH. IF I, uh, IF I EVER COMPLAIN ABOUT A BAD HAIR DAY AGAIN, SOMEBODY SLAP ME.
WELL, IT'S CLEAR NOW THAT APHRODITE COMPLETELY SCREWED UP WHAT THE DARK DAUGHTERS STOOD FOR.
I WAS DETERMINED THAT MY DARK DAUGHTERS WOULD BE NOTHING LIKE WHEN APHRODITE WAS THEIR LEADER.
NYX? I THINK I JUST LEARNED MY NEXT LESSON.
...NYX?

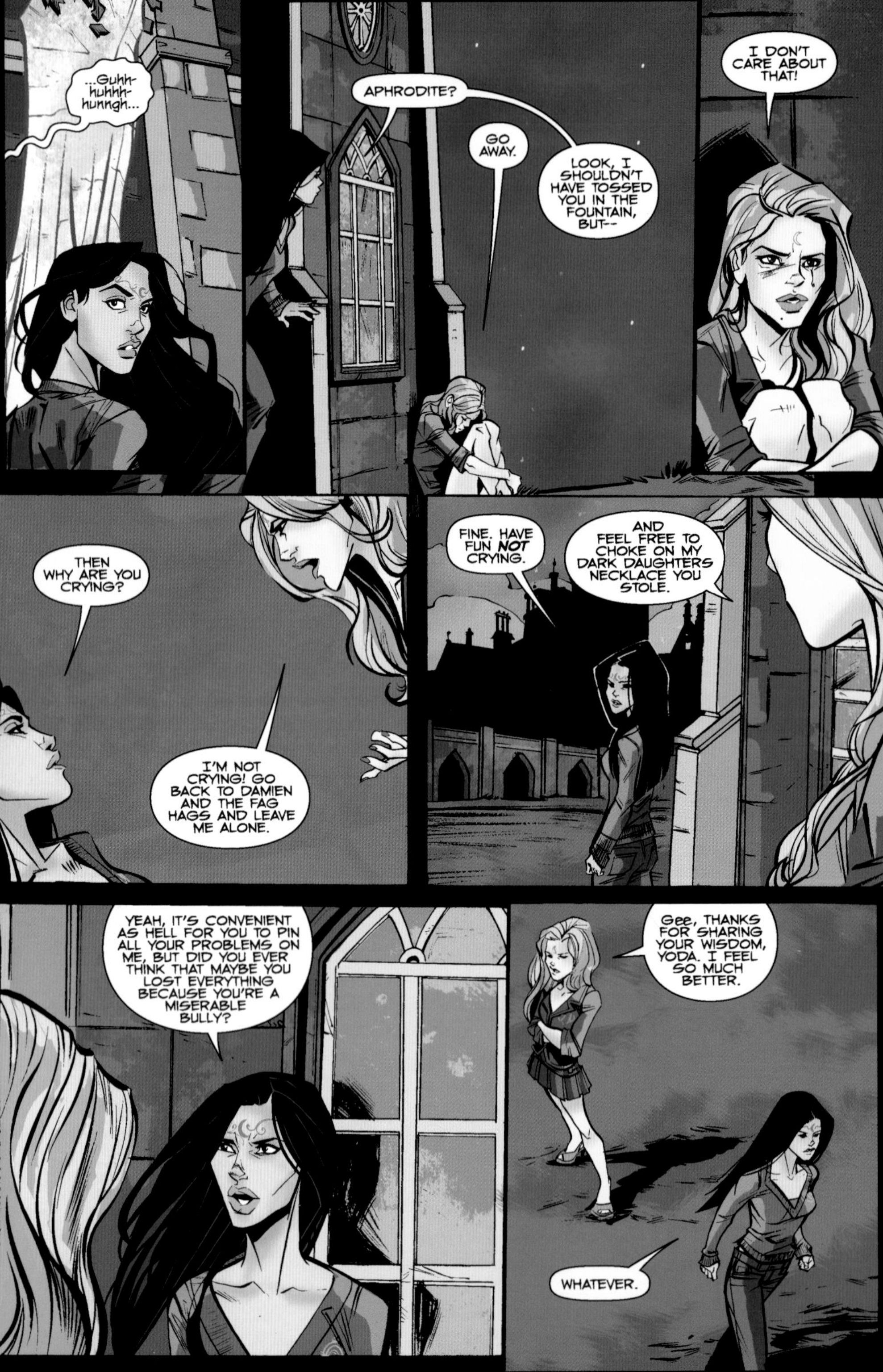
...Guhh-huhhh-hunngh...
APHRODITE?
GO AWAY.
LOOK, I SHOULDN'T HAVE TOSSED YOU IN THE FOUNTAIN, BUT--
I DON'T CARE ABOUT THAT!
THEN WHY ARE YOU CRYING?
I'M NOT CRYING! GO BACK TO DAMIEN AND THE FAG HAGS AND LEAVE ME ALONE.
FINE. HAVE FUN *NOT* CRYING.
AND FEEL FREE TO CHOKE ON MY DARK DAUGHTERS NECKLACE YOU STOLE.
YEAH, IT'S CONVENIENT AS HELL FOR YOU TO PIN ALL YOUR PROBLEMS ON ME, BUT DID YOU EVER THINK THAT MAYBE YOU LOST EVERYTHING BECAUSE YOU'RE A MISERABLE BULLY?
Gee, THANKS FOR SHARING YOUR WISDOM, YODA. I FEEL SO MUCH BETTER.
WHATEVER.

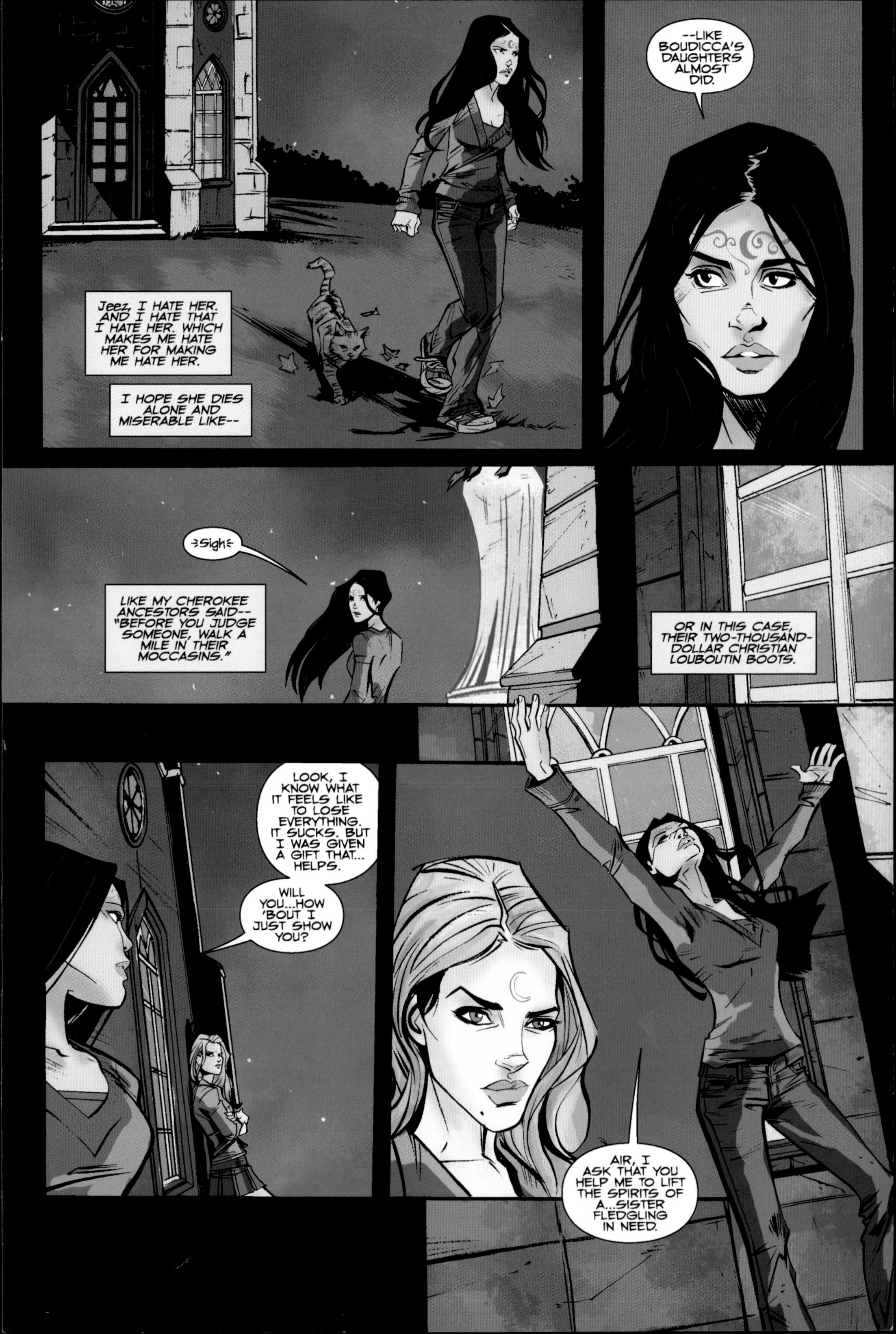
Jeez, I HATE HER. AND I HATE THAT I HATE HER. WHICH MAKES ME HATE HER FOR MAKING ME HATE HER.
I HOPE SHE DIES ALONE AND MISERABLE LIKE--
--LIKE BOUDICCA'S DAUGHTERS ALMOST DID.
Sigh
LIKE MY CHEROKEE ANCESTORS SAID-- "BEFORE YOU JUDGE SOMEONE, WALK A MILE IN THEIR MOCCASINS."
OR IN THIS CASE, THEIR TWO-THOUSAND-DOLLAR CHRISTIAN LOUBOUTIN BOOTS.
LOOK, I KNOW WHAT IT FEELS LIKE TO LOSE EVERYTHING. IT SUCKS. BUT I WAS GIVEN A GIFT THAT... HELPS.
WILL YOU...HOW 'BOUT I JUST SHOW YOU?
AIR, I ASK THAT YOU HELP ME TO LIFT THE SPIRITS OF A...SISTER FLEDGLING IN NEED.

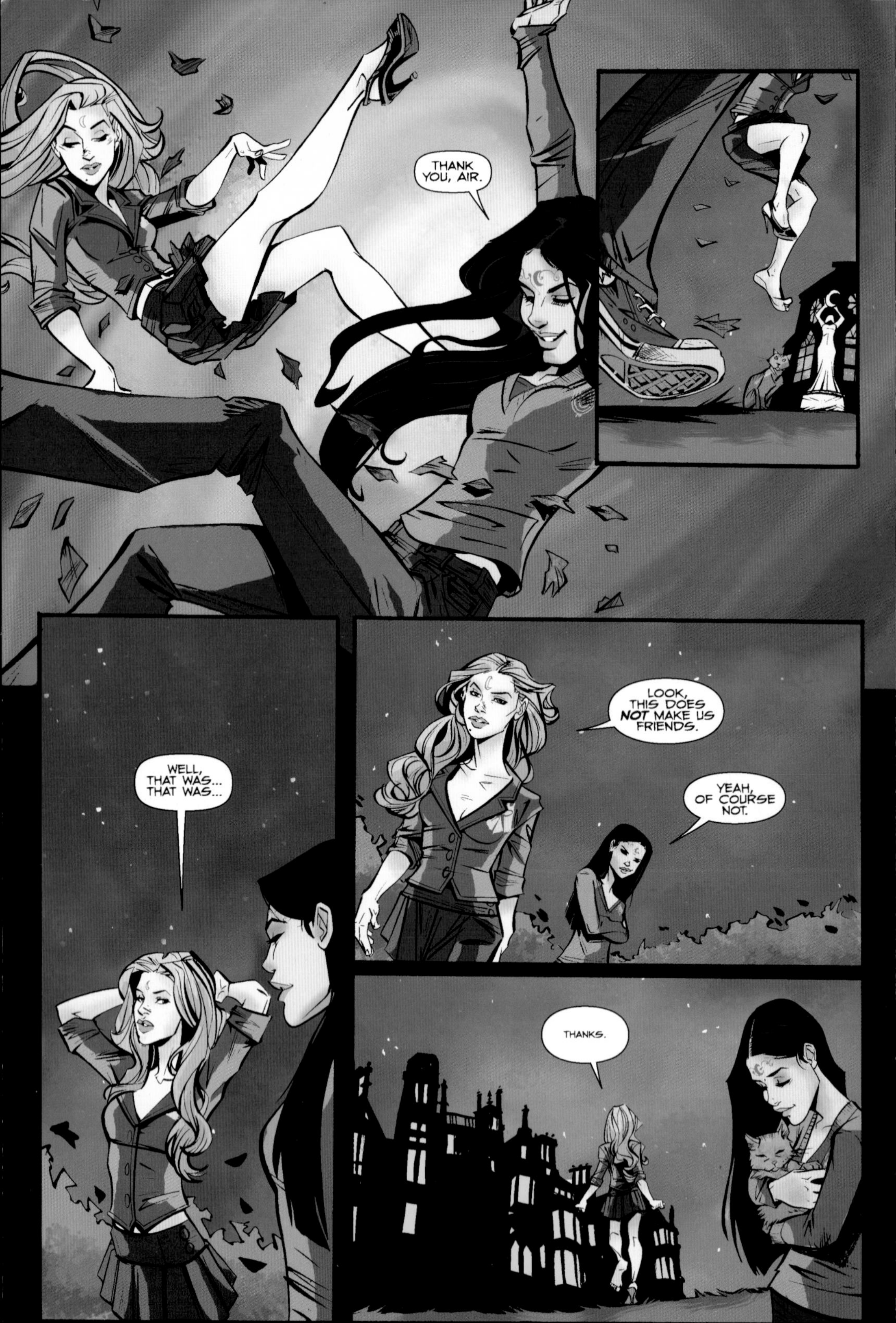
THANK YOU, AIR.
WELL, THAT WAS... THAT WAS...
LOOK, THIS DOES **NOT** MAKE US FRIENDS.
YEAH, OF COURSE NOT.
THANKS.

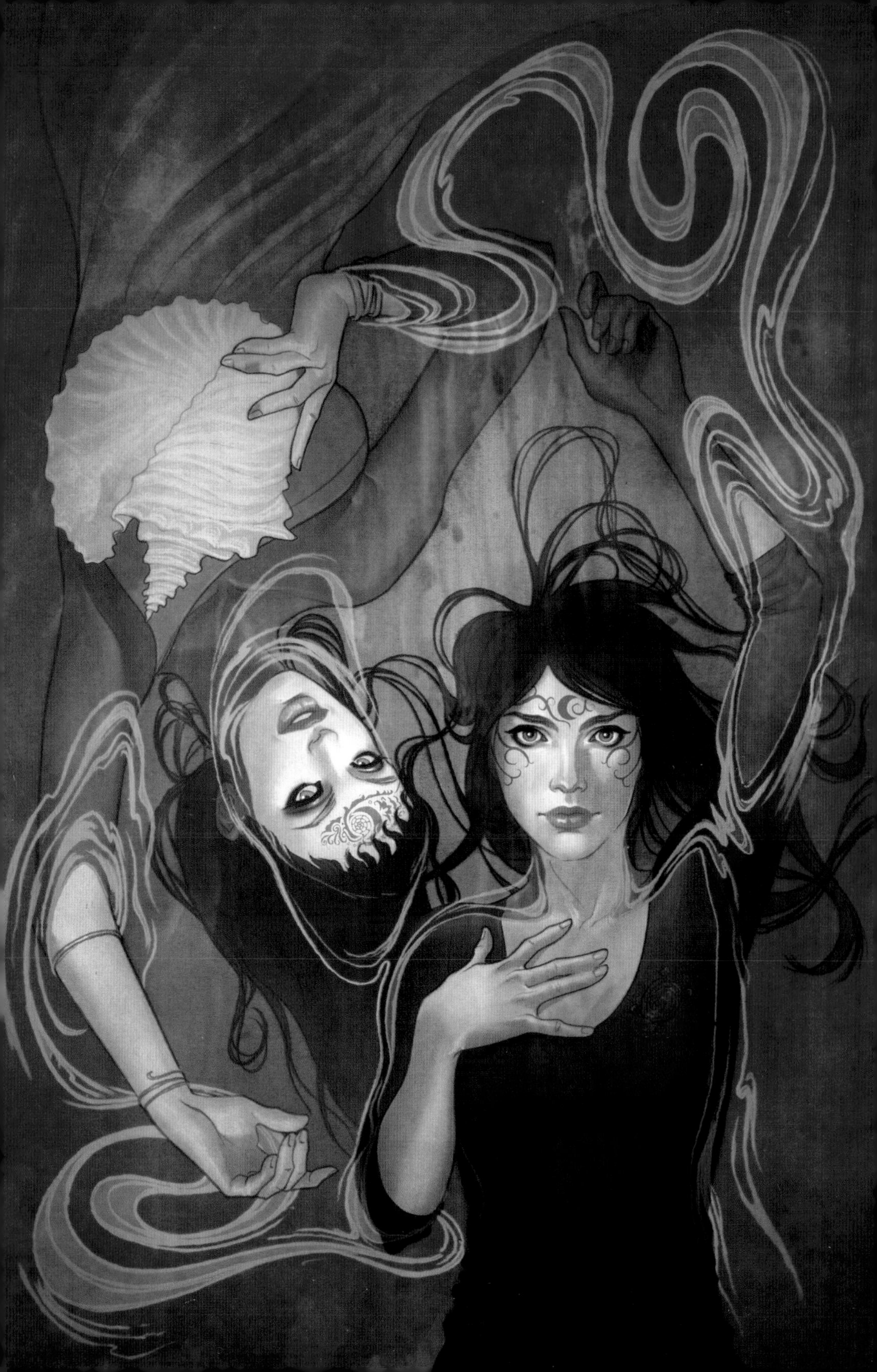

WATER

STORY BY
P. C. CAST
AND **KRISTIN CAST**

SCRIPT BY
KENT DALIAN

ART BY
JOËLLE JONES
AND **DANIEL KRALL**

COLORS BY
RYAN HILL
AND **DANIEL KRALL**

LETTERS BY
NATE PIEKOS OF **BLAMBOT®**

CHAPTER ILLUSTRATION BY
JENNY FRISON

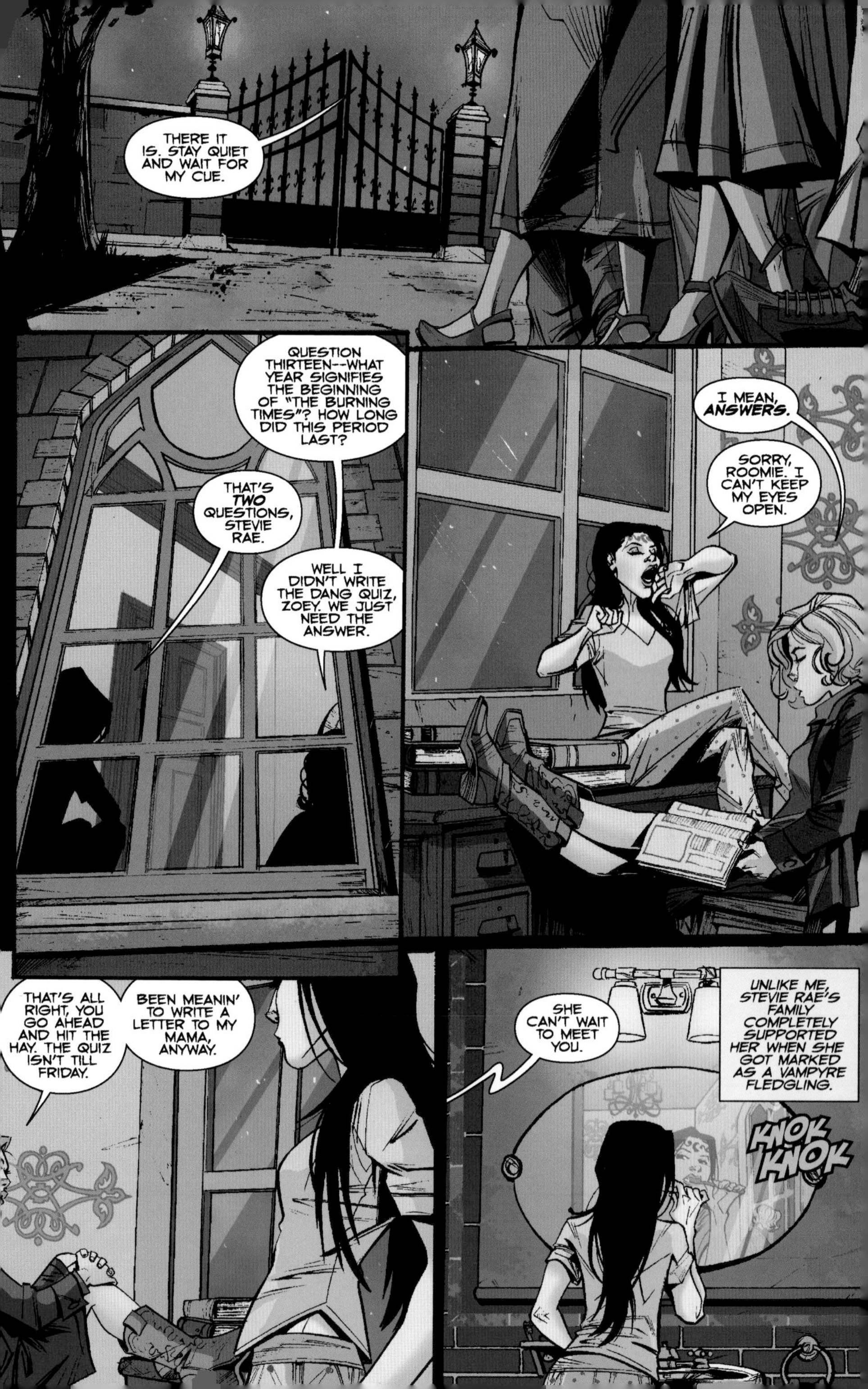
THERE IT IS. STAY QUIET AND WAIT FOR MY CUE.
QUESTION THIRTEEN--WHAT YEAR SIGNIFIES THE BEGINNING OF "THE BURNING TIMES"? HOW LONG DID THIS PERIOD LAST?
THAT'S *TWO* QUESTIONS, STEVIE RAE.
WELL I DIDN'T WRITE THE DANG QUIZ, ZOEY. WE JUST NEED THE ANSWER.
I MEAN, ***ANSWERS.***
SORRY, ROOMIE. I CAN'T KEEP MY EYES OPEN.
THAT'S ALL RIGHT, YOU GO AHEAD AND HIT THE HAY. THE QUIZ ISN'T TILL FRIDAY.
BEEN MEANIN' TO WRITE A LETTER TO MY MAMA, ANYWAY.
SHE CAN'T WAIT TO MEET YOU.
UNLIKE ME, STEVIE RAE'S FAMILY COMPLETELY SUPPORTED HER WHEN SHE GOT MARKED AS A VAMPYRE FLEDGLING.
KNOK KNOK

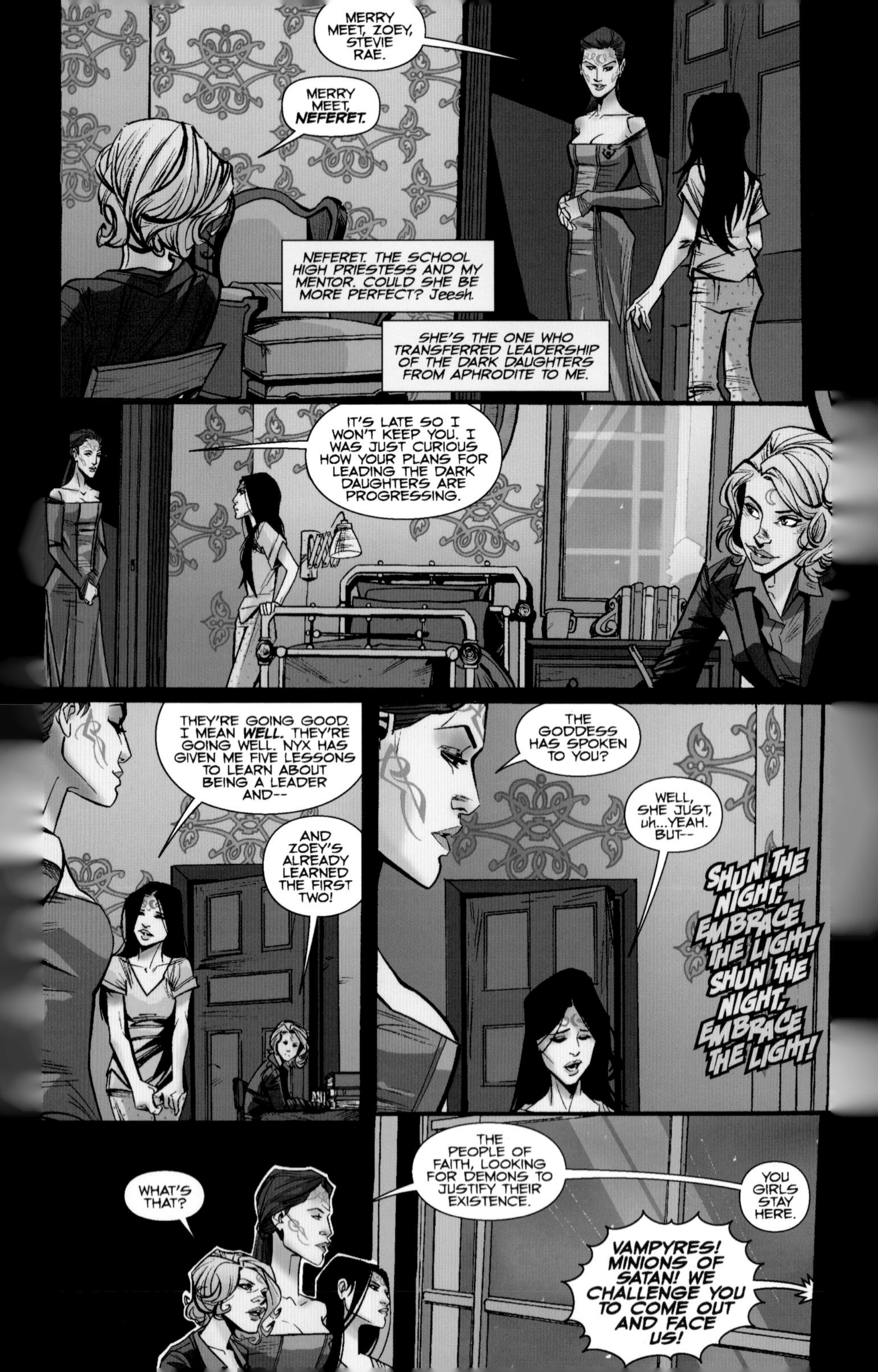
MERRY MEET, ZOEY, STEVIE RAE.
MERRY MEET, NEFERET.
NEFERET. THE SCHOOL HIGH PRIESTESS AND MY MENTOR. COULD SHE BE MORE PERFECT? Jeesh.
SHE'S THE ONE WHO TRANSFERRED LEADERSHIP OF THE DARK DAUGHTERS FROM APHRODITE TO ME.
IT'S LATE SO I WON'T KEEP YOU. I WAS JUST CURIOUS HOW YOUR PLANS FOR LEADING THE DARK DAUGHTERS ARE PROGRESSING.
THEY'RE GOING GOOD. I MEAN WELL. THEY'RE GOING WELL. NYX HAS GIVEN ME FIVE LESSONS TO LEARN ABOUT BEING A LEADER AND--
AND ZOEY'S ALREADY LEARNED THE FIRST TWO!
THE GODDESS HAS SPOKEN TO YOU?
WELL, SHE JUST, uh...YEAH. BUT--
SHUN THE NIGHT, EMBRACE THE LIGHT! SHUN THE NIGHT, EMBRACE THE LIGHT!
WHAT'S THAT?
THE PEOPLE OF FAITH, LOOKING FOR DEMONS TO JUSTIFY THEIR EXISTENCE.
YOU GIRLS STAY HERE.
VAMPYRES! MINIONS OF SATAN! WE CHALLENGE YOU TO COME OUT AND FACE US!

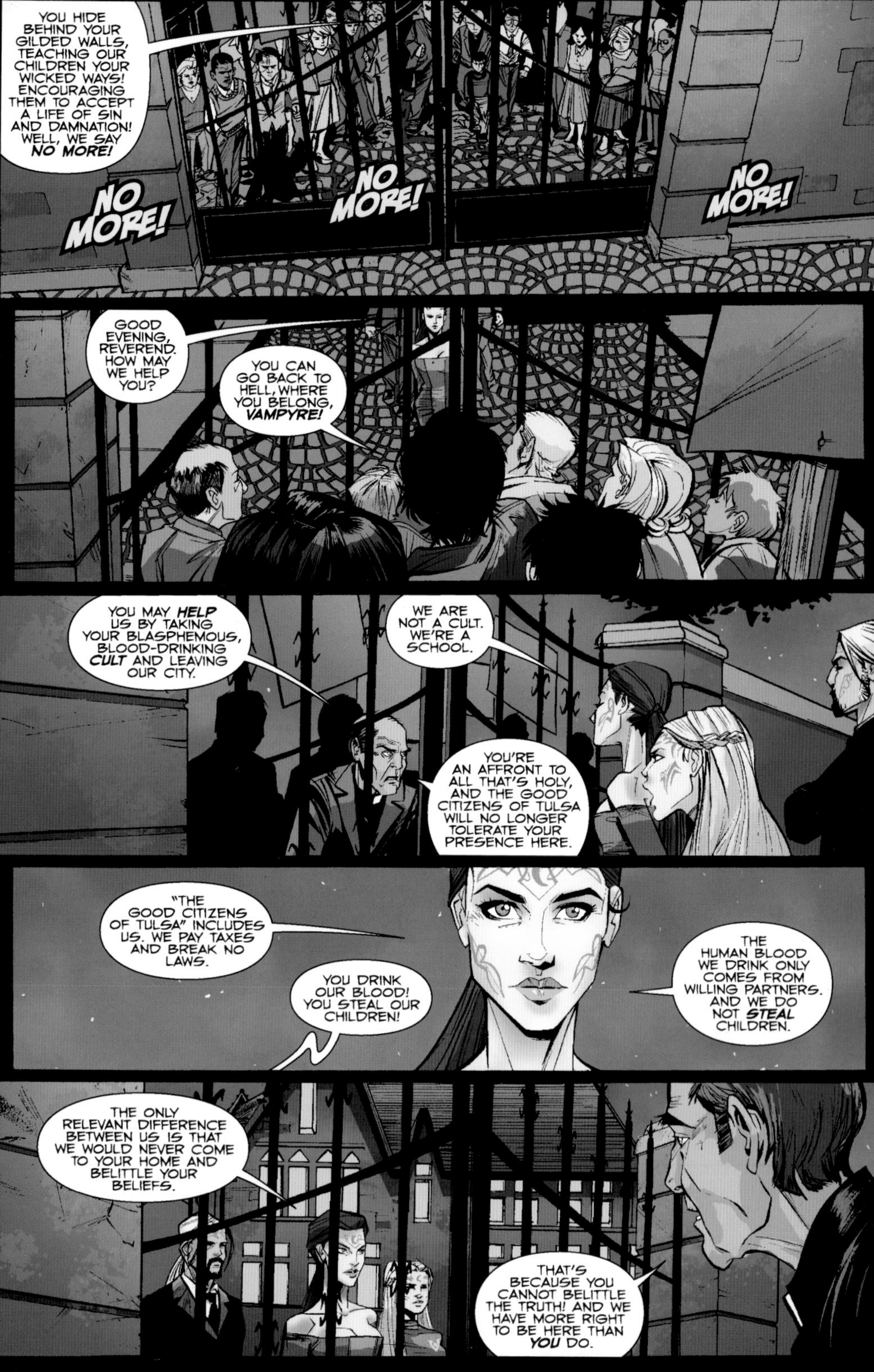
YOU HIDE BEHIND YOUR GILDED WALLS, TEACHING OUR CHILDREN YOUR WICKED WAYS! ENCOURAGING THEM TO ACCEPT A LIFE OF SIN AND DAMNATION! WELL, WE SAY *NO MORE!*
NO MORE!
NO MORE!
NO MORE!
GOOD EVENING, REVEREND. HOW MAY WE HELP YOU?
YOU CAN GO BACK TO HELL, WHERE YOU BELONG, *VAMPYRE!*
YOU MAY *HELP* US BY TAKING YOUR BLASPHEMOUS, BLOOD-DRINKING *CULT* AND LEAVING OUR CITY.
WE ARE NOT A CULT. WE'RE A SCHOOL.
YOU'RE AN AFFRONT TO ALL THAT'S HOLY, AND THE GOOD CITIZENS OF TULSA WILL NO LONGER TOLERATE YOUR PRESENCE HERE.
"THE GOOD CITIZENS OF TULSA" INCLUDES US. WE PAY TAXES AND BREAK NO LAWS.
YOU DRINK OUR BLOOD! YOU STEAL OUR CHILDREN!
THE HUMAN BLOOD WE DRINK ONLY COMES FROM WILLING PARTNERS. AND WE DO NOT *STEAL* CHILDREN.
THE ONLY RELEVANT DIFFERENCE BETWEEN US IS THAT WE WOULD NEVER COME TO YOUR HOME AND BELITTLE YOUR BELIEFS.
THAT'S BECAUSE YOU CANNOT BELITTLE THE TRUTH! AND WE HAVE MORE RIGHT TO BE HERE THAN *YOU* DO.

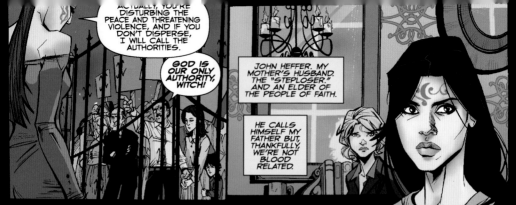

ACTUALLY, YOU'RE DISTURBING THE PEACE AND THREATENING VIOLENCE, AND IF YOU DON'T DISPERSE, I WILL CALL THE AUTHORITIES.

GOD IS OUR ONLY AUTHORITY, WITCH!

JOHN HEFFER. MY MOTHER'S HUSBAND. THE "STEPLOSER." AND AN ELDER OF THE PEOPLE OF FAITH.

HE CALLS HIMSELF MY FATHER BUT, THANKFULLY, WE'RE NOT BLOOD RELATED.

THE DAY I GOT MARKED, HE WAS A BIG HELP.

WELL, IT SEEMS YOUR WILLFUL BEHAVIOR AND BAD ATTITUDE HAVE FINALLY CAUGHT UP WITH YOU.

I DIDN'T CAUSE THIS. IT'S A BIOLOGICAL HORMONE THING THAT--

DO YOU REALIZE THAT YOU'VE BECOME THE VERY THING THAT I DEVOTE MY LIFE TO FIGHTING AGAINST?

AND NOW HERE YOU STAND, IN MY LIVING ROOM, UNDER MY ROOF!

MAMA? I NEED YOU TO--

DEAR LORD, WHAT WILL OUR FRIENDS THINK? AND THE CHURCH? WHAT ARE WE GOING TO DO?

WE'RE GOING TO GIVE THIS TO GOD.

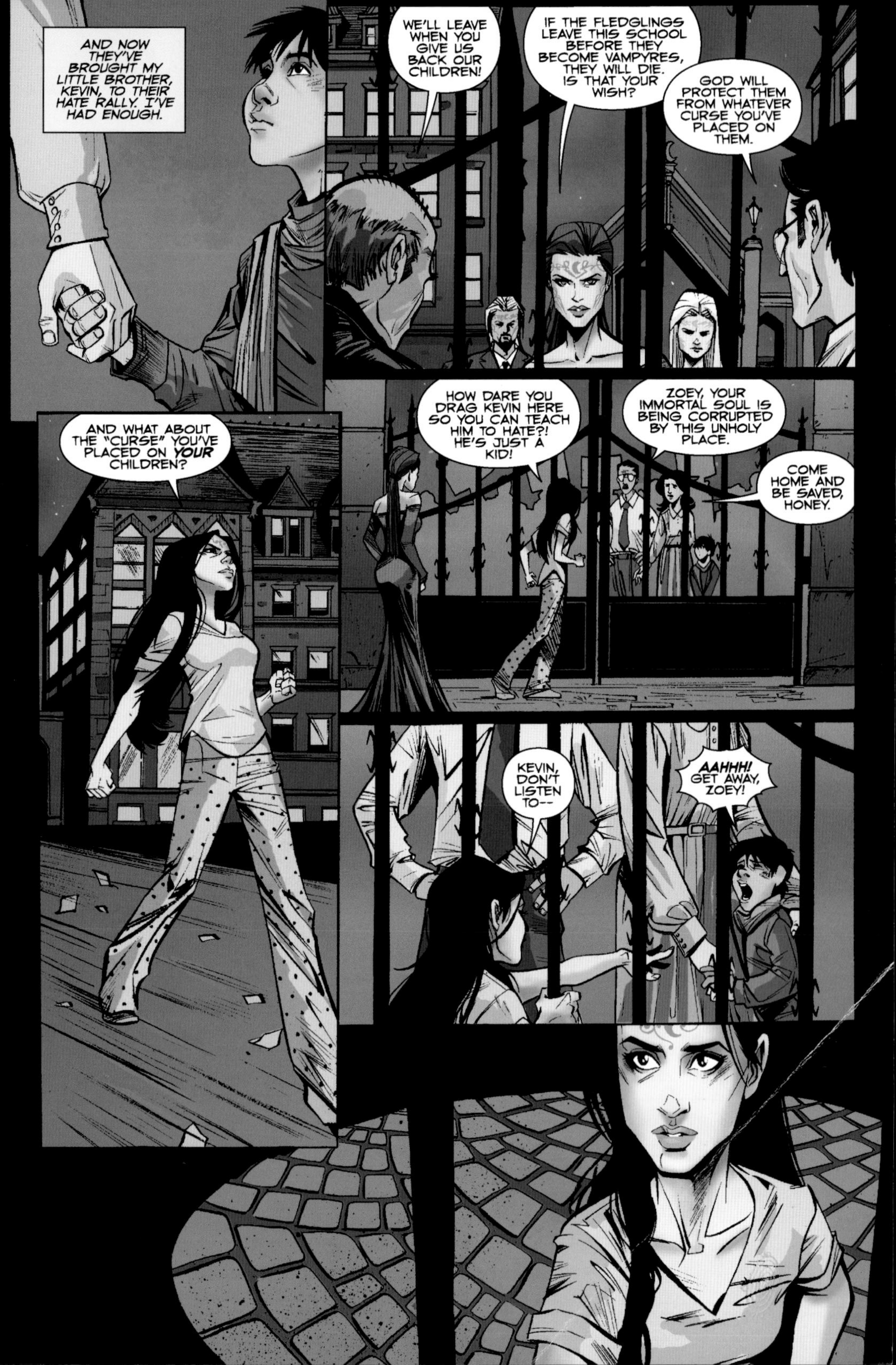
AND NOW THEY'VE BROUGHT MY LITTLE BROTHER, KEVIN, TO THEIR HATE RALLY. I'VE HAD ENOUGH.
WE'LL LEAVE WHEN YOU GIVE US BACK OUR CHILDREN!
IF THE FLEDGLINGS LEAVE THIS SCHOOL BEFORE THEY BECOME VAMPYRES, THEY WILL DIE. IS THAT YOUR WISH?
GOD WILL PROTECT THEM FROM WHATEVER CURSE YOU'VE PLACED ON THEM.
AND WHAT ABOUT THE "CURSE" YOU'VE PLACED ON YOUR CHILDREN?
HOW DARE YOU DRAG KEVIN HERE SO YOU CAN TEACH HIM TO HATE?! HE'S JUST A KID!
ZOEY, YOUR IMMORTAL SOUL IS BEING CORRUPTED BY THIS UNHOLY PLACE.
COME HOME AND BE SAVED, HONEY.
KEVIN, DON'T LISTEN TO--
AAHHH! GET AWAY, ZOEY!

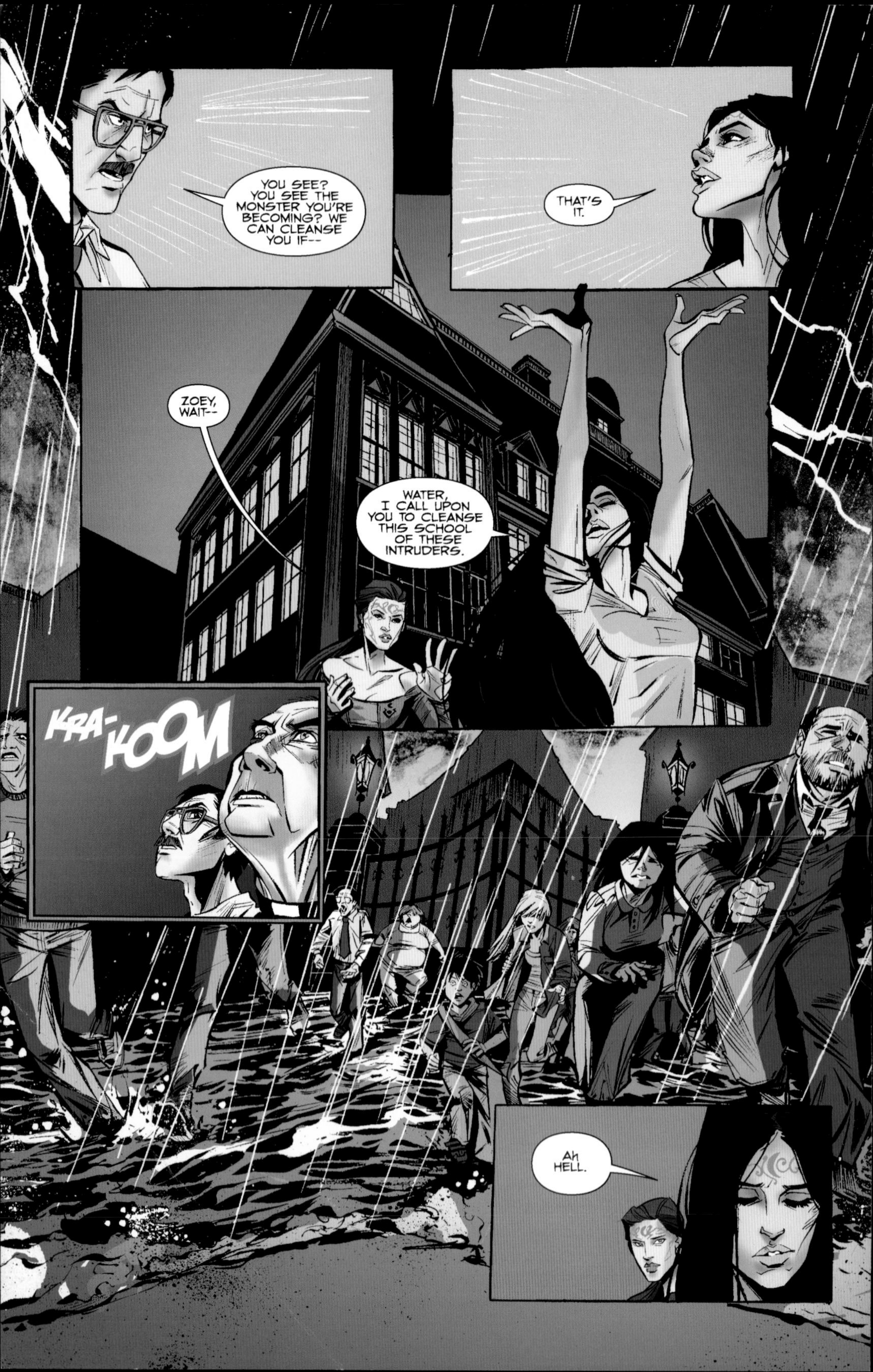
YOU SEE? YOU SEE THE MONSTER YOU'RE BECOMING? WE CAN CLEANSE YOU IF--
THAT'S IT.
ZOEY, WAIT--
WATER, I CALL UPON YOU TO CLEANSE THIS SCHOOL OF THESE INTRUDERS.
KRA-KOOM
Ah HELL.

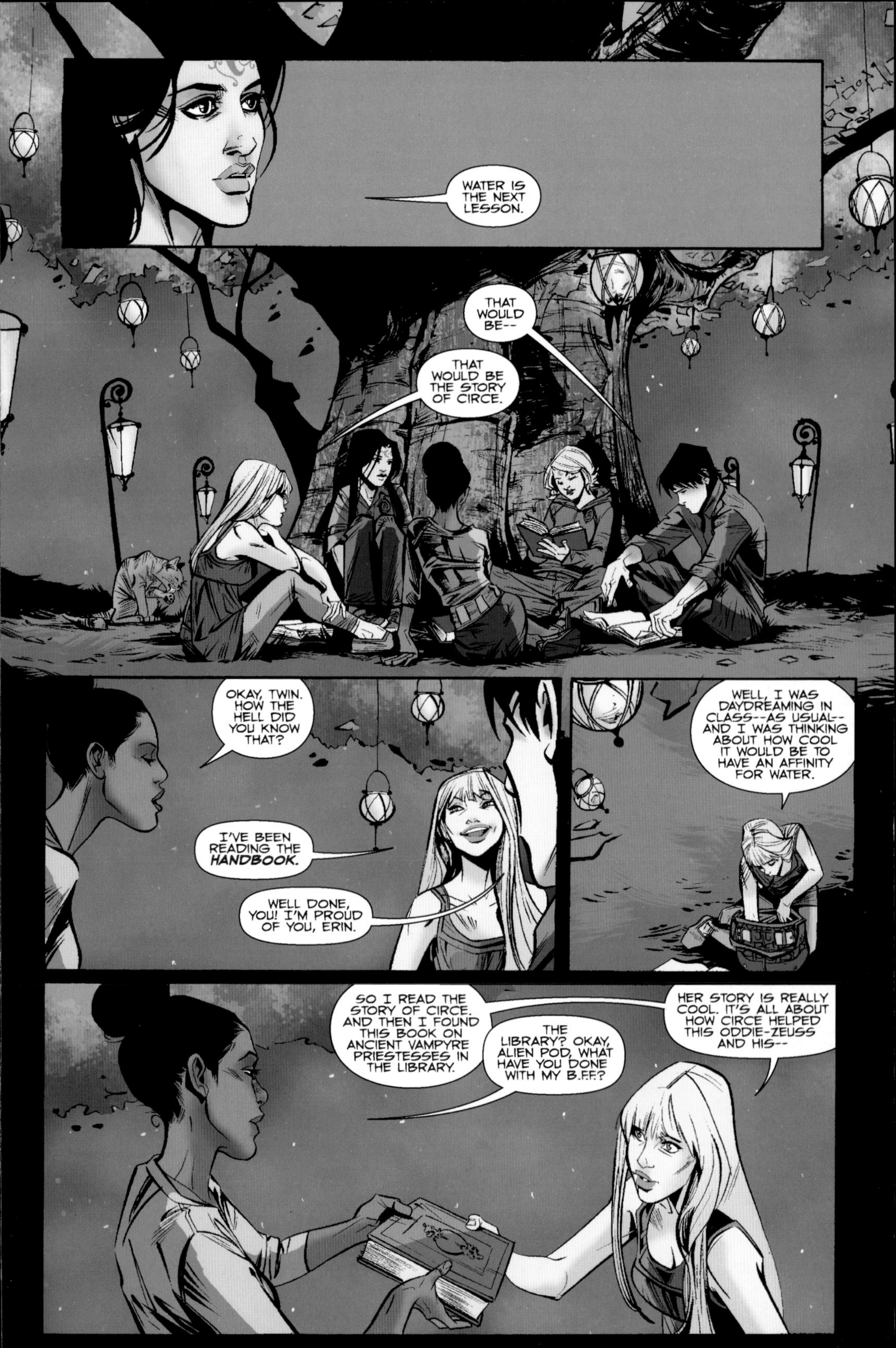
WATER IS THE NEXT LESSON.
THAT WOULD BE--
THAT WOULD BE THE STORY OF CIRCE.
OKAY, TWIN. HOW THE HELL DID YOU KNOW THAT?
I'VE BEEN READING THE HANDBOOK.
WELL DONE, YOU! I'M PROUD OF YOU, ERIN.
WELL, I WAS DAYDREAMING IN CLASS--AS USUAL--AND I WAS THINKING ABOUT HOW COOL IT WOULD BE TO HAVE AN AFFINITY FOR WATER.
SO I READ THE STORY OF CIRCE. AND THEN I FOUND THIS BOOK ON ANCIENT VAMPYRE PRIESTESSES IN THE LIBRARY.
THE LIBRARY? OKAY, ALIEN POD, WHAT HAVE YOU DONE WITH MY B.F.F.?
HER STORY IS REALLY COOL. IT'S ALL ABOUT HOW CIRCE HELPED THIS ODDIE-ZEUSS AND HIS--

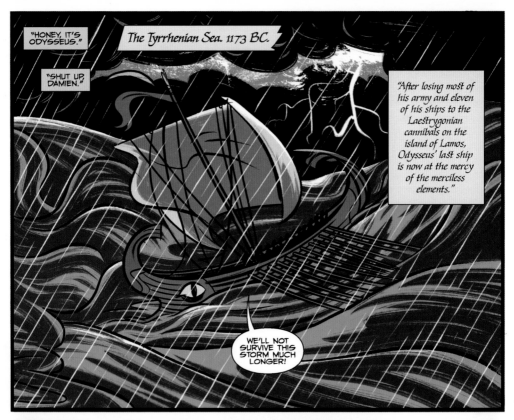

"HONEY, IT'S ODYSSEUS."

The Tyrrhenian Sea. 1173 BC.

"SHUT UP, DAMIEN."

"After losing most of his army and eleven of his ships to the Laestrygonian cannibals on the island of Lamos, Odysseus' last ship is now at the mercy of the merciless elements."

WE'LL NOT SURVIVE THIS STORM MUCH LONGER!

"Odysseus. Legendary champion of the Trojan War. Now questioning whether he ever should have left Ithaca--his beloved homeland."

WE MUST FIND LAND, ODYSSEUS, AND QUICKLY!

I AGREE, EURYLOCHUS.

AND I, IF ONLY TO REPLENISH OUR DWINDLING WINE AND FOOD STORES.

THERE IS LAND AHEAD. THE ISLAND OF AEAEA.

BUT COMMANDER, THAT'S THE HOME OF THE VAMPYRE WITCH, CIRCE!

DOES SHE HAVE WINE?

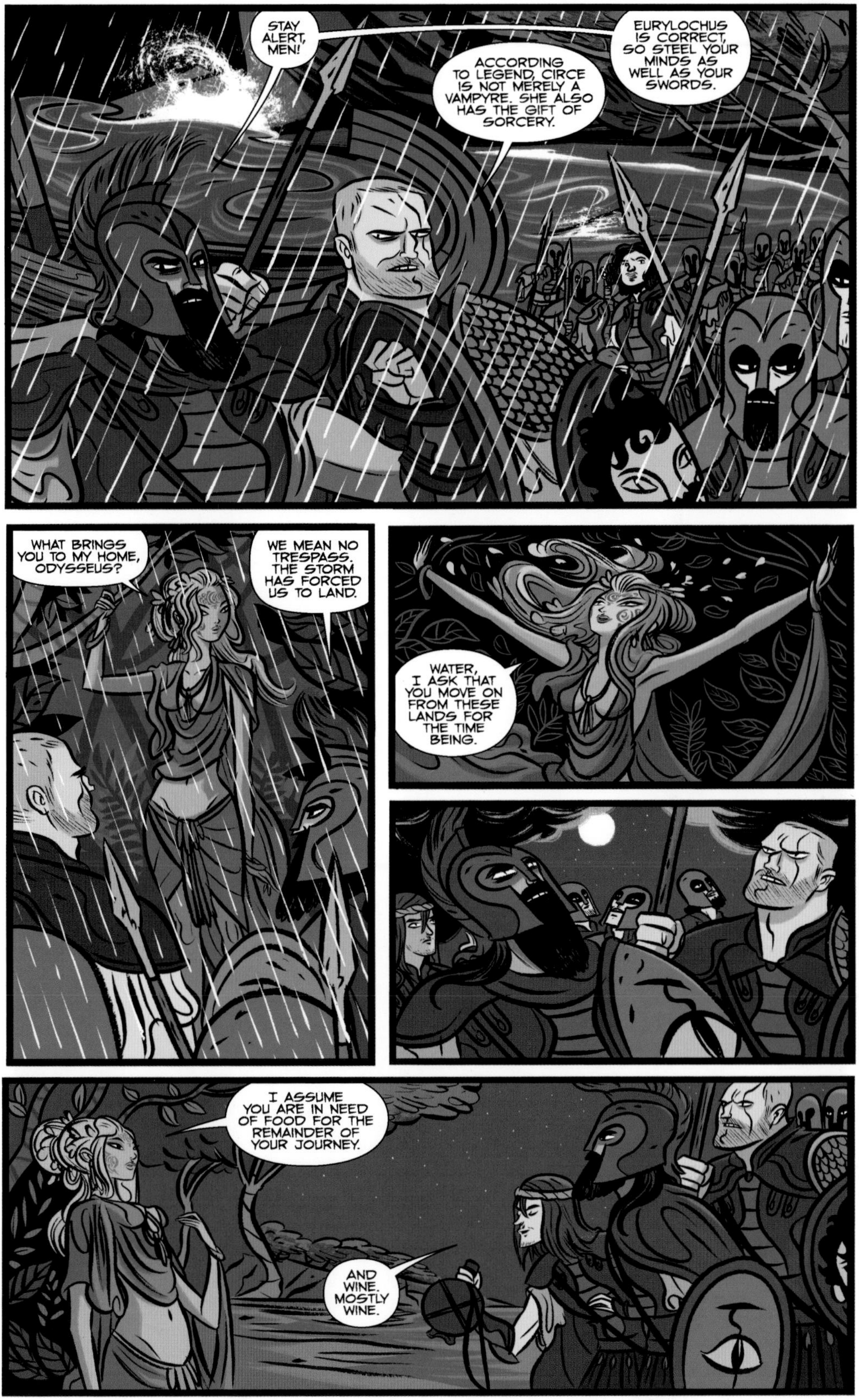

STAY ALERT, MEN!
ACCORDING TO LEGEND, CIRCE IS NOT MERELY A VAMPYRE. SHE ALSO HAS THE GIFT OF SORCERY.
EURYLOCHUS IS CORRECT, SO STEEL YOUR MINDS AS WELL AS YOUR SWORDS.
WHAT BRINGS YOU TO MY HOME, ODYSSEUS?
WE MEAN NO TRESPASS. THE STORM HAS FORCED US TO LAND.
WATER, I ASK THAT YOU MOVE ON FROM THESE LANDS FOR THE TIME BEING.
I ASSUME YOU ARE IN NEED OF FOOD FOR THE REMAINDER OF YOUR JOURNEY.
AND WINE. MOSTLY WINE.

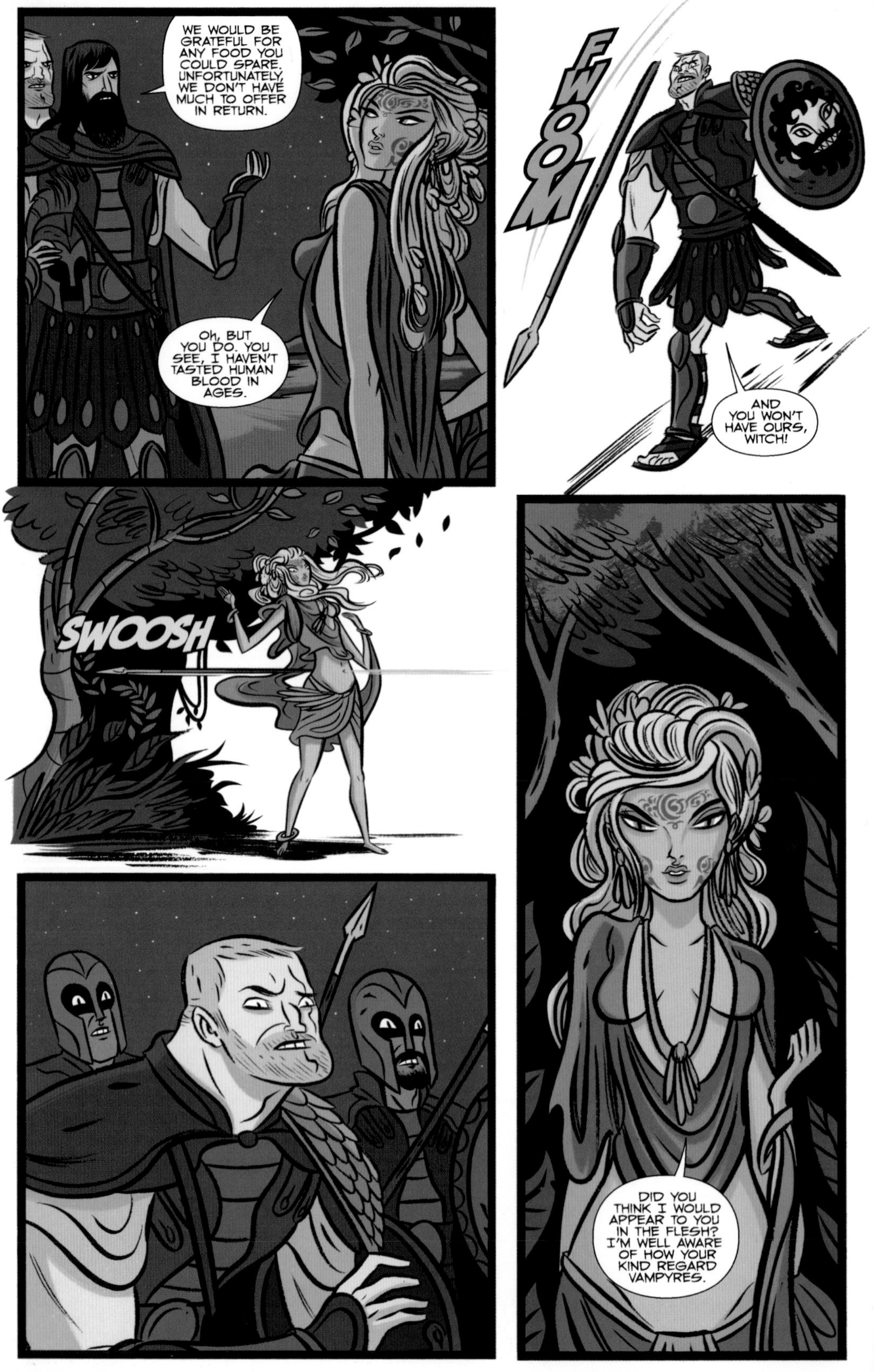
WE WOULD BE GRATEFUL FOR ANY FOOD YOU COULD SPARE. UNFORTUNATELY, WE DON'T HAVE MUCH TO OFFER IN RETURN.
OH, BUT YOU DO. YOU SEE, I HAVEN'T TASTED HUMAN BLOOD IN AGES.
FWOOM
AND YOU WON'T HAVE OURS, WITCH!
SWOOSH
DID YOU THINK I WOULD APPEAR TO YOU IN THE FLESH? I'M WELL AWARE OF HOW YOUR KIND REGARD VAMPYRES.

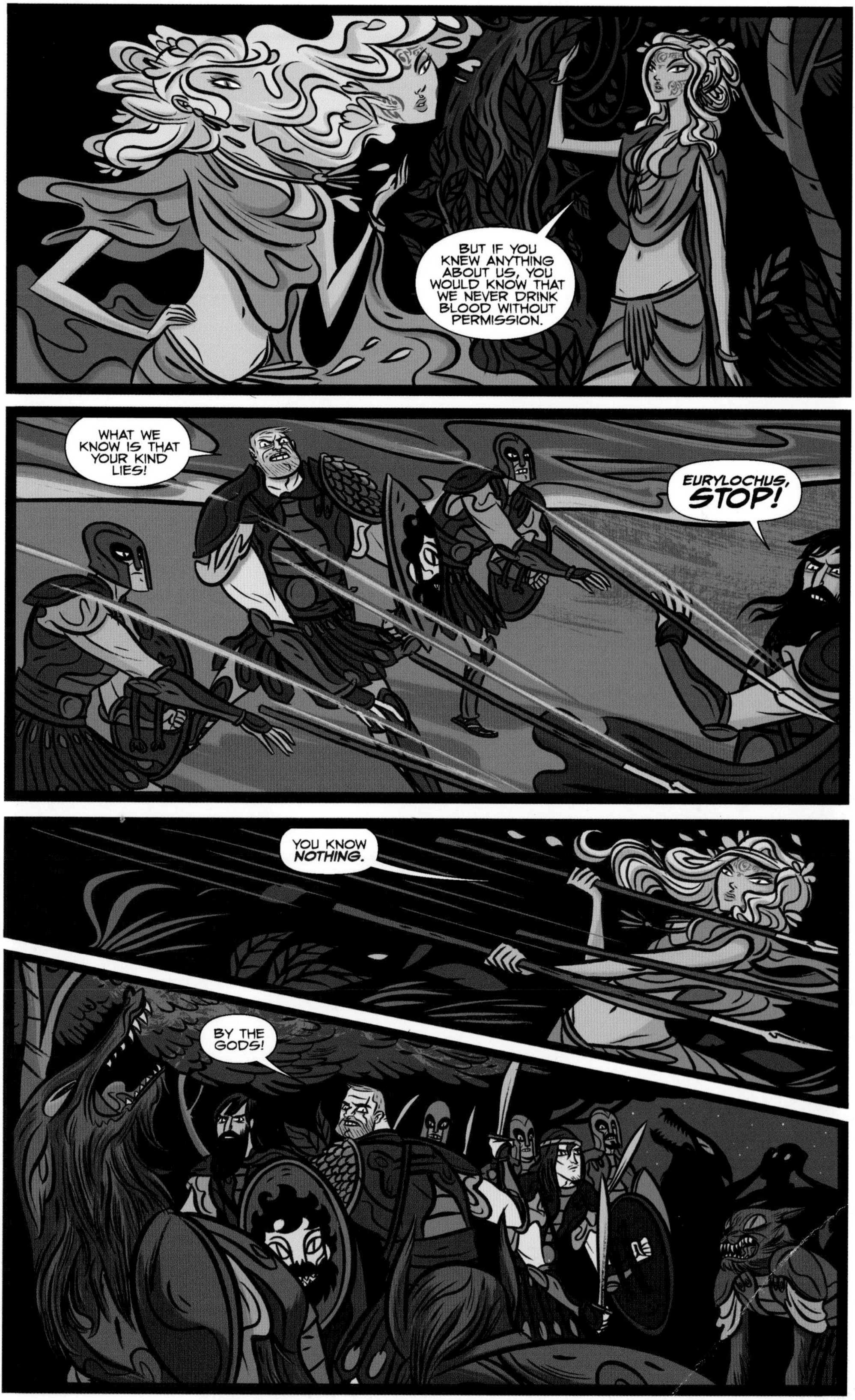

BUT IF YOU KNEW ANYTHING ABOUT US, YOU WOULD KNOW THAT WE NEVER DRINK BLOOD WITHOUT PERMISSION.
WHAT WE KNOW IS THAT YOUR KIND LIES!
EURYLOCHUS, STOP!
YOU KNOW NOTHING.
BY THE GODS!

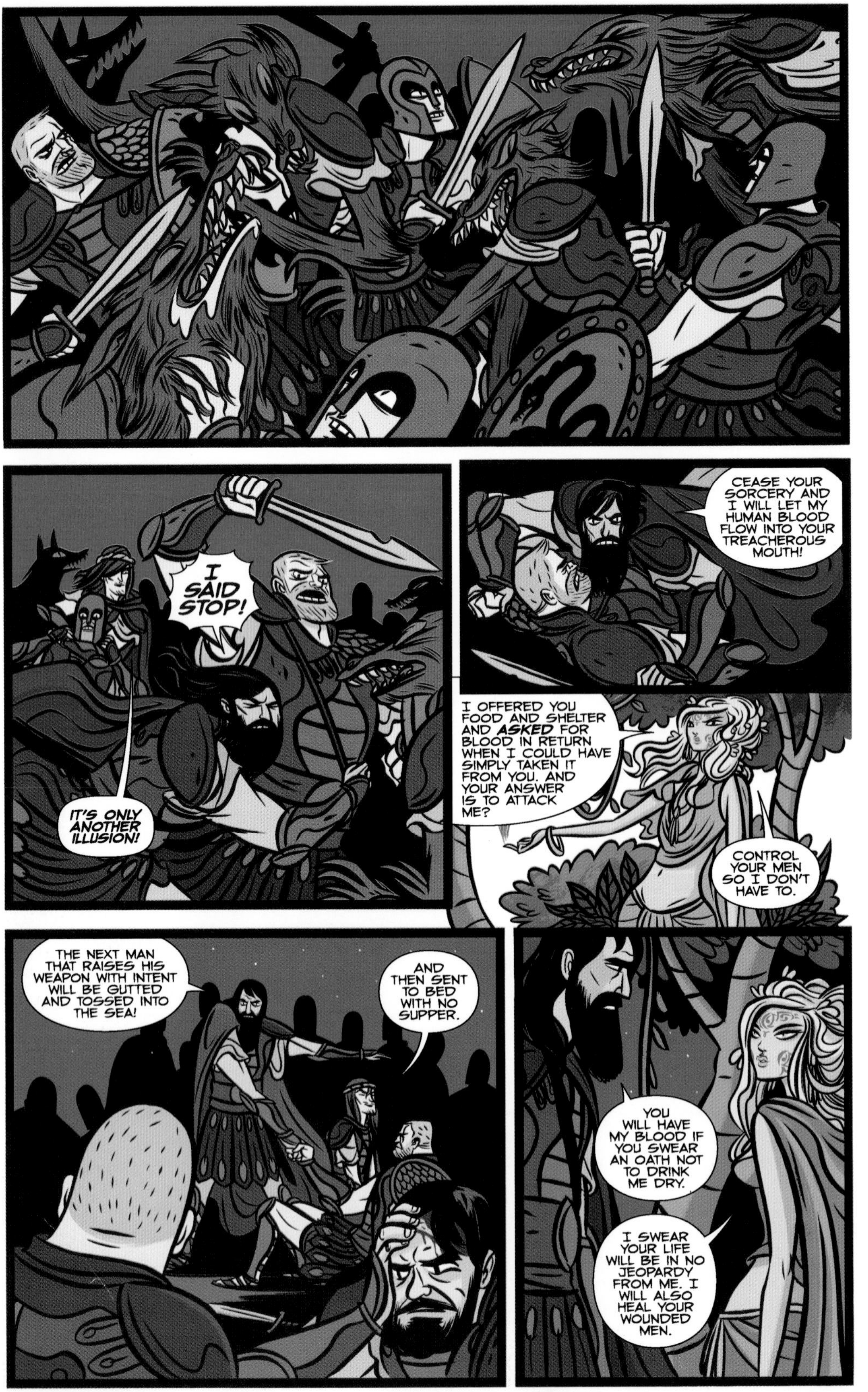
I SAID STOP!
IT'S ONLY ANOTHER ILLUSION!
CEASE YOUR SORCERY AND I WILL LET MY HUMAN BLOOD FLOW INTO YOUR TREACHEROUS MOUTH!
I OFFERED YOU FOOD AND SHELTER AND ASKED FOR BLOOD IN RETURN WHEN I COULD HAVE SIMPLY TAKEN IT FROM YOU. AND YOUR ANSWER IS TO ATTACK ME?
CONTROL YOUR MEN SO I DON'T HAVE TO.
THE NEXT MAN THAT RAISES HIS WEAPON WITH INTENT WILL BE GUTTED AND TOSSED INTO THE SEA!
AND THEN SENT TO BED WITH NO SUPPER.
YOU WILL HAVE MY BLOOD IF YOU SWEAR AN OATH NOT TO DRINK ME DRY.
I SWEAR YOUR LIFE WILL BE IN NO JEOPARDY FROM ME. I WILL ALSO HEAL YOUR WOUNDED MEN.

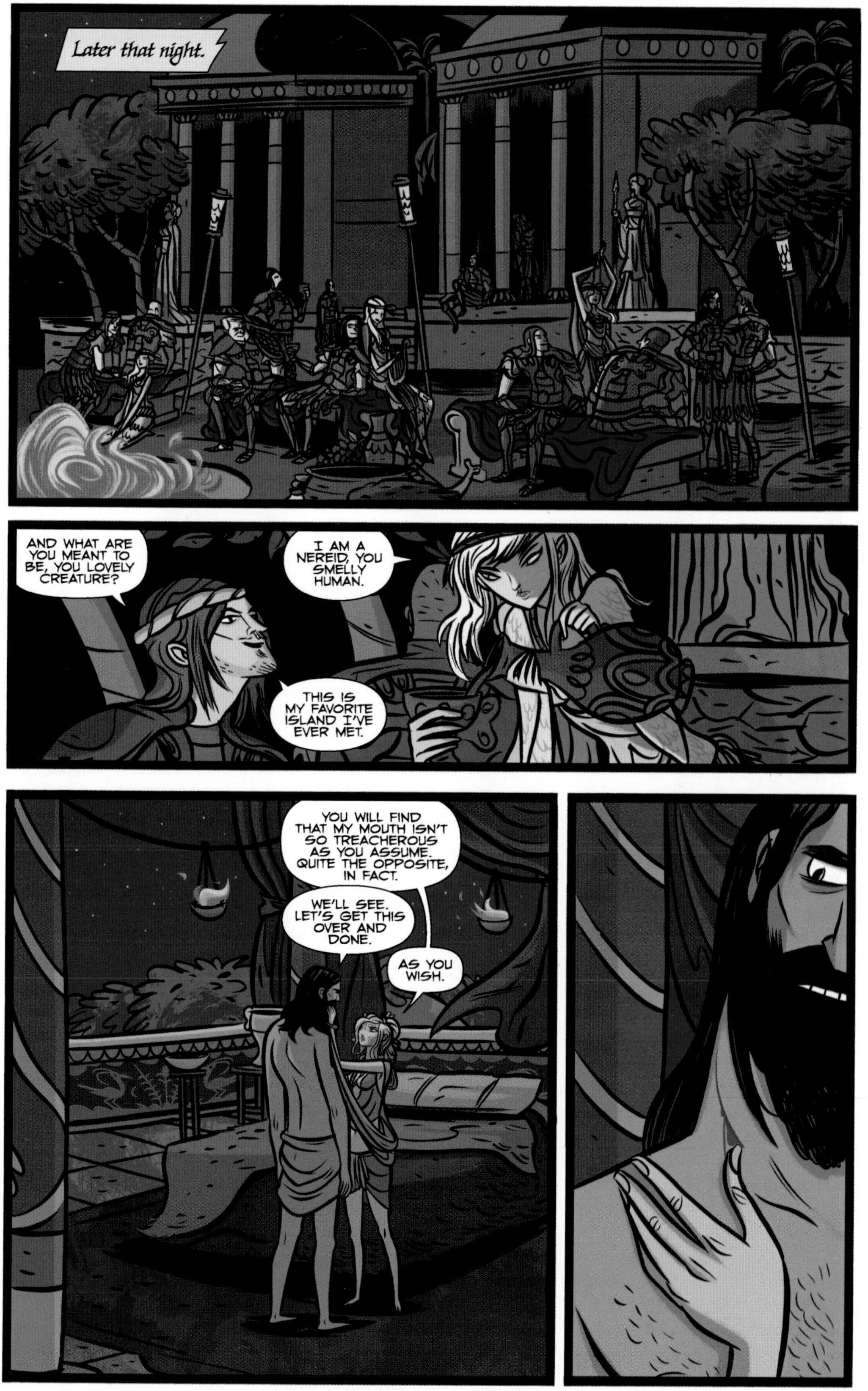

Later that night.
AND WHAT ARE YOU MEANT TO BE, YOU LOVELY CREATURE?
I AM A NEREID, YOU SMELLY HUMAN.
THIS IS MY FAVORITE ISLAND I'VE EVER MET.
YOU WILL FIND THAT MY MOUTH ISN'T SO TREACHEROUS AS YOU ASSUME. QUITE THE OPPOSITE, IN FACT.
WE'LL SEE. LET'S GET THIS OVER AND DONE.
AS YOU WISH.

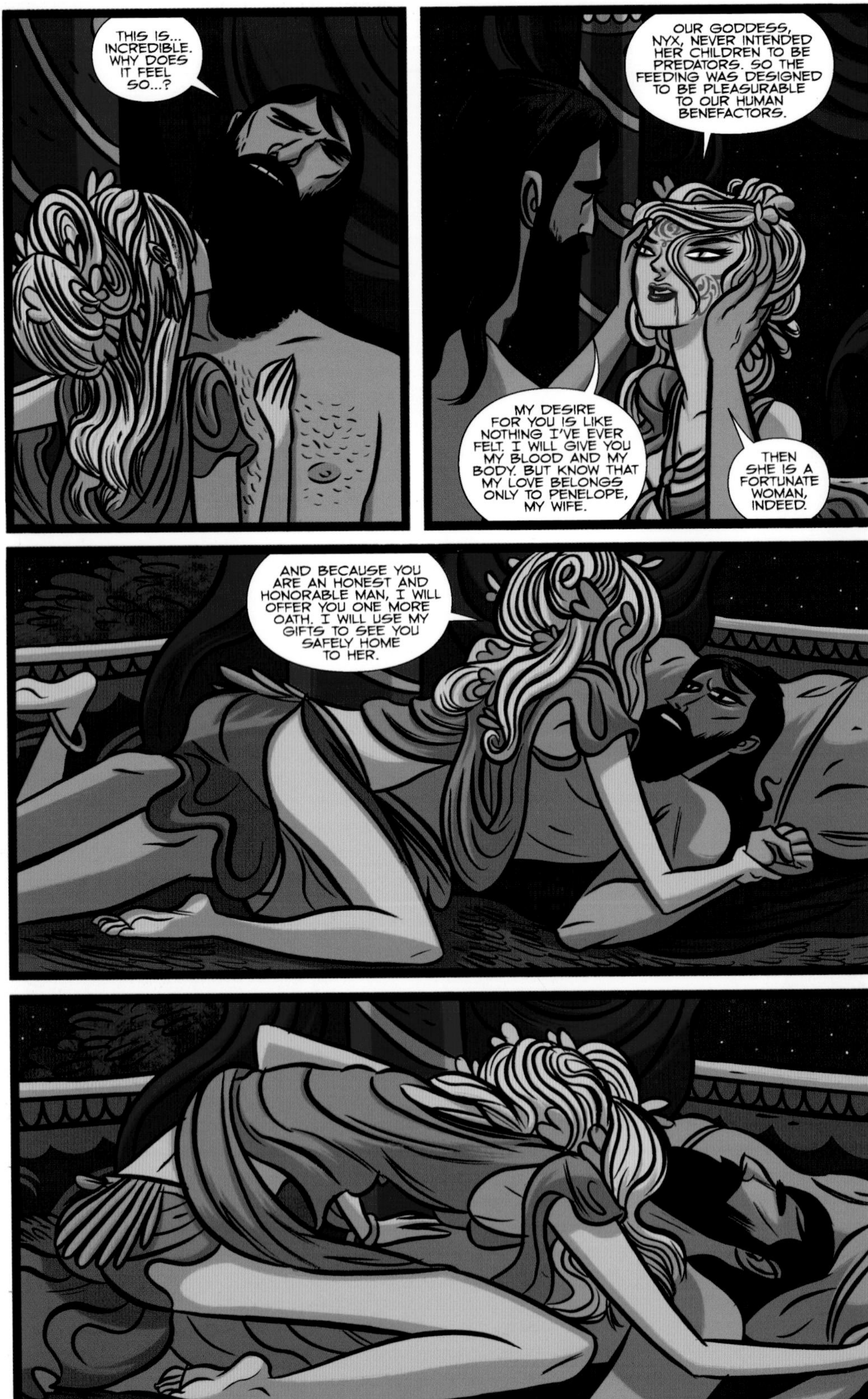
THIS IS... INCREDIBLE. WHY DOES IT FEEL SO...?
OUR GODDESS, NYX, NEVER INTENDED HER CHILDREN TO BE PREDATORS. SO THE FEEDING WAS DESIGNED TO BE PLEASURABLE TO OUR HUMAN BENEFACTORS.
MY DESIRE FOR YOU IS LIKE NOTHING I'VE EVER FELT. I WILL GIVE YOU MY BLOOD AND MY BODY. BUT KNOW THAT MY LOVE BELONGS ONLY TO PENELOPE, MY WIFE.
THEN SHE IS A FORTUNATE WOMAN, INDEED.
AND BECAUSE YOU ARE AN HONEST AND HONORABLE MAN, I WILL OFFER YOU ONE MORE OATH. I WILL USE MY GIFTS TO SEE YOU SAFELY HOME TO HER.

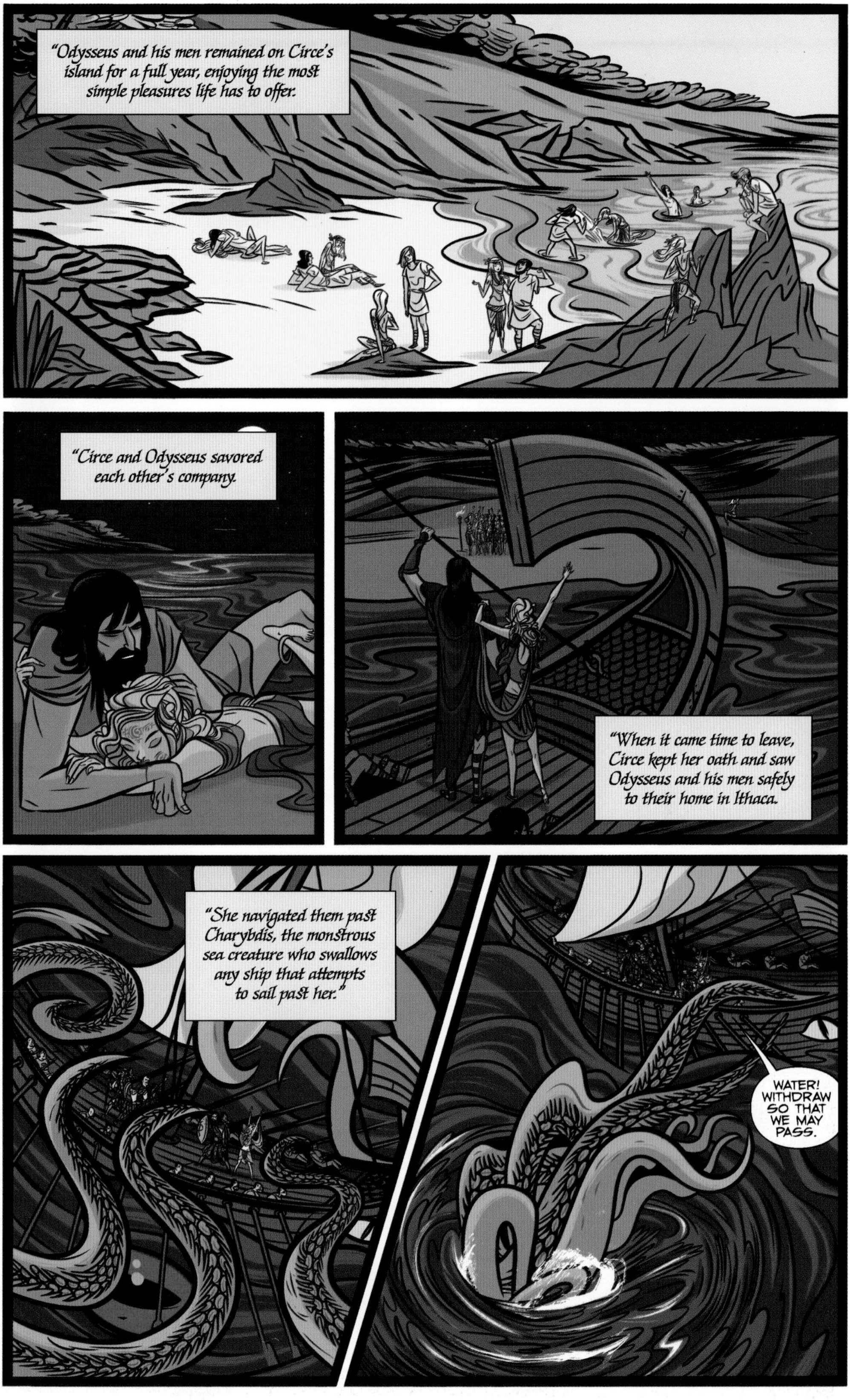
"Odysseus and his men remained on Circe's island for a full year, enjoying the most simple pleasures life has to offer.
"Circe and Odysseus savored each other's company.
"When it came time to leave, Circe kept her oath and saw Odysseus and his men safely to their home in Ithaca.
"She navigated them past Charybdis, the monstrous sea creature who swallows any ship that attempts to sail past her."
WATER! WITHDRAW SO THAT WE MAY PASS.

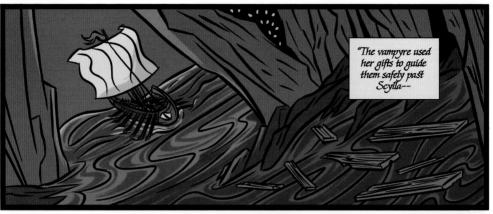

"The vampyre used her gifts to guide them safely past Scylla--"

"--the serpent who feasts on Charybdis's survivors.

WATER, SHIELD US!

"The final threat was the seductive, deathly song of the Sirens."

"The Siren's Song drove human men mad with passion. They had no choice but to answer its call..."

"No man, no matter his strength, had ever been able to resist it.

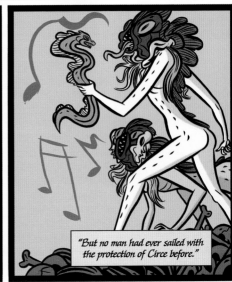

"But no man had ever sailed with the protection of Circe before."

ILLUSION!

CIRCE, YOU ACCURSED WITCH!!

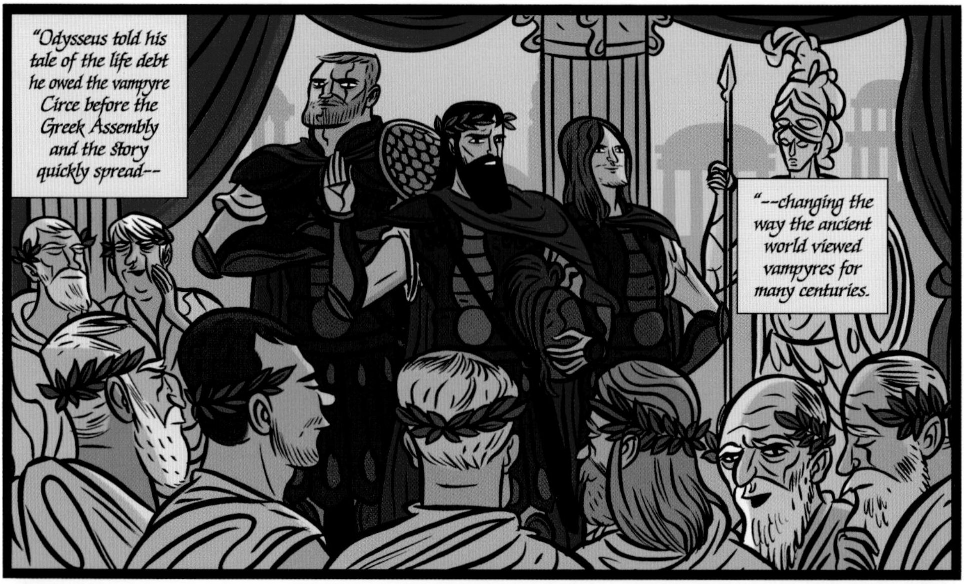
"Odysseus told his tale of the life debt he owed the vampyre Circe before the Greek Assembly and the story quickly spread--
"--changing the way the ancient world viewed vampyres for many centuries.

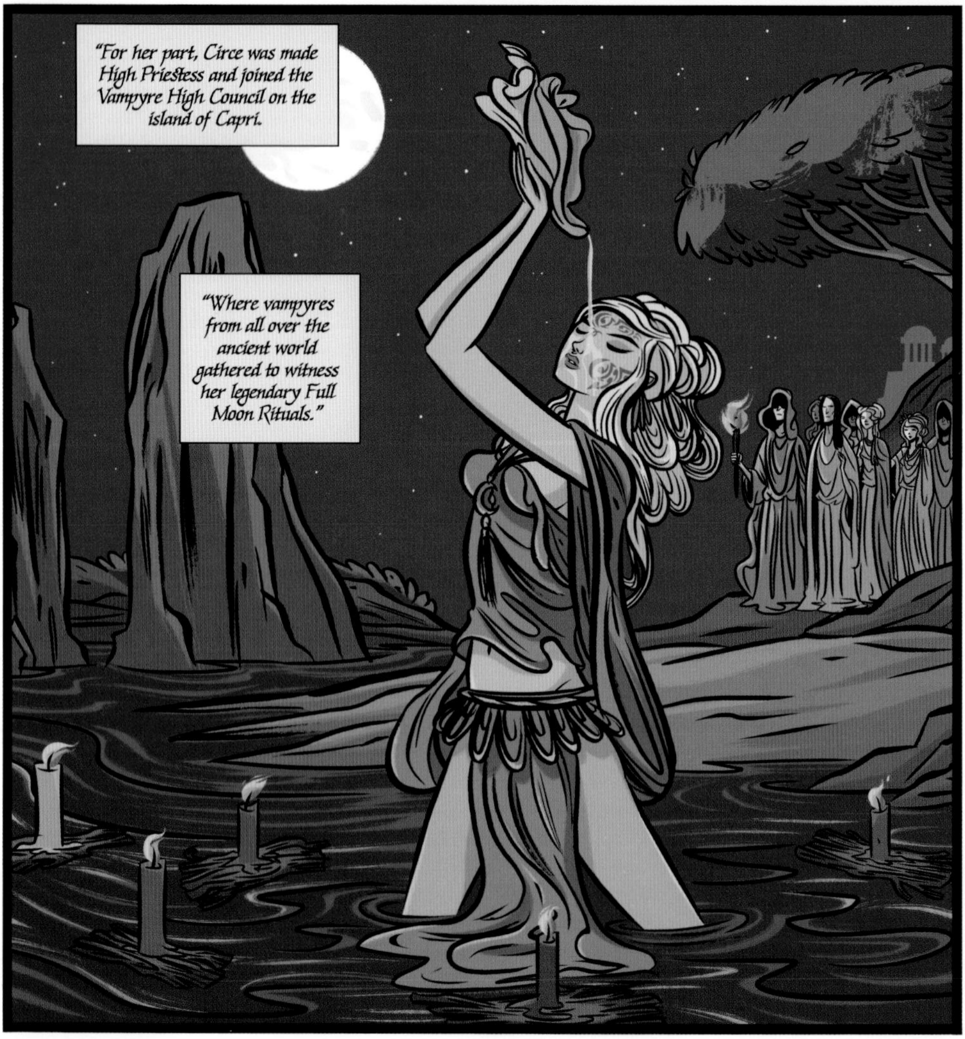
"For her part, Circe was made High Priestess and joined the Vampyre High Council on the island of Capri.
"Where vampyres from all over the ancient world gathered to witness her legendary Full Moon Rituals."

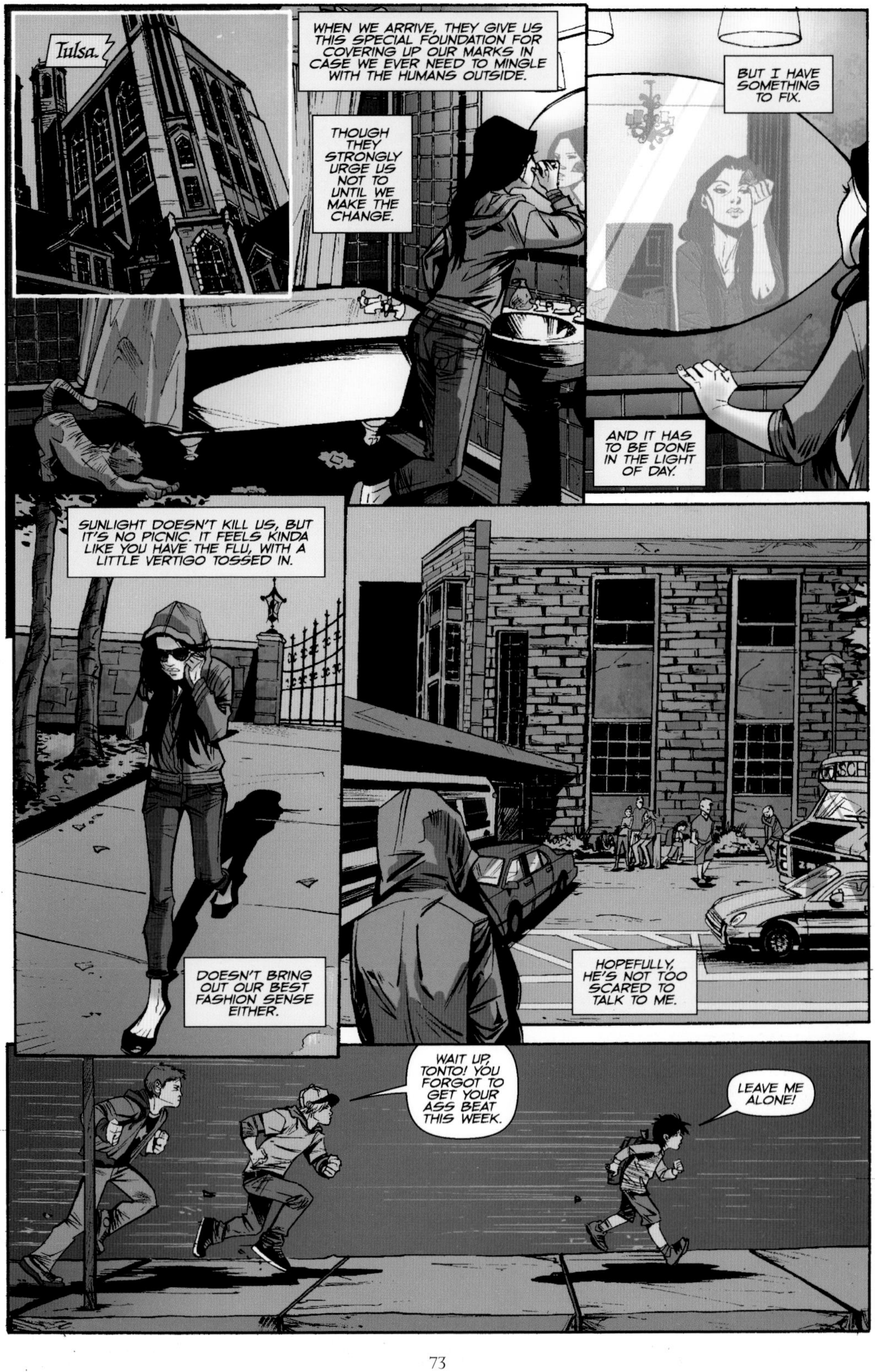
Tulsa.
WHEN WE ARRIVE, THEY GIVE US THIS SPECIAL FOUNDATION FOR COVERING UP OUR MARKS IN CASE WE EVER NEED TO MINGLE WITH THE HUMANS OUTSIDE.
THOUGH THEY STRONGLY URGE US NOT TO UNTIL WE MAKE THE CHANGE.
BUT I HAVE SOMETHING TO FIX.
AND IT HAS TO BE DONE IN THE LIGHT OF DAY.
SUNLIGHT DOESN'T KILL US, BUT IT'S NO PICNIC. IT FEELS KINDA LIKE YOU HAVE THE FLU, WITH A LITTLE VERTIGO TOSSED IN.
DOESN'T BRING OUT OUR BEST FASHION SENSE EITHER.
HOPEFULLY, HE'S NOT TOO SCARED TO TALK TO ME.
WAIT UP, TONTO! YOU FORGOT TO GET YOUR ASS BEAT THIS WEEK.
LEAVE ME ALONE!

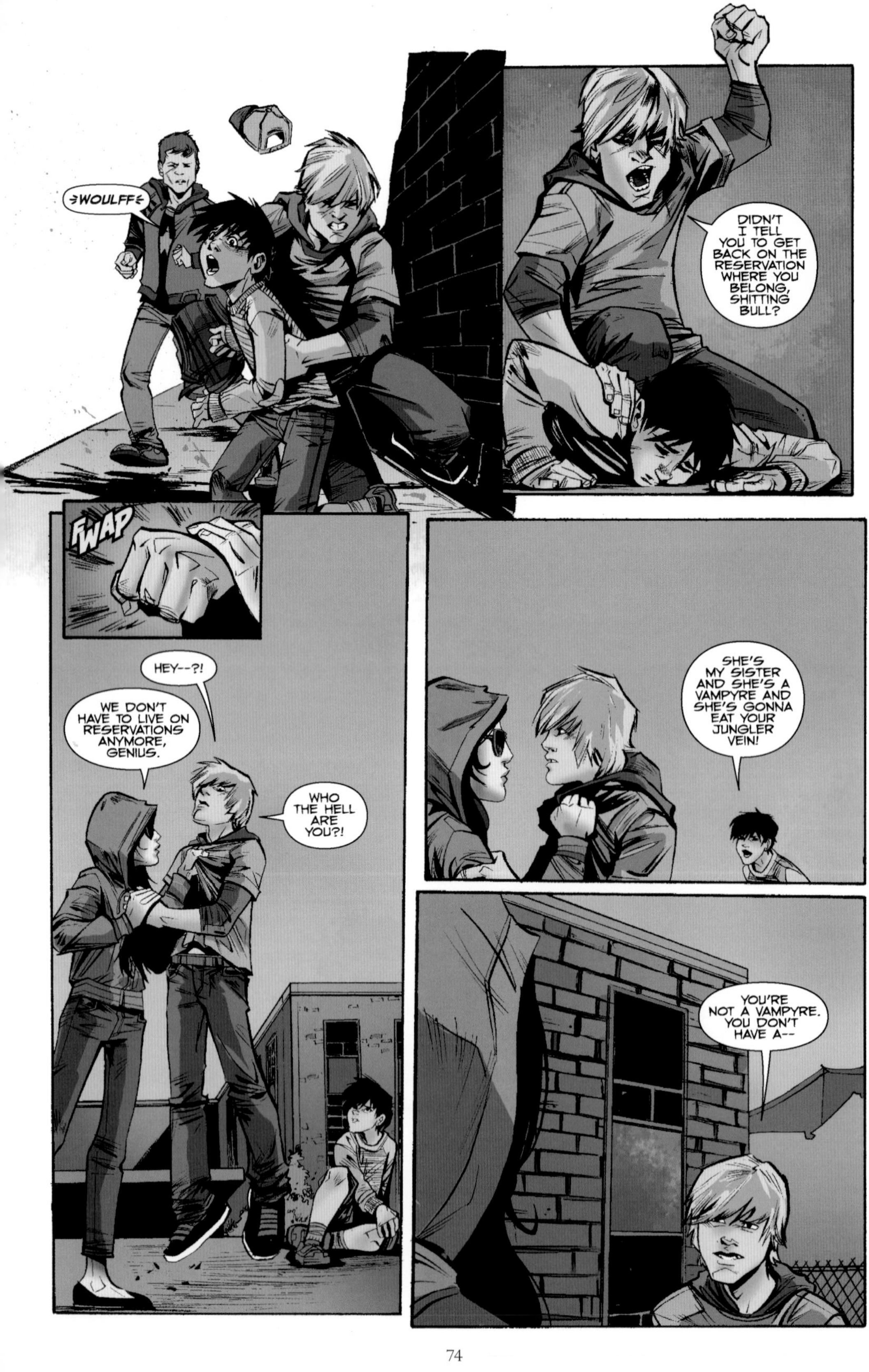
WOULFF
DIDN'T I TELL YOU TO GET BACK ON THE RESERVATION WHERE YOU BELONG, SHITTING BULL?
FWAP
HEY--?!
WE DON'T HAVE TO LIVE ON RESERVATIONS ANYMORE, GENIUS.
WHO THE HELL ARE YOU?!
SHE'S MY SISTER AND SHE'S A VAMPYRE AND SHE'S GONNA EAT YOUR JUNGLER VEIN!
YOU'RE NOT A VAMPYRE. YOU DON'T HAVE A--

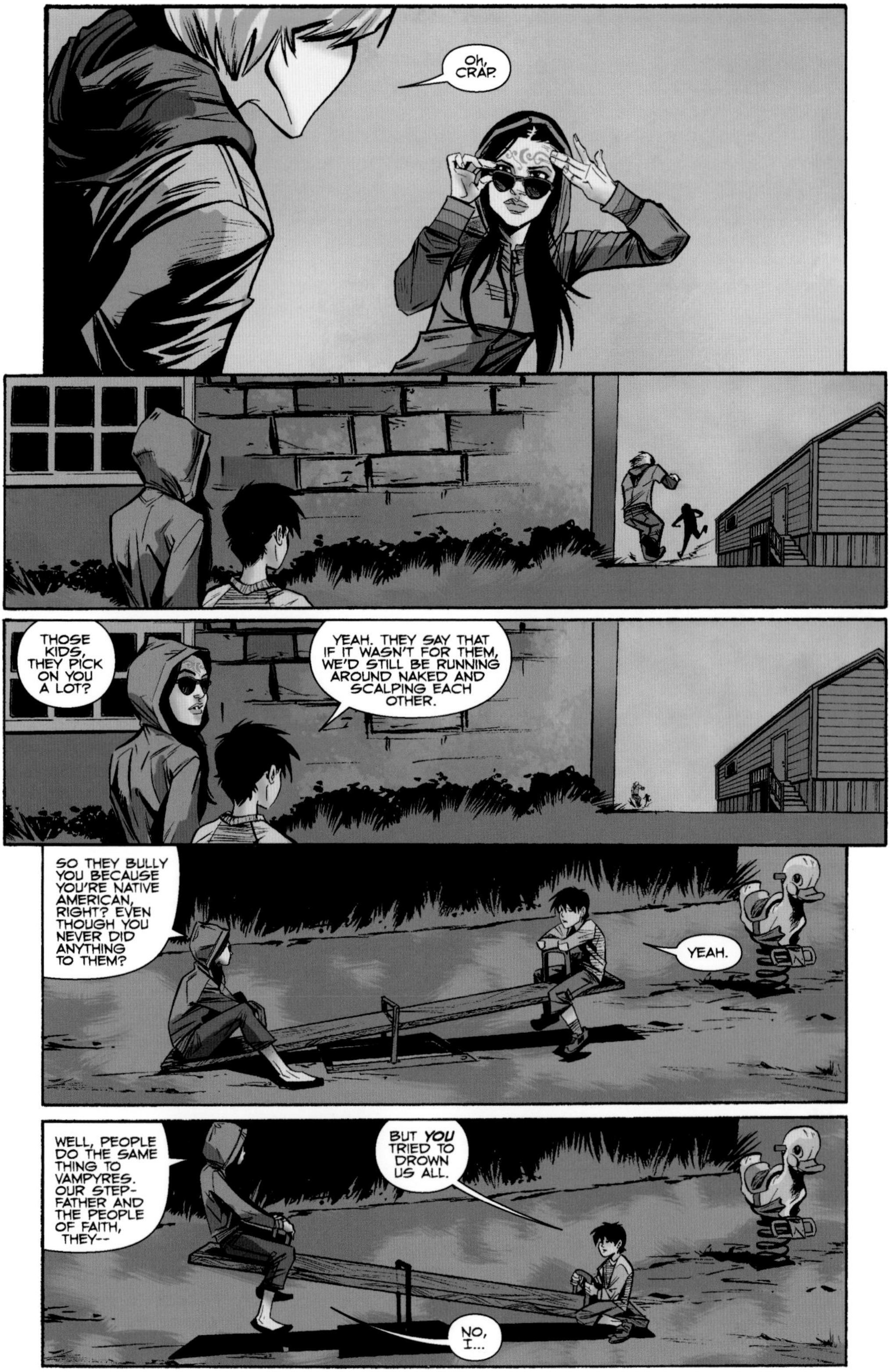
Oh, CRAP.
THOSE KIDS, THEY PICK ON YOU A LOT?
YEAH. THEY SAY THAT IF IT WASN'T FOR THEM, WE'D STILL BE RUNNING AROUND NAKED AND SCALPING EACH OTHER.
SO THEY BULLY YOU BECAUSE YOU'RE NATIVE AMERICAN, RIGHT? EVEN THOUGH YOU NEVER DID ANYTHING TO THEM?
YEAH.
WELL, PEOPLE DO THE SAME THING TO VAMPYRES. OUR STEP-FATHER AND THE PEOPLE OF FAITH, THEY--
BUT YOU TRIED TO DROWN US ALL.
NO, I...

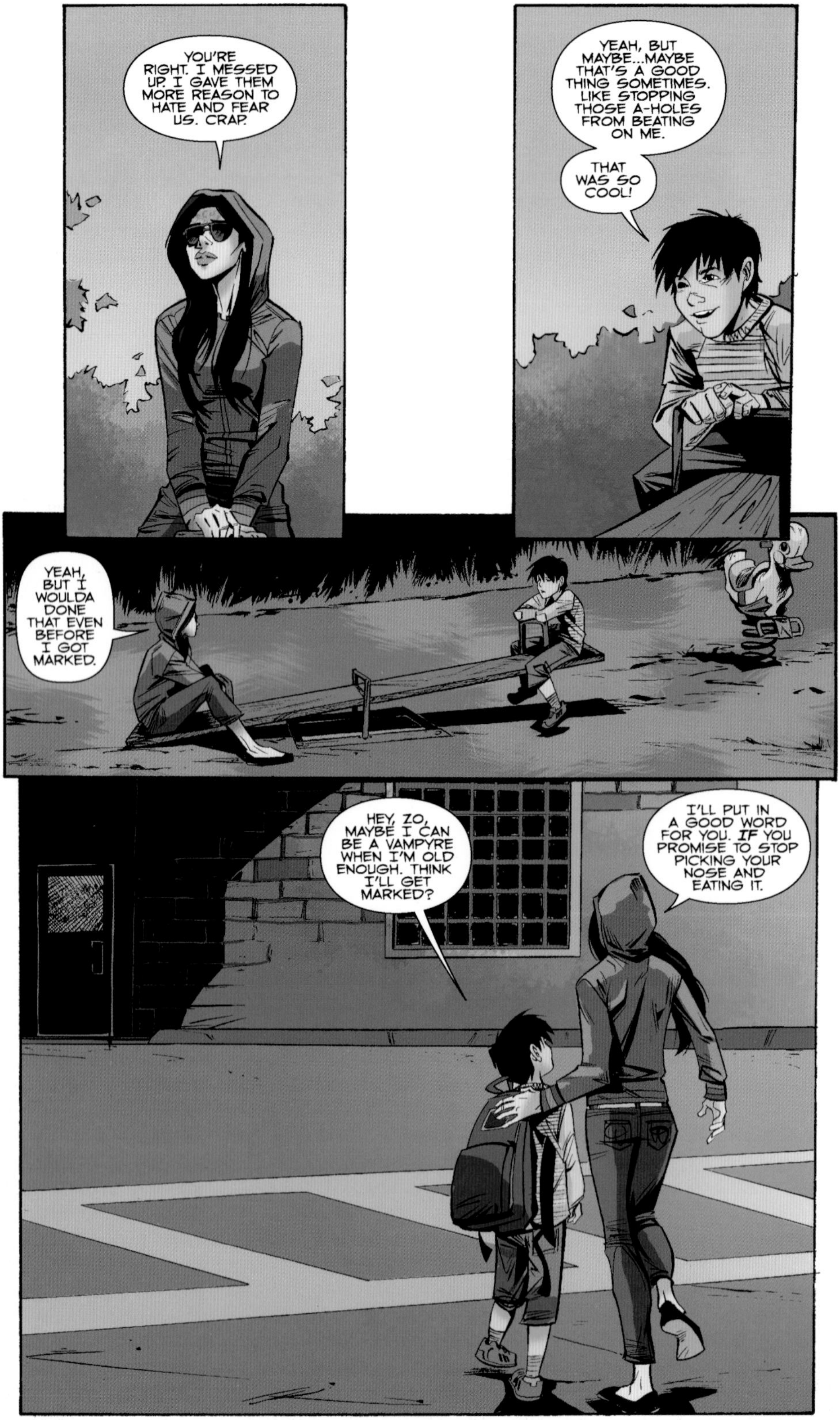
YOU'RE RIGHT. I MESSED UP. I GAVE THEM MORE REASON TO HATE AND FEAR US. CRAP.
YEAH, BUT MAYBE...MAYBE THAT'S A GOOD THING SOMETIMES. LIKE STOPPING THOSE A-HOLES FROM BEATING ON ME.
THAT WAS SO COOL!
YEAH, BUT I WOULDA DONE THAT EVEN BEFORE I GOT MARKED.
HEY, ZO, MAYBE I CAN BE A VAMPYRE WHEN I'M OLD ENOUGH. THINK I'LL GET MARKED?
I'LL PUT IN A GOOD WORD FOR YOU. IF YOU PROMISE TO STOP PICKING YOUR NOSE AND EATING IT.

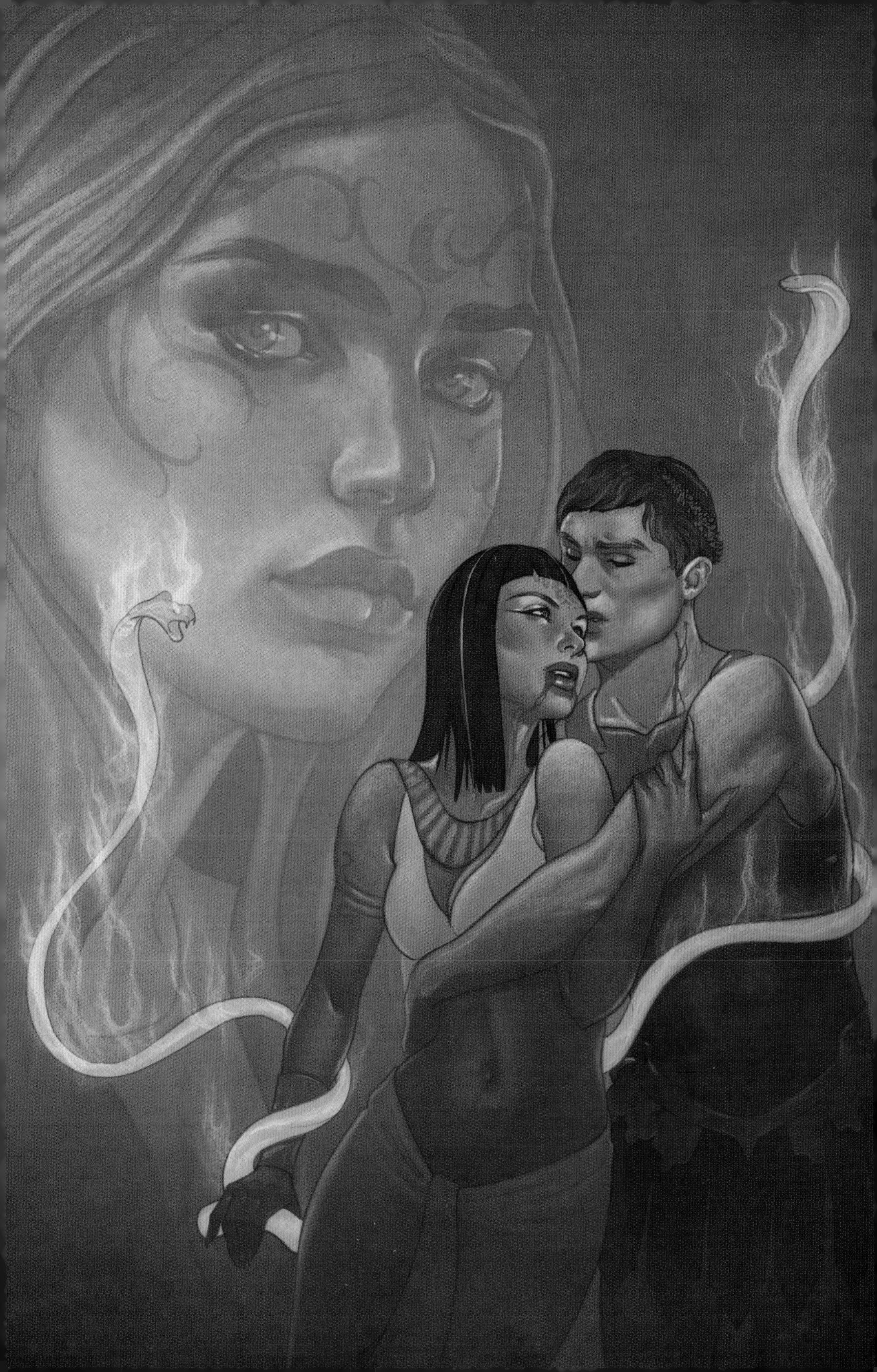

FIRE

STORY BY
P. C. CAST
AND **KRISTIN CAST**

SCRIPT BY
KENT DALIAN

ART BY
JOËLLE JONES
AND **JONATHAN CASE**

COLORS BY
RYAN HILL
AND **JONATHAN CASE**

LETTERS BY
NATE PIEKOS OF **BLAMBOT®**

CHAPTER ILLUSTRATION BY
JENNY FRISON

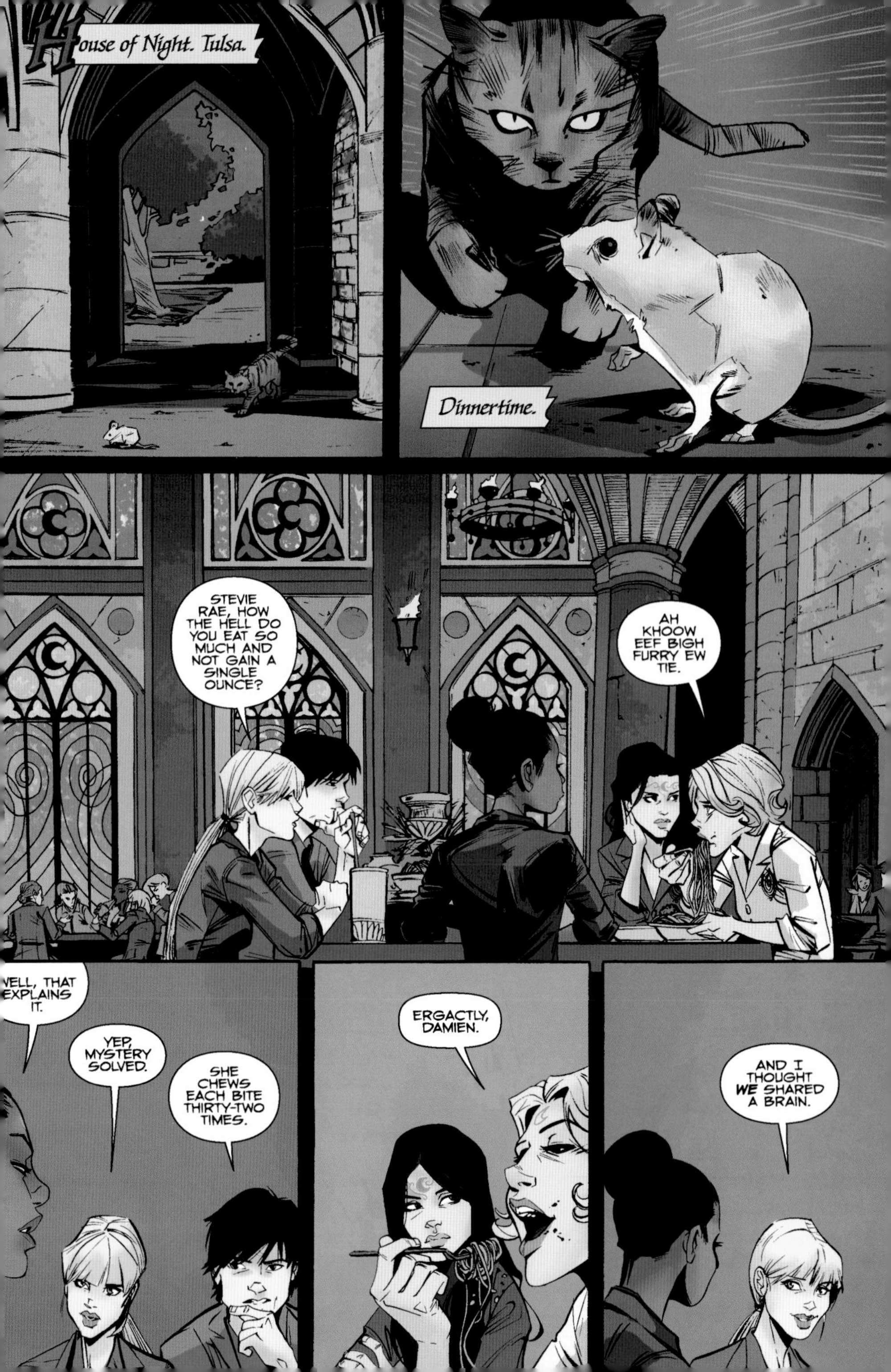
House of Night. Tulsa.
Dinnertime.
STEVIE RAE, HOW THE HELL DO YOU EAT SO MUCH AND NOT GAIN A SINGLE OUNCE?
AH KHOOW EEF BIGH FURRY EW TIE.
WELL, THAT EXPLAINS IT.
YEP, MYSTERY SOLVED.
SHE CHEWS EACH BITE THIRTY-TWO TIMES.
ERGACTLY, DAMIEN.
AND I THOUGHT **WE** SHARED A BRAIN.

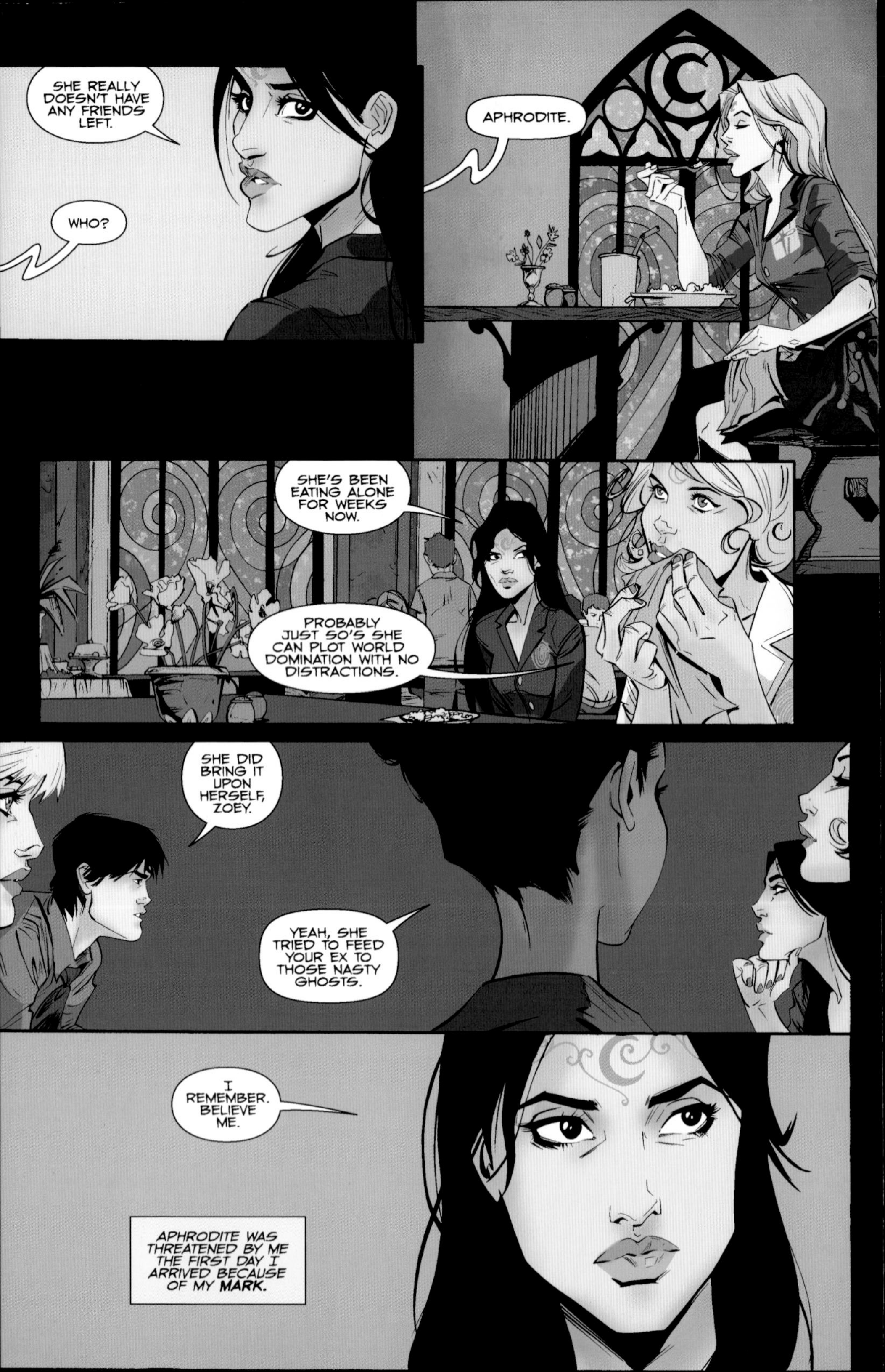
SHE REALLY DOESN'T HAVE ANY FRIENDS LEFT.
WHO?
APHRODITE.
SHE'S BEEN EATING ALONE FOR WEEKS NOW.
PROBABLY JUST SO'S SHE CAN PLOT WORLD DOMINATION WITH NO DISTRACTIONS.
SHE DID BRING IT UPON HERSELF, ZOEY.
YEAH, SHE TRIED TO FEED YOUR EX TO THOSE NASTY GHOSTS.
I REMEMBER. BELIEVE ME.
APHRODITE WAS THREATENED BY ME THE FIRST DAY I ARRIVED BECAUSE OF MY MARK.

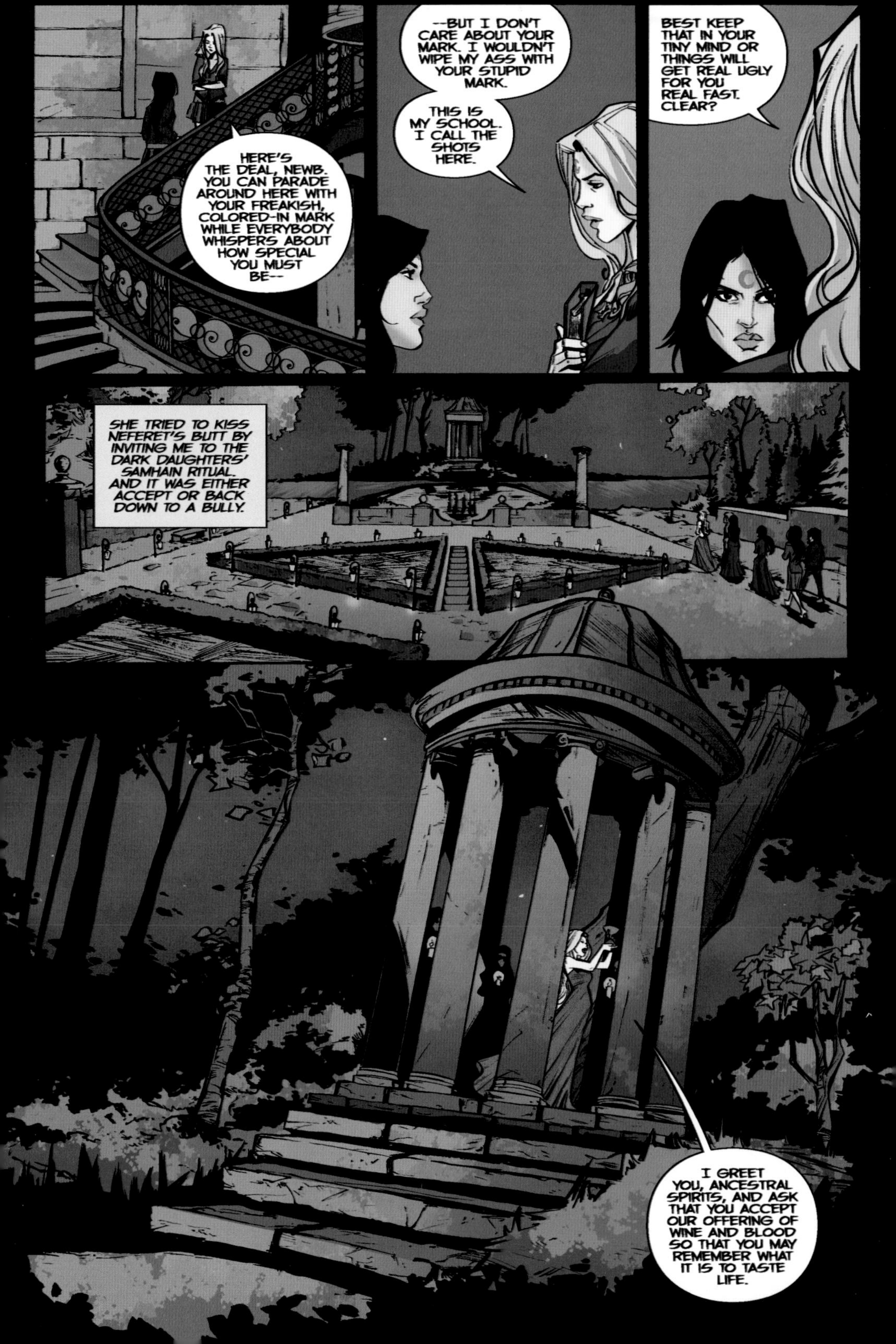
HERE'S THE DEAL, NEWB. YOU CAN PARADE AROUND HERE WITH YOUR FREAKISH, COLORED-IN MARK WHILE EVERYBODY WHISPERS ABOUT HOW SPECIAL YOU MUST BE--
--BUT I DON'T CARE ABOUT YOUR MARK. I WOULDN'T WIPE MY ASS WITH YOUR STUPID MARK.
THIS IS MY SCHOOL. I CALL THE SHOTS HERE.
BEST KEEP THAT IN YOUR TINY MIND OR THINGS WILL GET REAL UGLY FOR YOU REAL FAST. CLEAR?
SHE TRIED TO KISS NEFERET'S BUTT BY INVITING ME TO THE DARK DAUGHTERS' SAMHAIN RITUAL. AND IT WAS EITHER ACCEPT OR BACK DOWN TO A BULLY.
I GREET YOU, ANCESTRAL SPIRITS, AND ASK THAT YOU ACCEPT OUR OFFERING OF WINE AND BLOOD SO THAT YOU MAY REMEMBER WHAT IT IS TO TASTE LIFE.

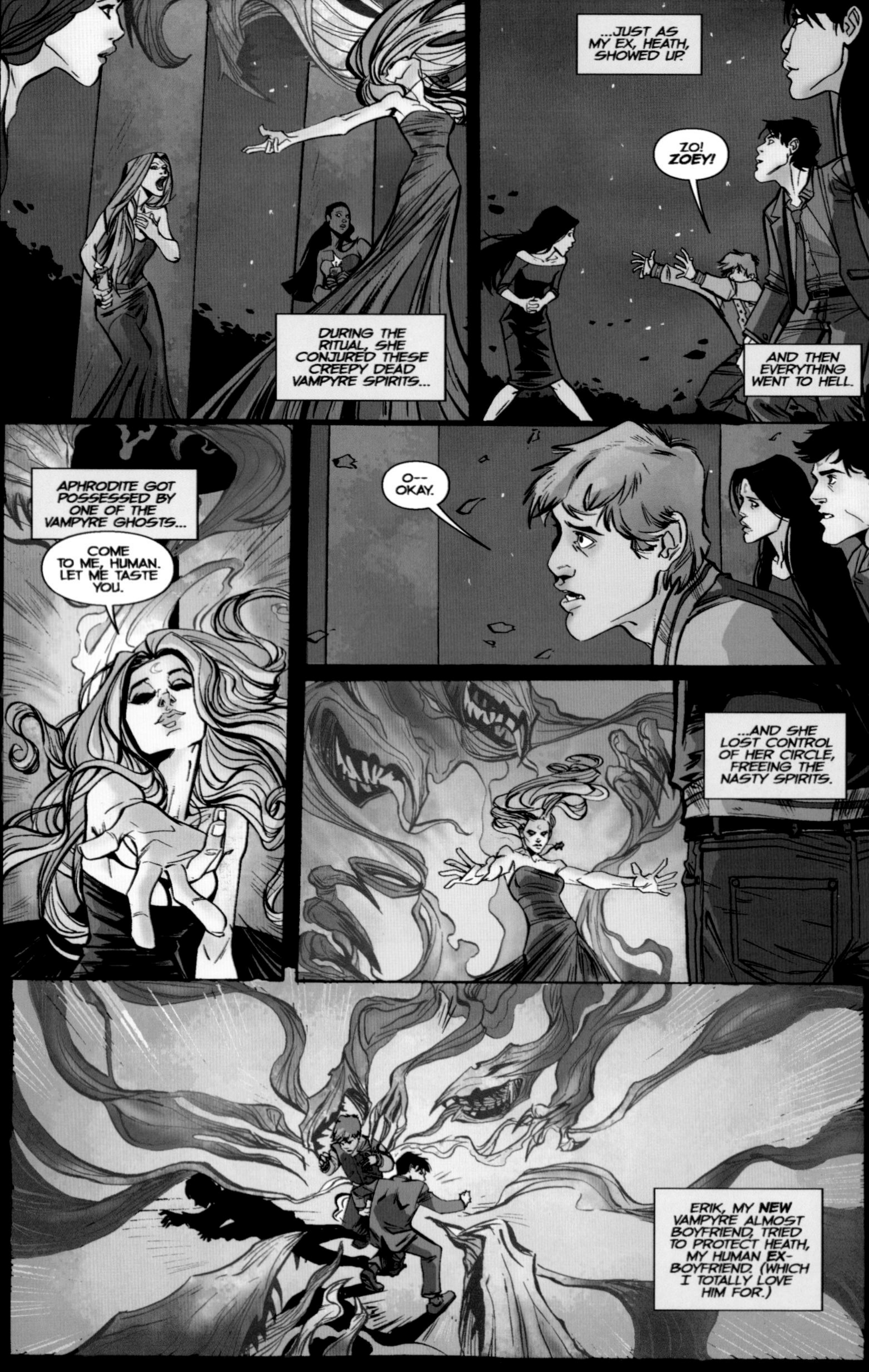
DURING THE RITUAL, SHE CONJURED THESE CREEPY DEAD VAMPYRE SPIRITS...
...JUST AS MY EX, HEATH, SHOWED UP.
ZO! ZOEY!
AND THEN EVERYTHING WENT TO HELL.
APHRODITE GOT POSSESSED BY ONE OF THE VAMPYRE GHOSTS...
COME TO ME, HUMAN. LET ME TASTE YOU.
O-- OKAY.
...AND SHE LOST CONTROL OF HER CIRCLE, FREEING THE NASTY SPIRITS.
ERIK, MY NEW VAMPYRE ALMOST BOYFRIEND, TRIED TO PROTECT HEATH, MY HUMAN EX-BOYFRIEND. (WHICH I TOTALLY LOVE HIM FOR.)

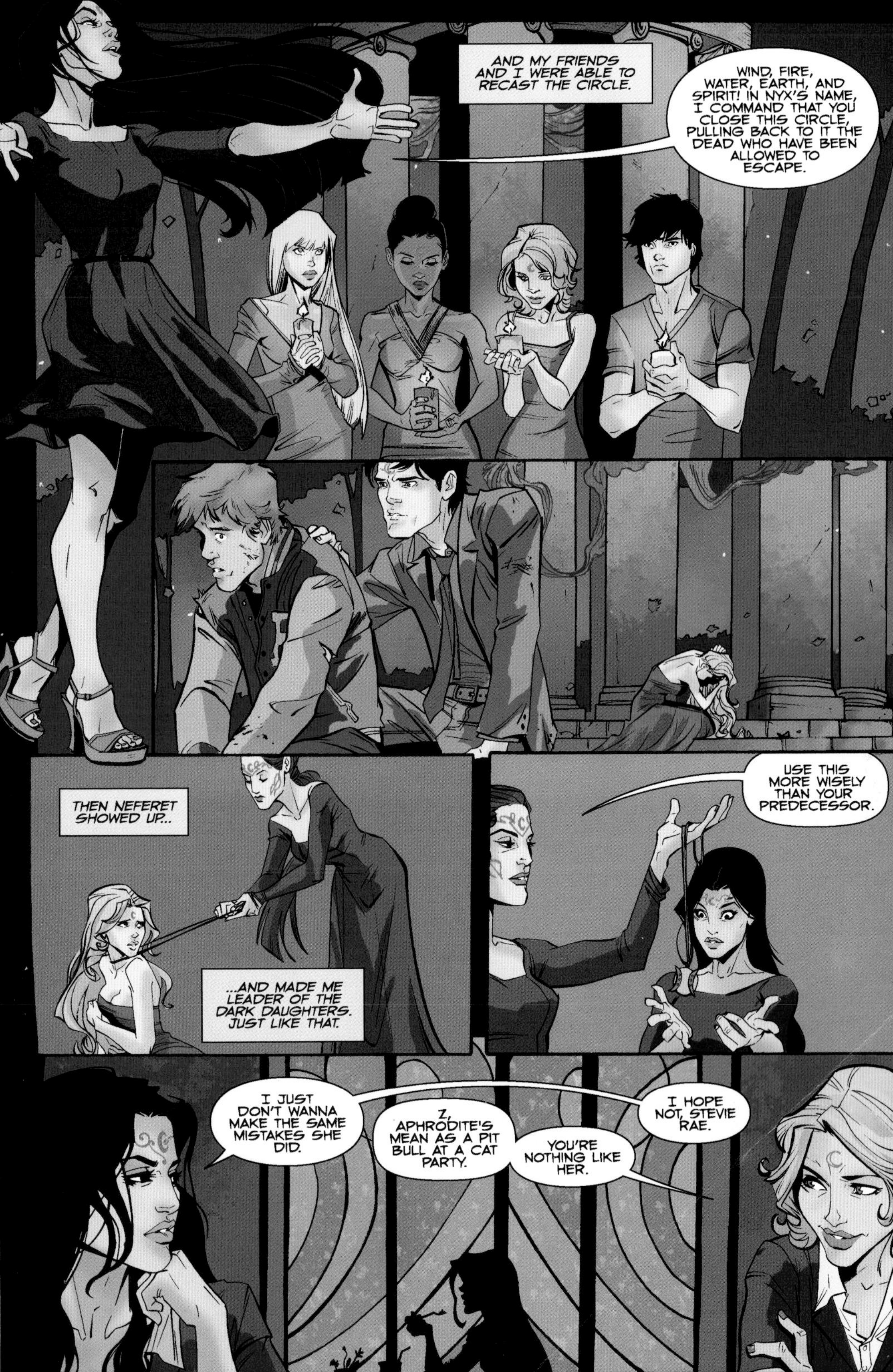
AND MY FRIENDS AND I WERE ABLE TO RECAST THE CIRCLE.
WIND, FIRE, WATER, EARTH, AND SPIRIT! IN NYX'S NAME, I COMMAND THAT YOU CLOSE THIS CIRCLE, PULLING BACK TO IT THE DEAD WHO HAVE BEEN ALLOWED TO ESCAPE.
THEN NEFERET SHOWED UP...
...AND MADE ME LEADER OF THE DARK DAUGHTERS. JUST LIKE THAT.
USE THIS MORE WISELY THAN YOUR PREDECESSOR.
I JUST DON'T WANNA MAKE THE SAME MISTAKES SHE DID.
Z, APHRODITE'S MEAN AS A PIT BULL AT A CAT PARTY.
YOU'RE NOTHING LIKE HER.
I HOPE NOT, STEVIE RAE.

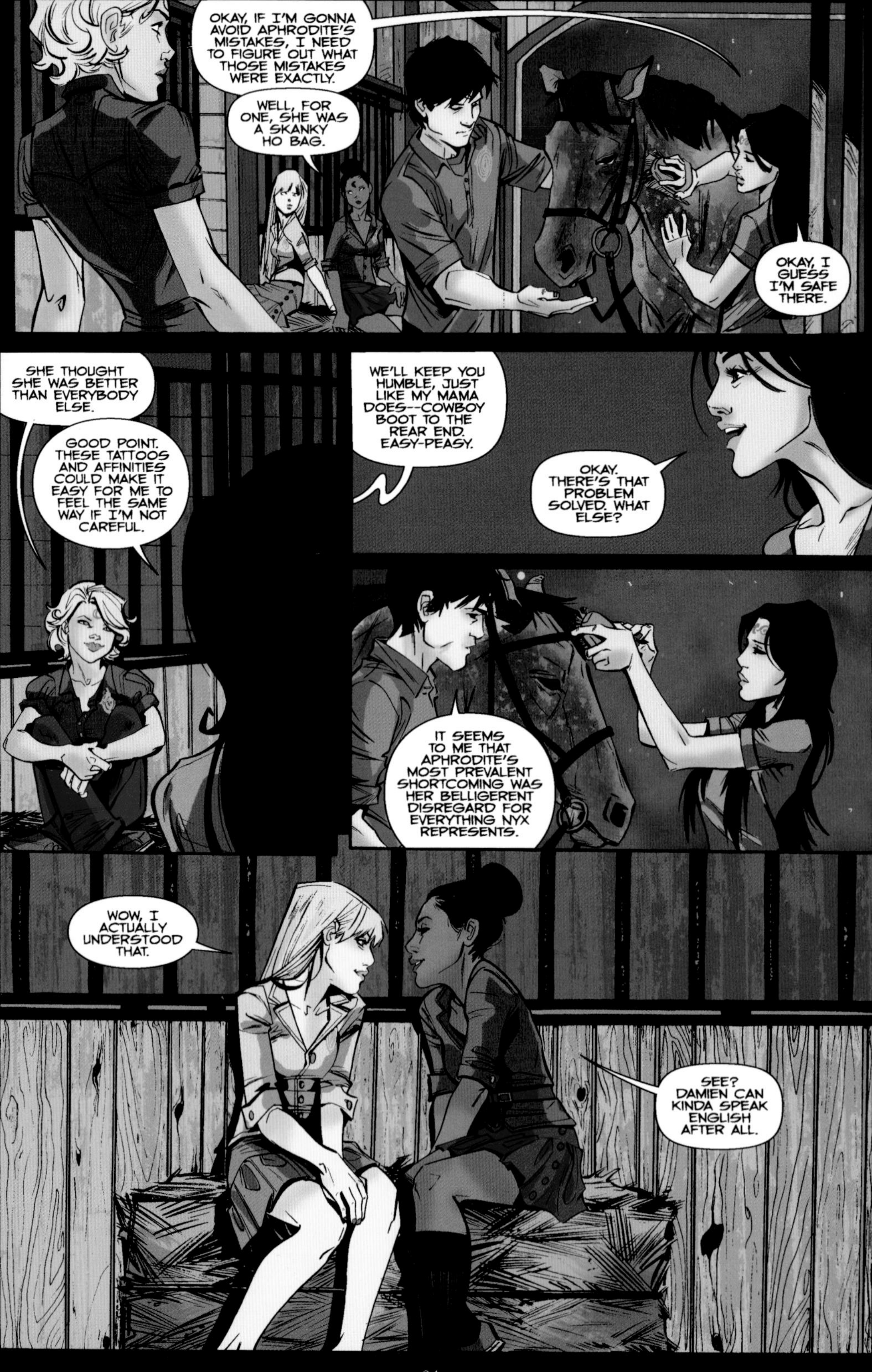
OKAY, IF I'M GONNA AVOID APHRODITE'S MISTAKES, I NEED TO FIGURE OUT WHAT THOSE MISTAKES WERE EXACTLY.
WELL, FOR ONE, SHE WAS A SKANKY HO BAG.
OKAY, I GUESS I'M SAFE THERE.
SHE THOUGHT SHE WAS BETTER THAN EVERYBODY ELSE.
GOOD POINT. THESE TATTOOS AND AFFINITIES COULD MAKE IT EASY FOR ME TO FEEL THE SAME WAY IF I'M NOT CAREFUL.
WE'LL KEEP YOU HUMBLE, JUST LIKE MY MAMA DOES--COWBOY BOOT TO THE REAR END. EASY-PEASY.
OKAY. THERE'S THAT PROBLEM SOLVED. WHAT ELSE?
IT SEEMS TO ME THAT APHRODITE'S MOST PREVALENT SHORTCOMING WAS HER BELLIGERENT DISREGARD FOR EVERYTHING NYX REPRESENTS.
WOW, I ACTUALLY UNDERSTOOD THAT.
SEE? DAMIEN CAN KINDA SPEAK ENGLISH AFTER ALL.

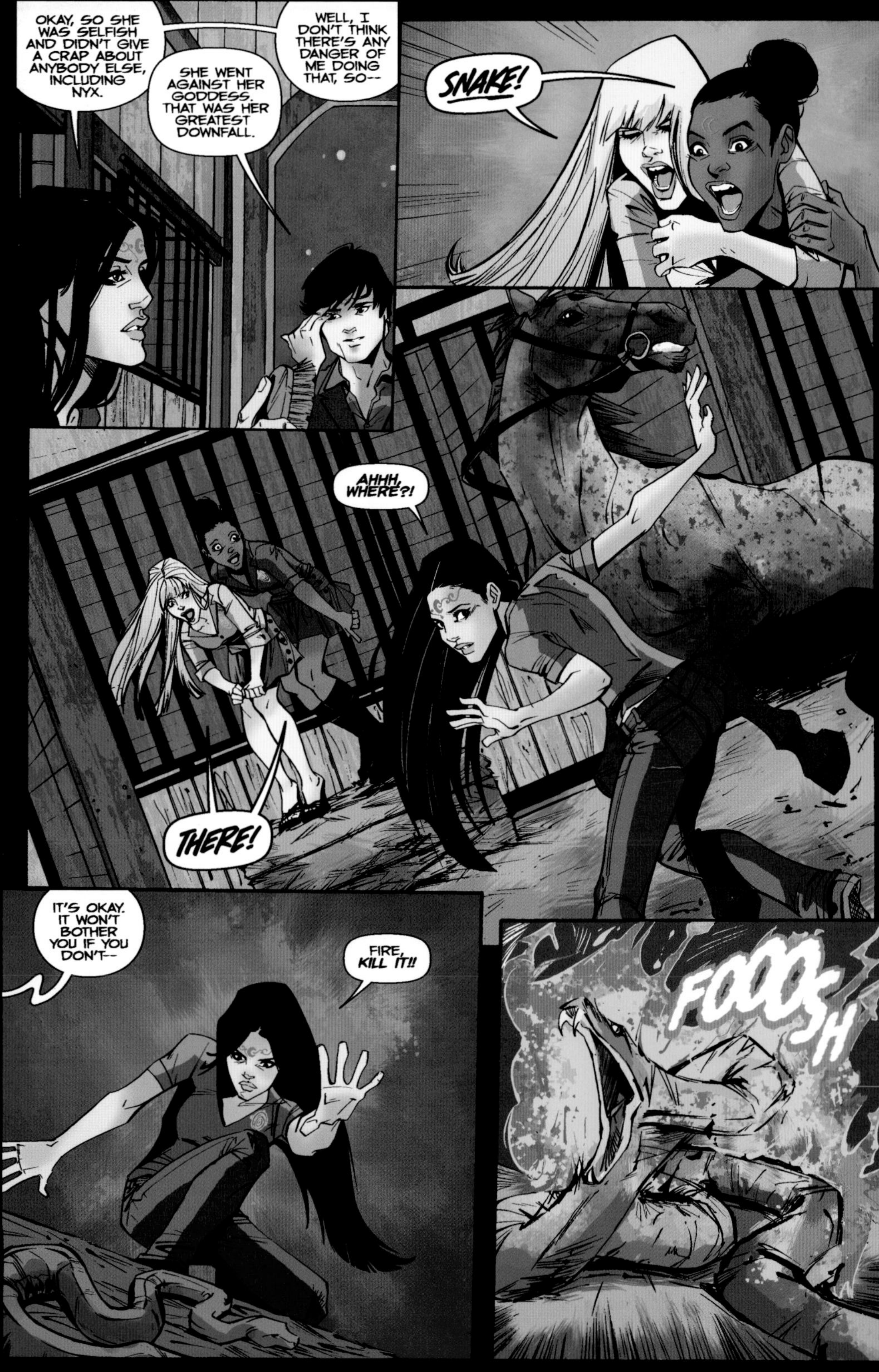
OKAY, SO SHE WAS SELFISH AND DIDN'T GIVE A CRAP ABOUT ANYBODY ELSE, INCLUDING NYX.
SHE WENT AGAINST HER GODDESS. THAT WAS HER GREATEST DOWNFALL.
WELL, I DON'T THINK THERE'S ANY DANGER OF ME DOING THAT, SO--
SNAKE!
AHHH, WHERE?!
THERE!
IT'S OKAY. IT WON'T BOTHER YOU IF YOU DON'T--
FIRE, KILL IT!!
FOOOSH

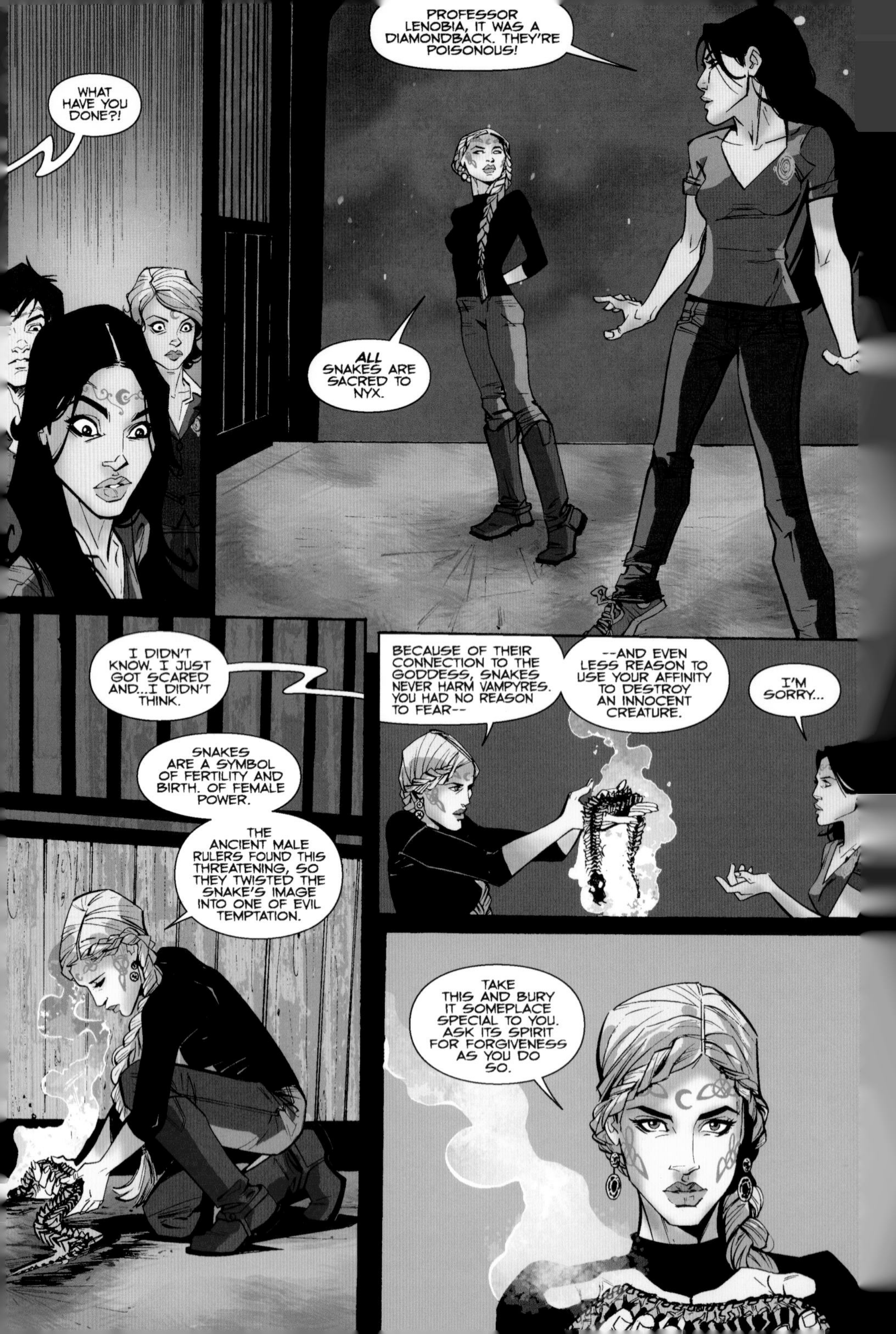
WHAT HAVE YOU DONE?!
PROFESSOR LENOBIA, IT WAS A DIAMONDBACK. THEY'RE POISONOUS!
ALL SNAKES ARE SACRED TO NYX.
I DIDN'T KNOW. I JUST GOT SCARED AND...I DIDN'T THINK.
SNAKES ARE A SYMBOL OF FERTILITY AND BIRTH. OF FEMALE POWER.
THE ANCIENT MALE RULERS FOUND THIS THREATENING, SO THEY TWISTED THE SNAKE'S IMAGE INTO ONE OF EVIL TEMPTATION.
BECAUSE OF THEIR CONNECTION TO THE GODDESS, SNAKES NEVER HARM VAMPYRES. YOU HAD NO REASON TO FEAR--
--AND EVEN LESS REASON TO USE YOUR AFFINITY TO DESTROY AN INNOCENT CREATURE.
I'M SORRY...
TAKE THIS AND BURY IT SOMEPLACE SPECIAL TO YOU. ASK ITS SPIRIT FOR FORGIVENESS AS YOU DO SO.

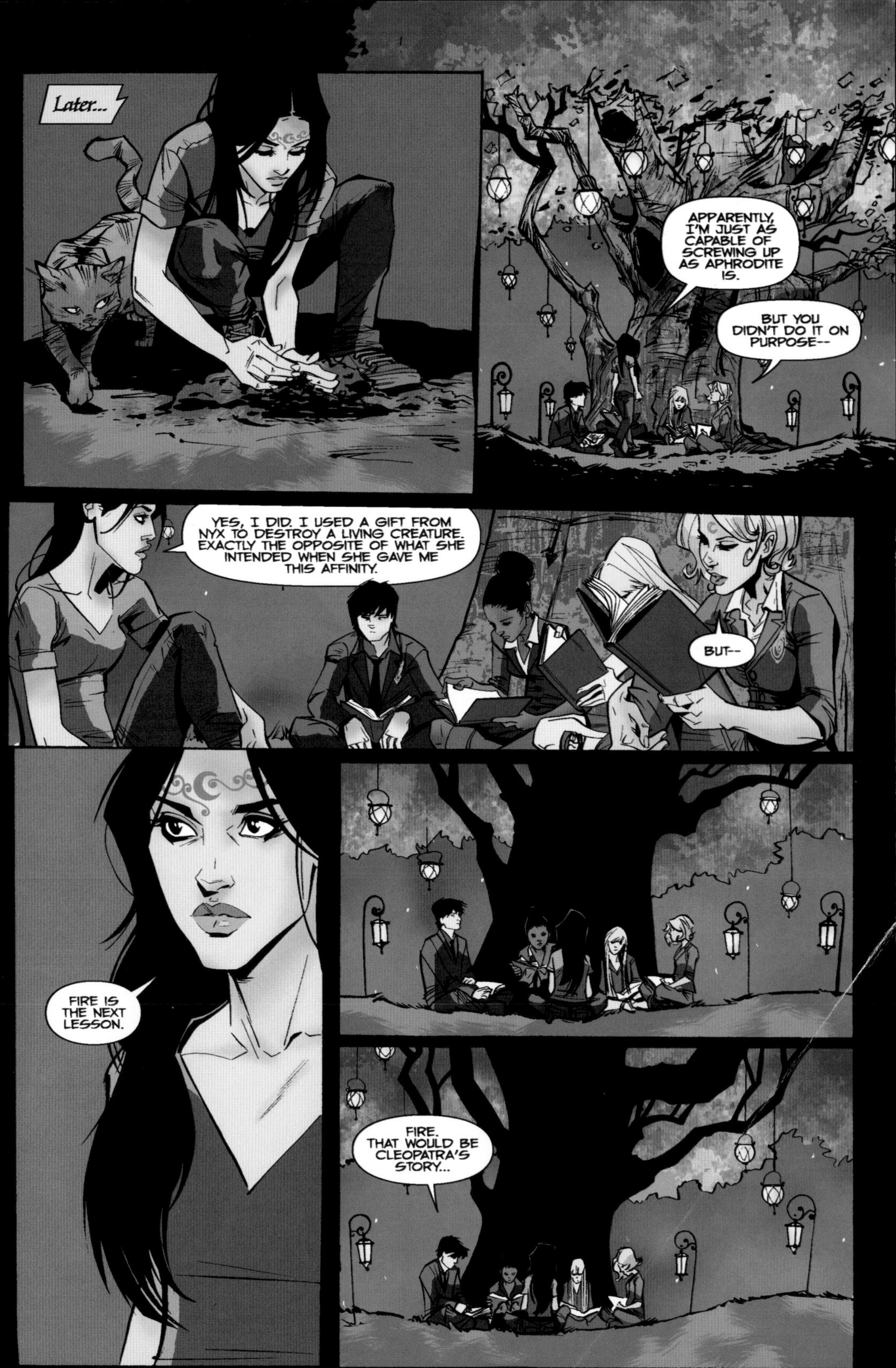
Later...
APPARENTLY, I'M JUST AS CAPABLE OF SCREWING UP AS APHRODITE IS.
BUT YOU DIDN'T DO IT ON PURPOSE--
YES, I DID. I USED A GIFT FROM NYX TO DESTROY A LIVING CREATURE. EXACTLY THE OPPOSITE OF WHAT SHE INTENDED WHEN SHE GAVE ME THIS AFFINITY.
BUT--
FIRE IS THE NEXT LESSON.
FIRE. THAT WOULD BE CLEOPATRA'S STORY...

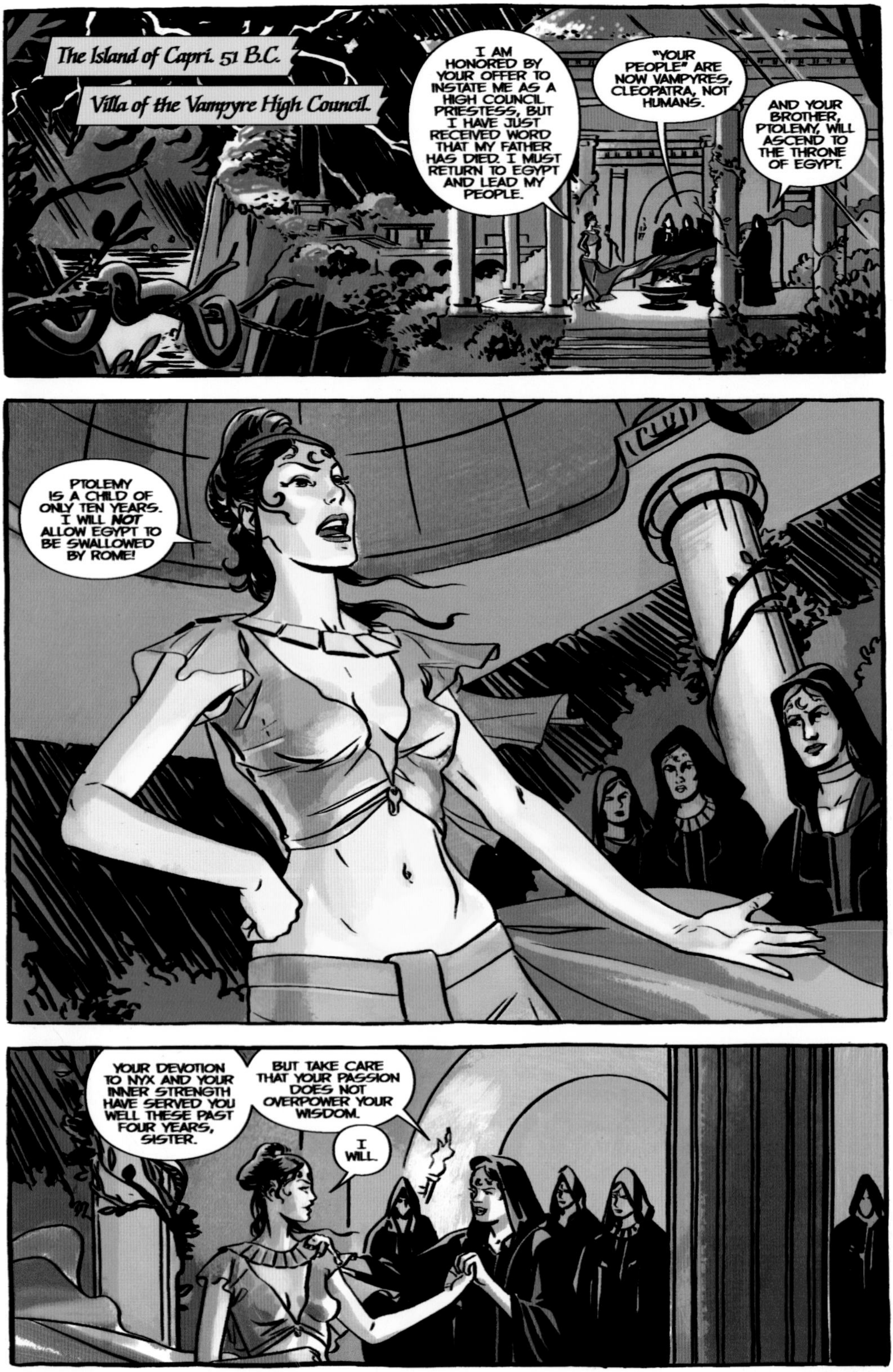
The Island of Capri. 51 B.C.
Villa of the Vampyre High Council.
I AM HONORED BY YOUR OFFER TO INSTATE ME AS A HIGH COUNCIL PRIESTESS, BUT I HAVE JUST RECEIVED WORD THAT MY FATHER HAS DIED. I MUST RETURN TO EGYPT AND LEAD MY PEOPLE.
"YOUR PEOPLE" ARE NOW VAMPYRES, CLEOPATRA, NOT HUMANS.
AND YOUR BROTHER, PTOLEMY, WILL ASCEND TO THE THRONE OF EGYPT.
PTOLEMY IS A CHILD OF ONLY TEN YEARS. I WILL *NOT* ALLOW EGYPT TO BE SWALLOWED BY ROME!
YOUR DEVOTION TO NYX AND YOUR INNER STRENGTH HAVE SERVED YOU WELL THESE PAST FOUR YEARS, SISTER.
BUT TAKE CARE THAT YOUR PASSION DOES NOT OVERPOWER YOUR WISDOM.
I WILL.

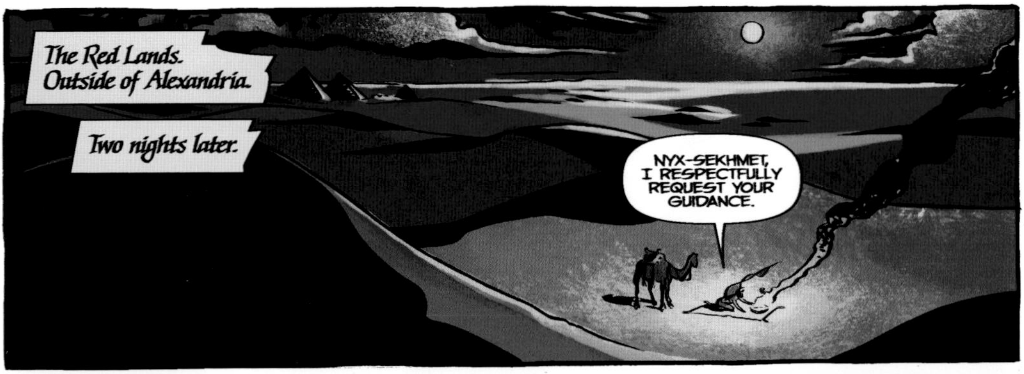
The Red Lands.
Outside of Alexandria.
Two nights later.
NYX-SEKHMET, I RESPECTFULLY REQUEST YOUR GUIDANCE.

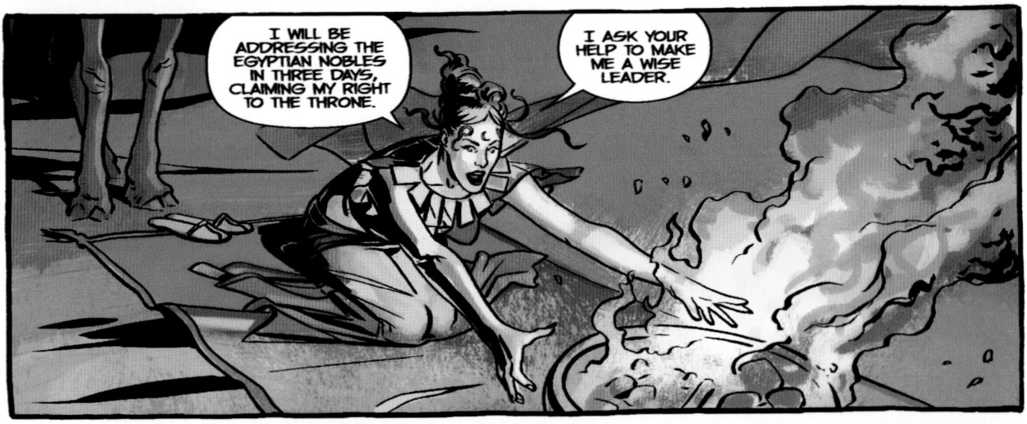
I WILL BE ADDRESSING THE EGYPTIAN NOBLES IN THREE DAYS, CLAIMING MY RIGHT TO THE THRONE.
I ASK YOUR HELP TO MAKE ME A WISE LEADER.

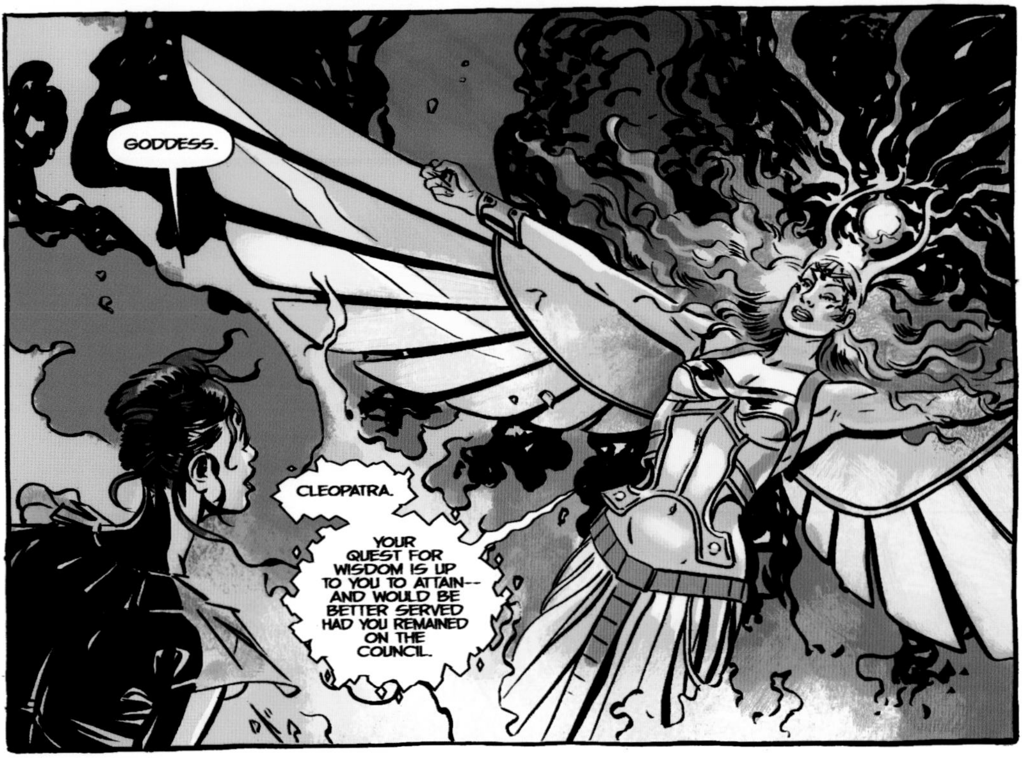
GODDESS.
CLEOPATRA.
YOUR QUEST FOR WISDOM IS UP TO YOU TO ATTAIN-- AND WOULD BE BETTER SERVED HAD YOU REMAINED ON THE COUNCIL.

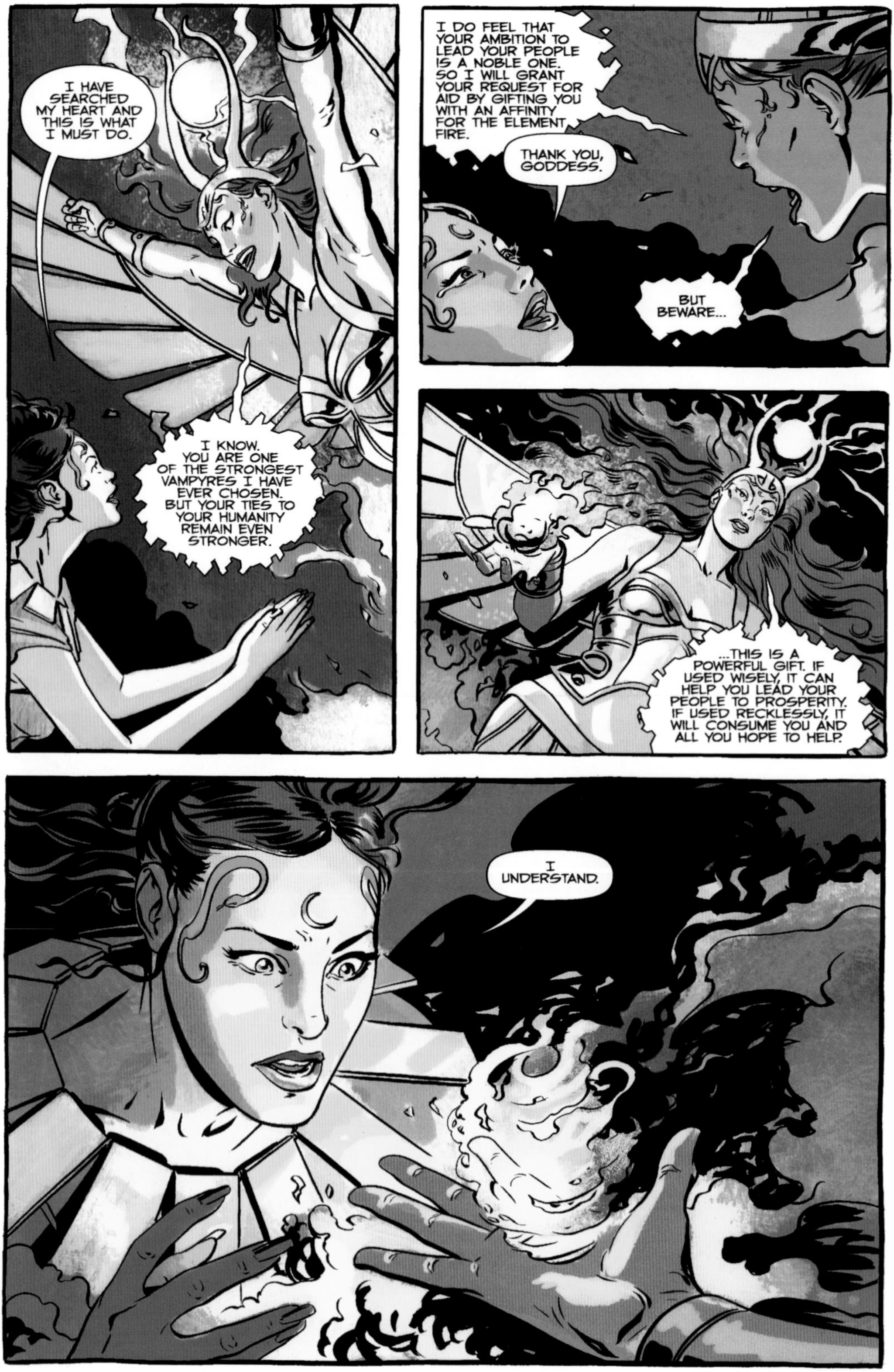
I HAVE SEARCHED MY HEART AND THIS IS WHAT I MUST DO.
I KNOW. YOU ARE ONE OF THE STRONGEST VAMPYRES I HAVE EVER CHOSEN. BUT YOUR TIES TO YOUR HUMANITY REMAIN EVEN STRONGER.
I DO FEEL THAT YOUR AMBITION TO LEAD YOUR PEOPLE IS A NOBLE ONE. SO I WILL GRANT YOUR REQUEST FOR AID BY GIFTING YOU WITH AN AFFINITY FOR THE ELEMENT FIRE.
THANK YOU, GODDESS.
BUT BEWARE...
...THIS IS A POWERFUL GIFT. IF USED WISELY, IT CAN HELP YOU LEAD YOUR PEOPLE TO PROSPERITY. IF USED RECKLESSLY, IT WILL CONSUME YOU AND ALL YOU HOPE TO HELP.
I UNDERSTAND.

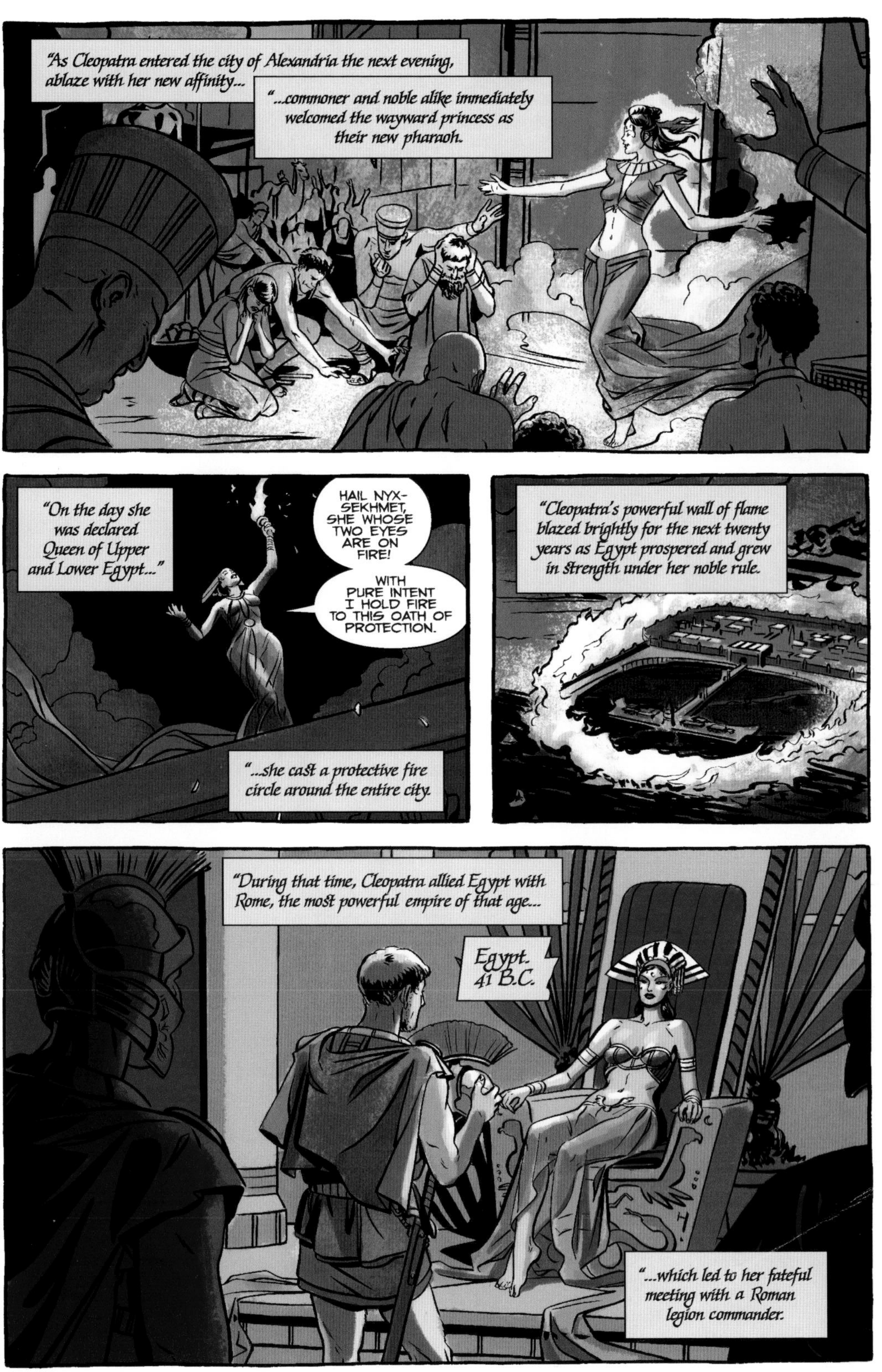
"As Cleopatra entered the city of Alexandria the next evening, ablaze with her new affinity...
"...commoner and noble alike immediately welcomed the wayward princess as their new pharaoh.
"On the day she was declared Queen of Upper and Lower Egypt..."
HAIL NYX-SEKHMET, SHE WHOSE TWO EYES ARE ON FIRE!
WITH PURE INTENT I HOLD FIRE TO THIS OATH OF PROTECTION.
"...she cast a protective fire circle around the entire city.
"Cleopatra's powerful wall of flame blazed brightly for the next twenty years as Egypt prospered and grew in strength under her noble rule.
"During that time, Cleopatra allied Egypt with Rome, the most powerful empire of that age...
Egypt. 41 B.C.
"...which led to her fateful meeting with a Roman legion commander.

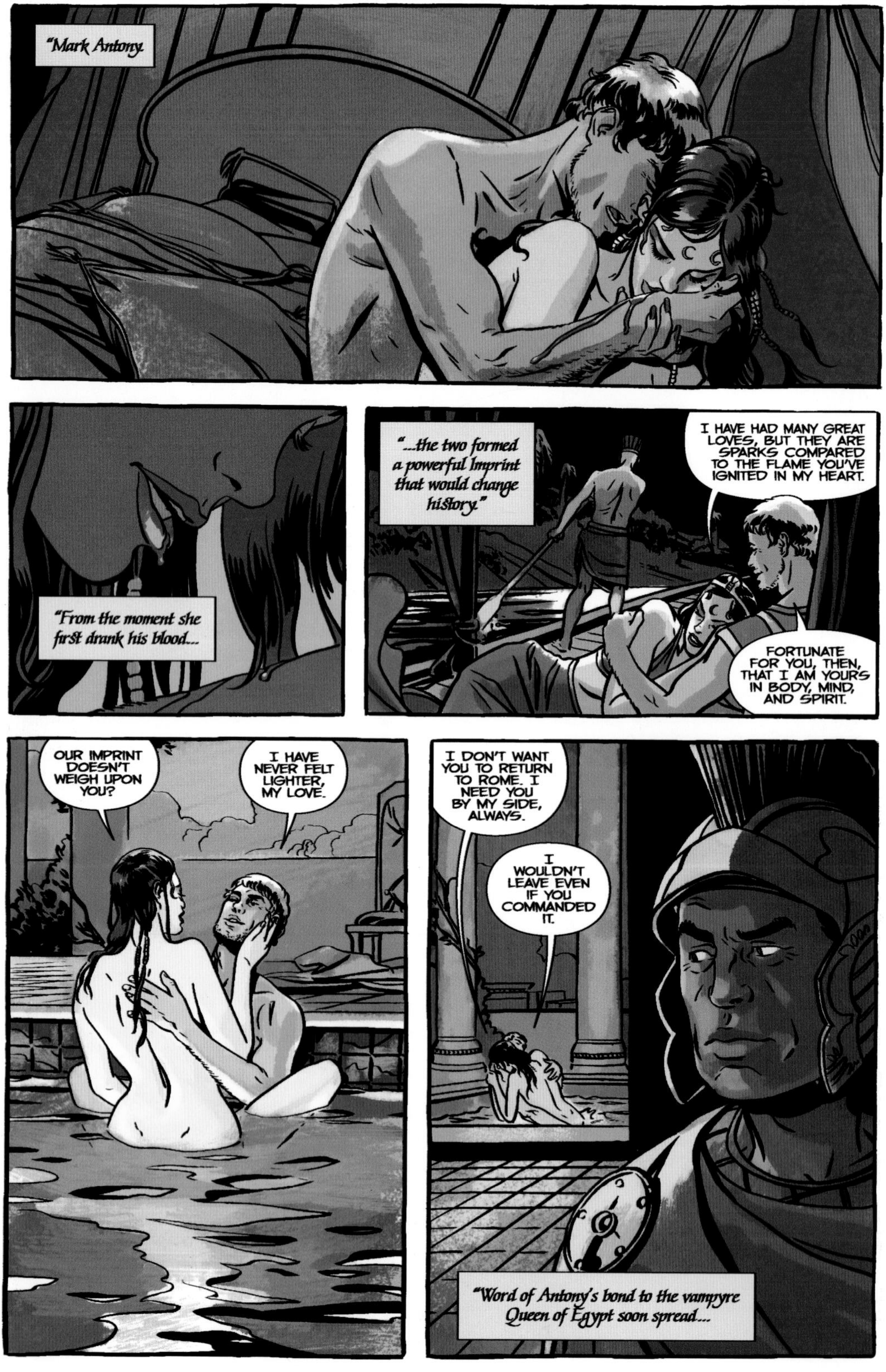

"Mark Antony.
"From the moment she first drank his blood...
"...the two formed a powerful Imprint that would change history."
I HAVE HAD MANY GREAT LOVES, BUT THEY ARE SPARKS COMPARED TO THE FLAME YOU'VE IGNITED IN MY HEART.
FORTUNATE FOR YOU, THEN, THAT I AM YOURS IN BODY, MIND, AND SPIRIT.
OUR IMPRINT DOESN'T WEIGH UPON YOU?
I HAVE NEVER FELT LIGHTER, MY LOVE.
I DON'T WANT YOU TO RETURN TO ROME. I NEED YOU BY MY SIDE, ALWAYS.
I WOULDN'T LEAVE EVEN IF YOU COMMANDED IT.
"Word of Antony's bond to the vampyre Queen of Egypt soon spread...

"...reaching the ear of his power-hungry rival in Rome, Octavian."

IT WOULD SEEM THAT MARK ANTONY MAY HAVE **IMPRINTED** WITH THE VAMPYRE PHARAOH.

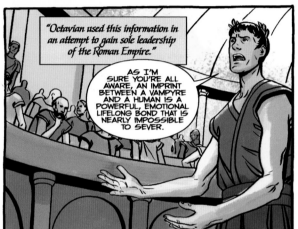

"Octavian used this information in an attempt to gain sole leadership of the Roman Empire."

AS I'M SURE YOU'RE ALL AWARE, AN IMPRINT BETWEEN A VAMPYRE AND A HUMAN IS A POWERFUL, EMOTIONAL, LIFELONG BOND THAT IS NEARLY IMPOSSIBLE TO SEVER.

MARK ANTONY HAS MADE IT OBVIOUS WHERE HIS LOYALTIES LIE, AND THEY ARE CLEARLY NOT WITH ROME.

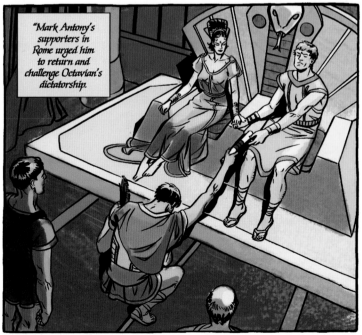

"Mark Antony's supporters in Rome urged him to return and challenge Octavian's dictatorship.

"But he would not leave Cleopatra.

93

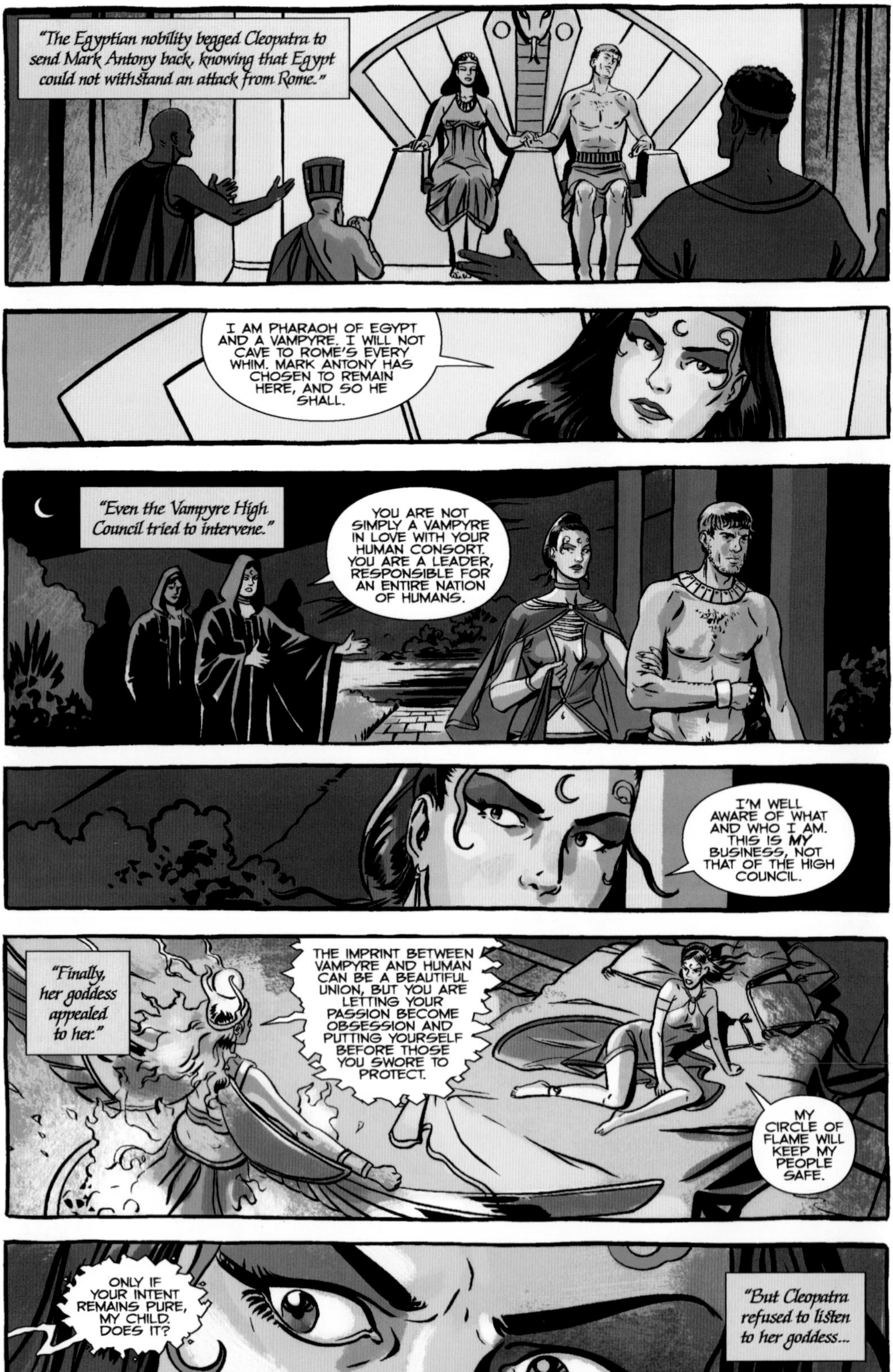
"The Egyptian nobility begged Cleopatra to send Mark Antony back, knowing that Egypt could not withstand an attack from Rome."
I AM PHARAOH OF EGYPT AND A VAMPYRE. I WILL NOT CAVE TO ROME'S EVERY WHIM. MARK ANTONY HAS CHOSEN TO REMAIN HERE, AND SO HE SHALL.
"Even the Vampyre High Council tried to intervene."
YOU ARE NOT SIMPLY A VAMPYRE IN LOVE WITH YOUR HUMAN CONSORT. YOU ARE A LEADER, RESPONSIBLE FOR AN ENTIRE NATION OF HUMANS.
I'M WELL AWARE OF WHAT AND WHO I AM. THIS IS MY BUSINESS, NOT THAT OF THE HIGH COUNCIL.
"Finally, her goddess appealed to her."
THE IMPRINT BETWEEN VAMPYRE AND HUMAN CAN BE A BEAUTIFUL UNION, BUT YOU ARE LETTING YOUR PASSION BECOME OBSESSION AND PUTTING YOURSELF BEFORE THOSE YOU SWORE TO PROTECT.
MY CIRCLE OF FLAME WILL KEEP MY PEOPLE SAFE.
ONLY IF YOUR INTENT REMAINS PURE, MY CHILD. DOES IT?
"But Cleopatra refused to listen to her goddess...

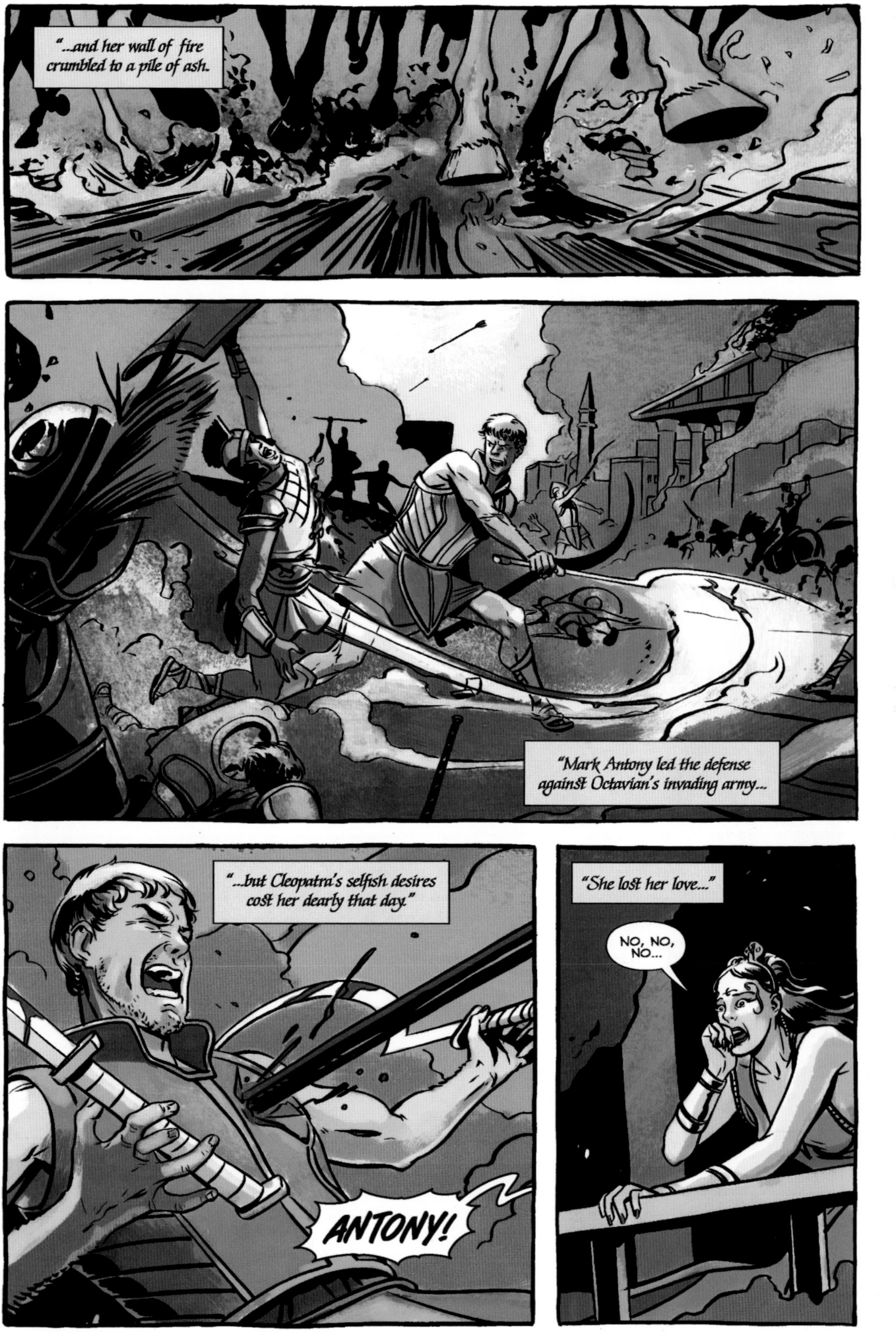
"...and her wall of fire crumbled to a pile of ash.
"Mark Antony led the defense against Octavian's invading army...
"...but Cleopatra's selfish desires cost her dearly that day."
ANTONY!
"She lost her love..."
NO, NO, NO...

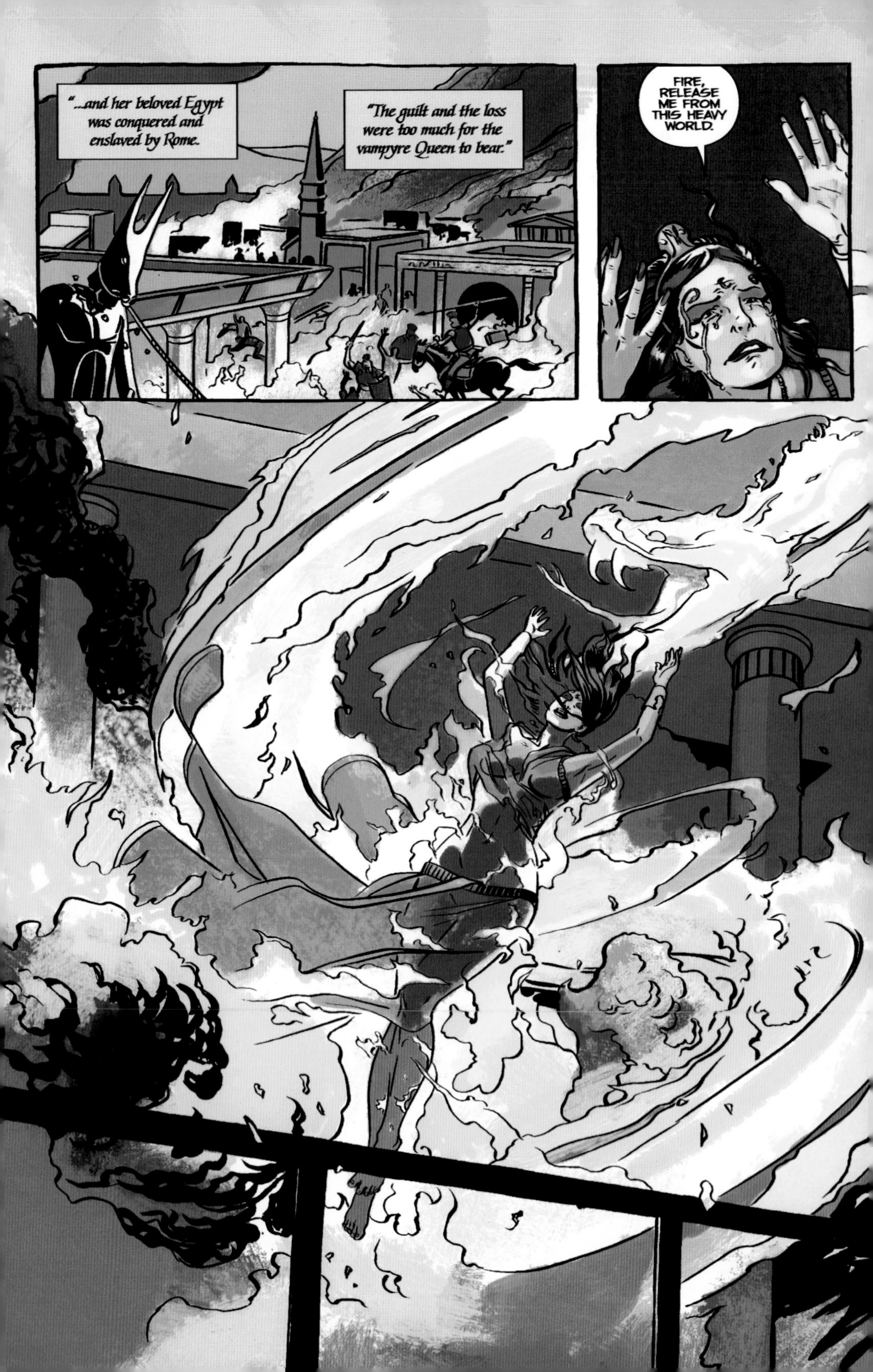
"...and her beloved Egypt was conquered and enslaved by Rome.
"The guilt and the loss were too much for the vampyre Queen to bear."
FIRE, RELEASE ME FROM THIS HEAVY WORLD.

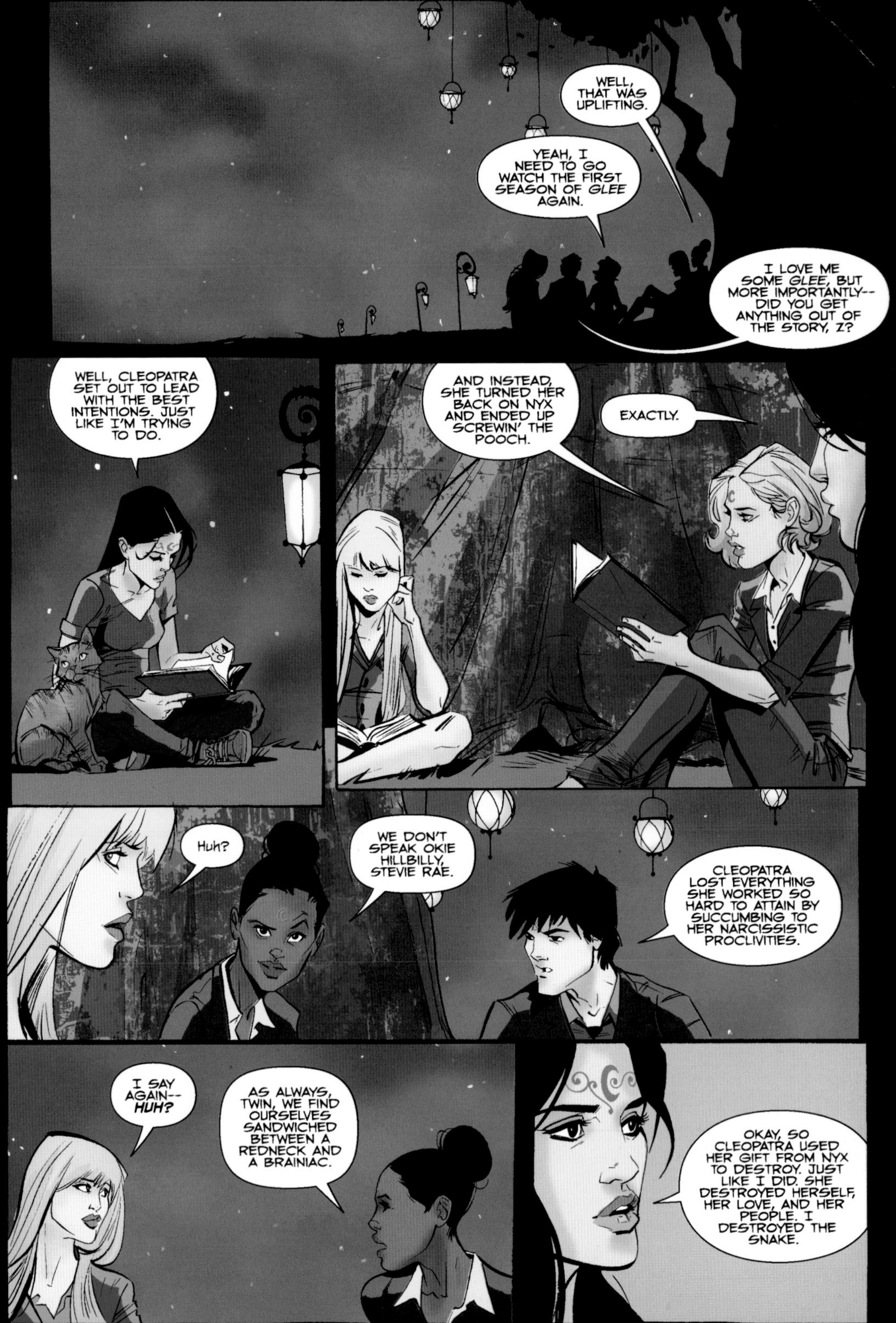
WELL, THAT WAS UPLIFTING.
YEAH, I NEED TO GO WATCH THE FIRST SEASON OF *GLEE* AGAIN.
I LOVE ME SOME *GLEE*, BUT MORE IMPORTANTLY-- DID YOU GET ANYTHING OUT OF THE STORY, Z?
WELL, CLEOPATRA SET OUT TO LEAD WITH THE BEST INTENTIONS. JUST LIKE I'M TRYING TO DO.
AND INSTEAD, SHE TURNED HER BACK ON NYX AND ENDED UP SCREWIN' THE POOCH.
EXACTLY.
Huh?
WE DON'T SPEAK OKIE HILLBILLY, STEVIE RAE.
CLEOPATRA LOST EVERYTHING SHE WORKED SO HARD TO ATTAIN BY SUCCUMBING TO HER NARCISSISTIC PROCLIVITIES.
I SAY AGAIN-- ***HUH?***
AS ALWAYS, TWIN, WE FIND OURSELVES SANDWICHED BETWEEN A REDNECK AND A BRAINIAC.
OKAY, SO CLEOPATRA USED HER GIFT FROM NYX TO DESTROY. JUST LIKE I DID. SHE DESTROYED HERSELF, HER LOVE, AND HER PEOPLE. I DESTROYED THE SNAKE.

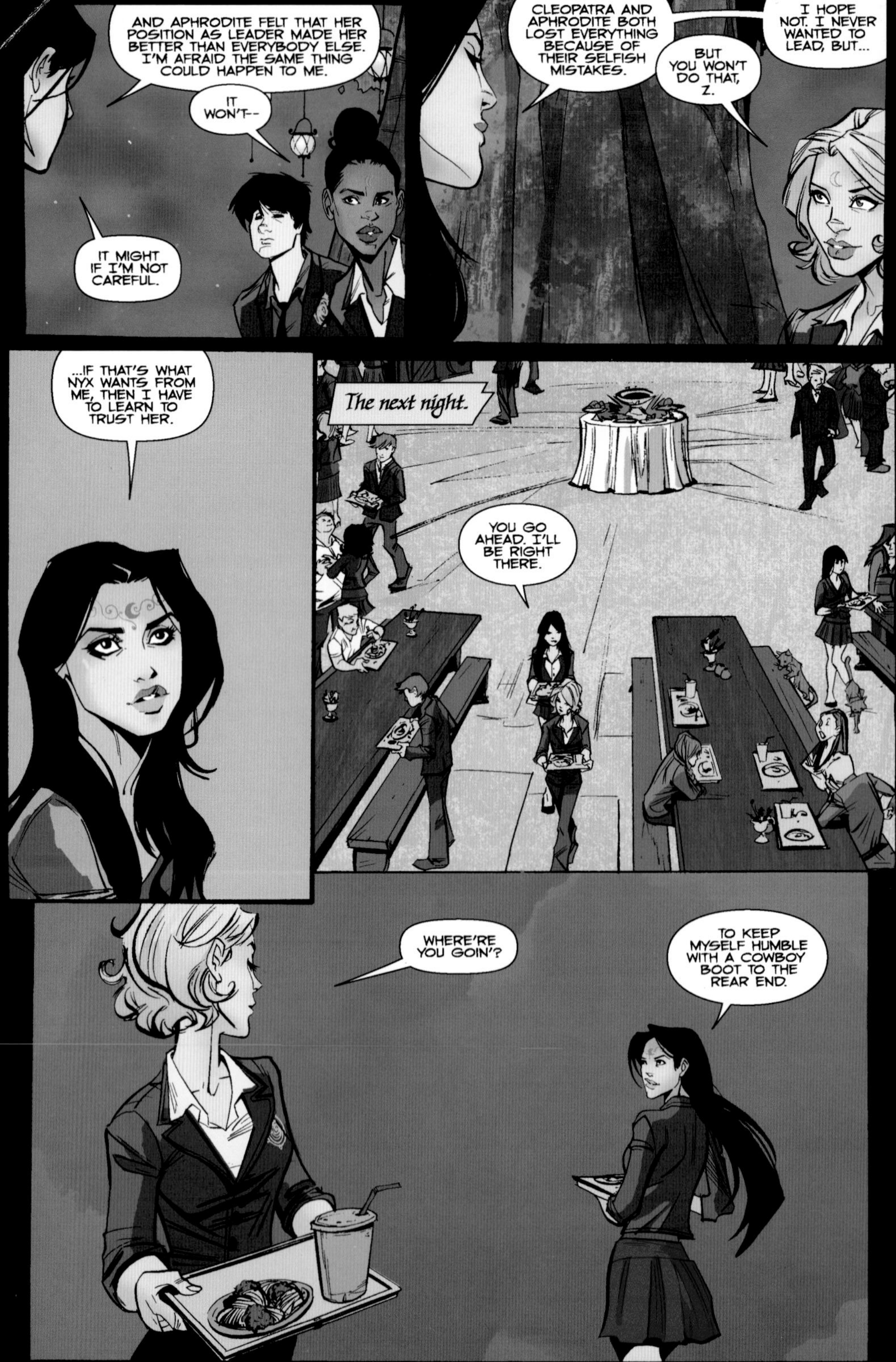
AND APHRODITE FELT THAT HER POSITION AS LEADER MADE HER BETTER THAN EVERYBODY ELSE. I'M AFRAID THE SAME THING COULD HAPPEN TO ME.
IT WON'T--
IT MIGHT IF I'M NOT CAREFUL.
CLEOPATRA AND APHRODITE BOTH LOST EVERYTHING BECAUSE OF THEIR SELFISH MISTAKES.
BUT YOU WON'T DO THAT, Z.
I HOPE NOT. I NEVER WANTED TO LEAD, BUT...
...IF THAT'S WHAT NYX WANTS FROM ME, THEN I HAVE TO LEARN TO TRUST HER.
The next night.
YOU GO AHEAD. I'LL BE RIGHT THERE.
WHERE'RE YOU GOIN'?
TO KEEP MYSELF HUMBLE WITH A COWBOY BOOT TO THE REAR END.

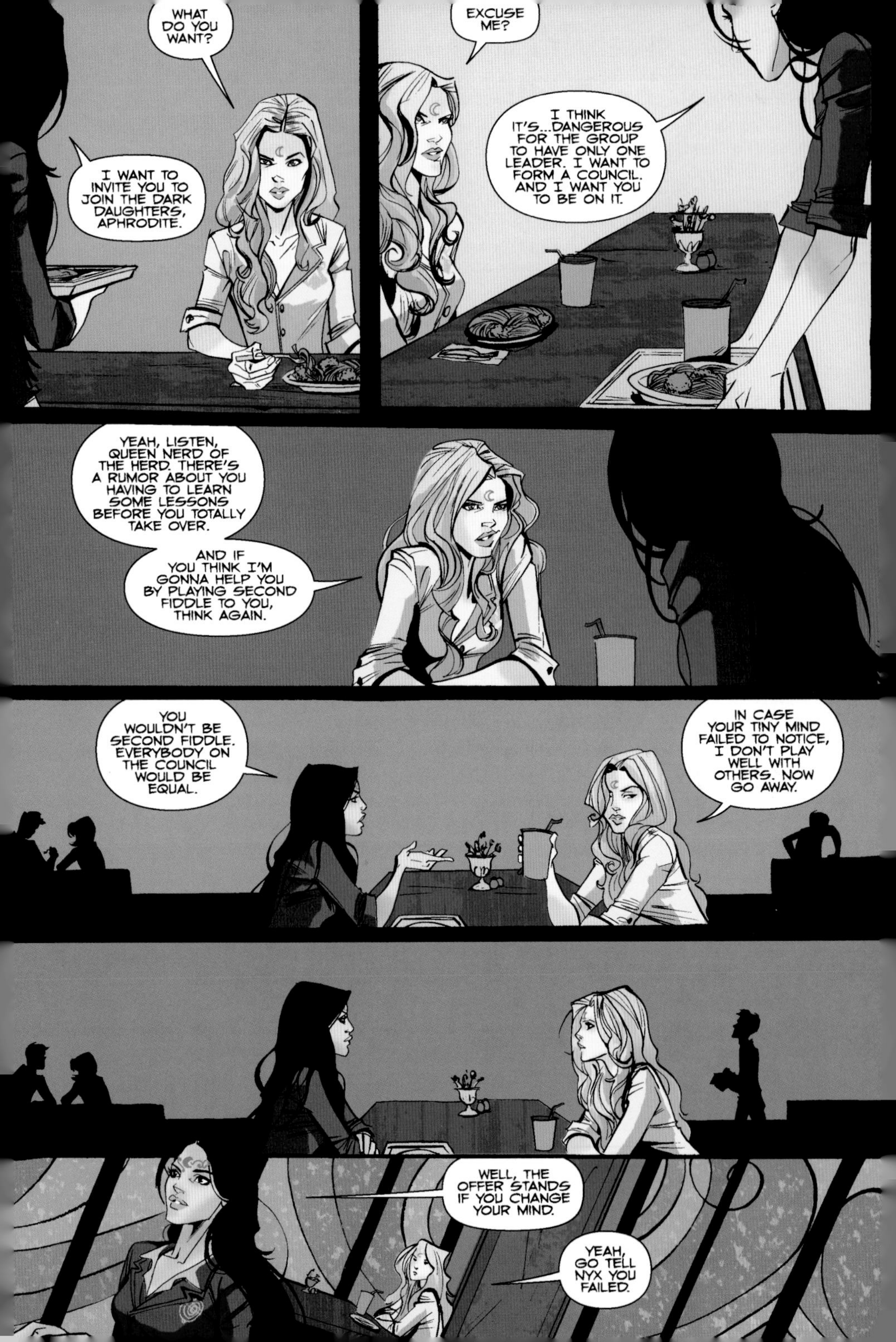
WHAT DO YOU WANT?
I WANT TO INVITE YOU TO JOIN THE DARK DAUGHTERS, APHRODITE.
EXCUSE ME?
I THINK IT'S...DANGEROUS FOR THE GROUP TO HAVE ONLY ONE LEADER. I WANT TO FORM A COUNCIL. AND I WANT YOU TO BE ON IT.
YEAH, LISTEN, QUEEN NERD OF THE HERD. THERE'S A RUMOR ABOUT YOU HAVING TO LEARN SOME LESSONS BEFORE YOU TOTALLY TAKE OVER.
AND IF YOU THINK I'M GONNA HELP YOU BY PLAYING SECOND FIDDLE TO YOU, THINK AGAIN.
YOU WOULDN'T BE SECOND FIDDLE. EVERYBODY ON THE COUNCIL WOULD BE EQUAL.
IN CASE YOUR TINY MIND FAILED TO NOTICE, I DON'T PLAY WELL WITH OTHERS. NOW GO AWAY.
WELL, THE OFFER STANDS IF YOU CHANGE YOUR MIND.
YEAH, GO TELL NYX YOU FAILED.

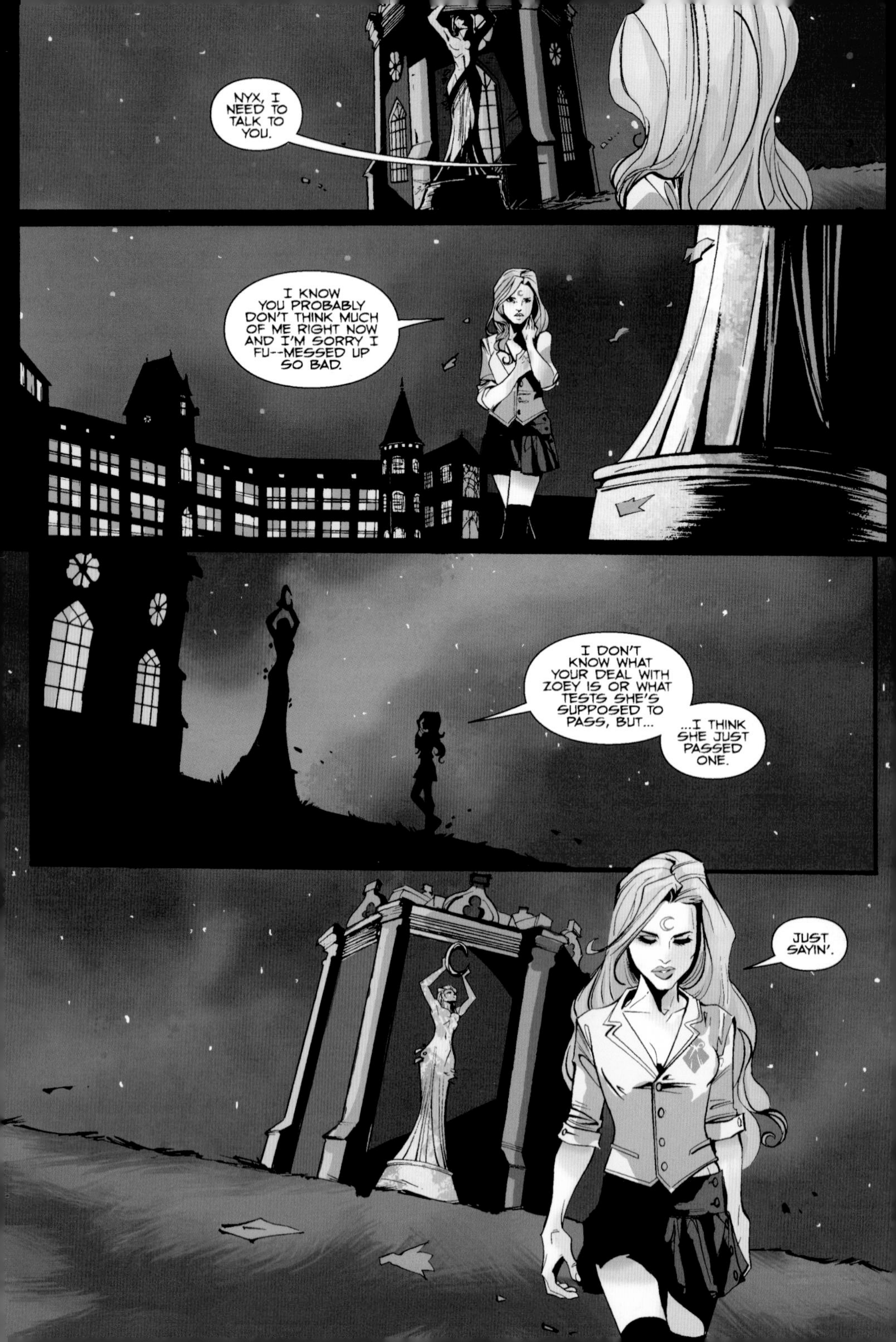
NYX, I NEED TO TALK TO YOU.
I KNOW YOU PROBABLY DON'T THINK MUCH OF ME RIGHT NOW AND I'M SORRY I FU--MESSED UP SO BAD.
I DON'T KNOW WHAT YOUR DEAL WITH ZOEY IS OR WHAT TESTS SHE'S SUPPOSED TO PASS, BUT...
...I THINK SHE JUST PASSED ONE.
JUST SAYIN'.

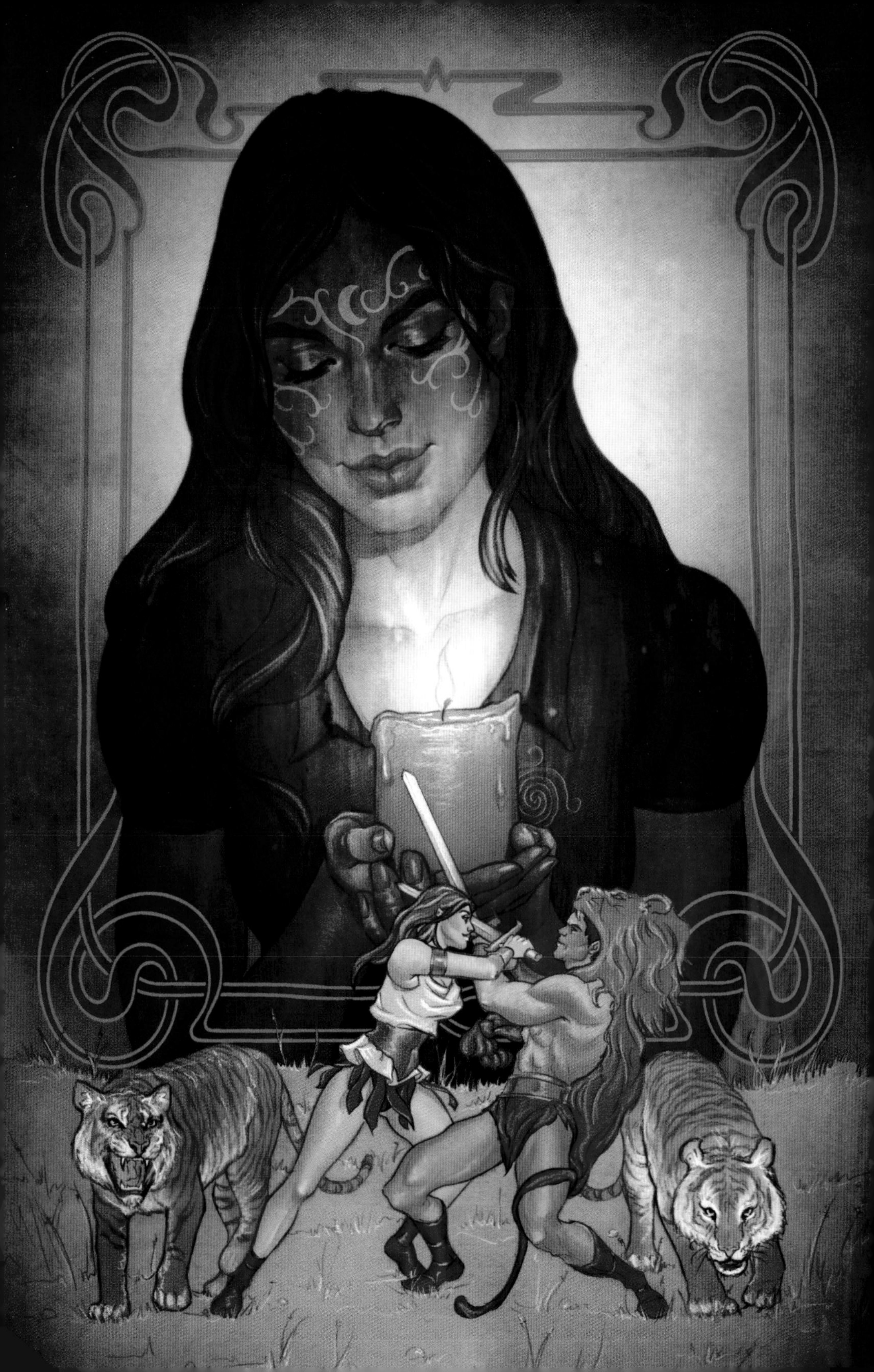

SPIRIT

STORY BY
P. C. CAST
AND **KRISTIN CAST**

SCRIPT BY
KENT DALIAN

ART BY
JOËLLE JONES
AND **ERIC CANETE**

COLORS BY
RYAN HILL
AND **ERIC CANETE**

LETTERS BY
NATE PIEKOS OF **BLAMBOT®**

CHAPTER ILLUSTRATION BY
JENNY FRISON

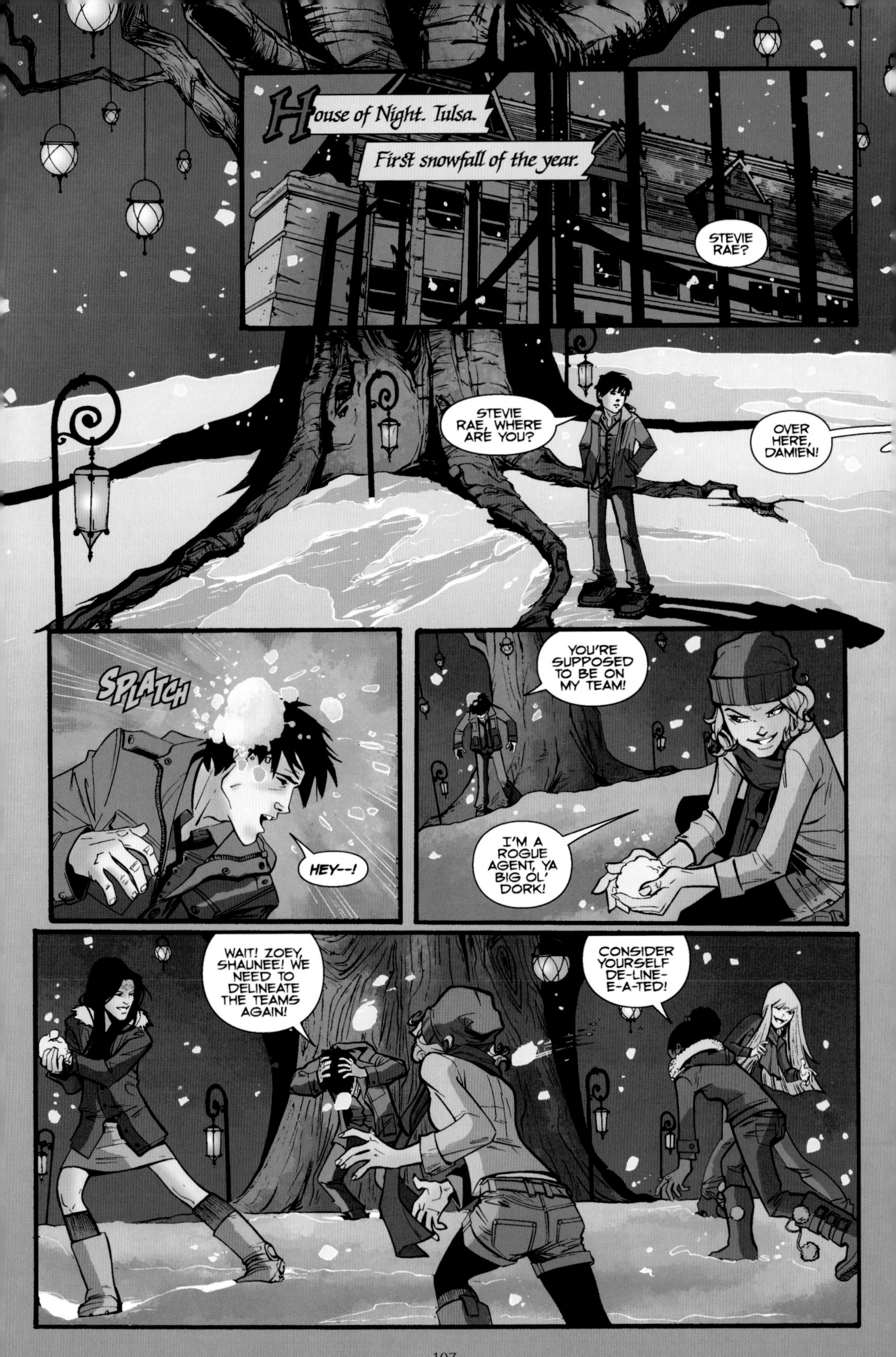

House of Night. Tulsa.
First snowfall of the year.
STEVIE RAE?
STEVIE RAE, WHERE ARE YOU?
OVER HERE, DAMIEN!
SPLATCH
HEY--!
YOU'RE SUPPOSED TO BE ON MY TEAM!
I'M A ROGUE AGENT, YA BIG OL' DORK!
WAIT! ZOEY, SHAUNEE! WE NEED TO DELINEATE THE TEAMS AGAIN!
CONSIDER YOURSELF DE-LINE-E-A-TED!

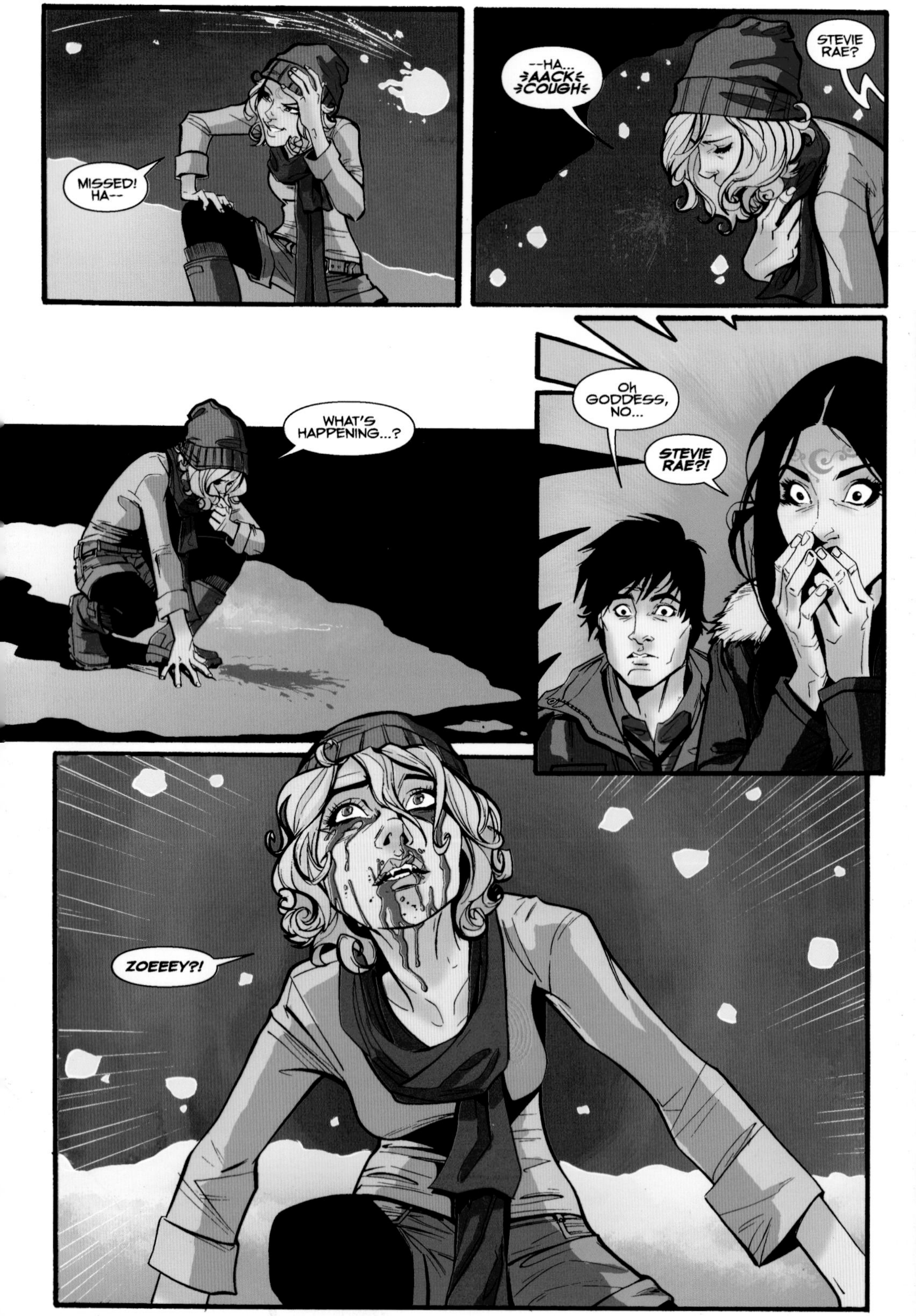
MISSED! HA--
--HA... AACK COUGH
STEVIE RAE?
WHAT'S HAPPENING...?
Oh GODDESS, NO...
STEVIE RAE?!
ZOEEEY?!

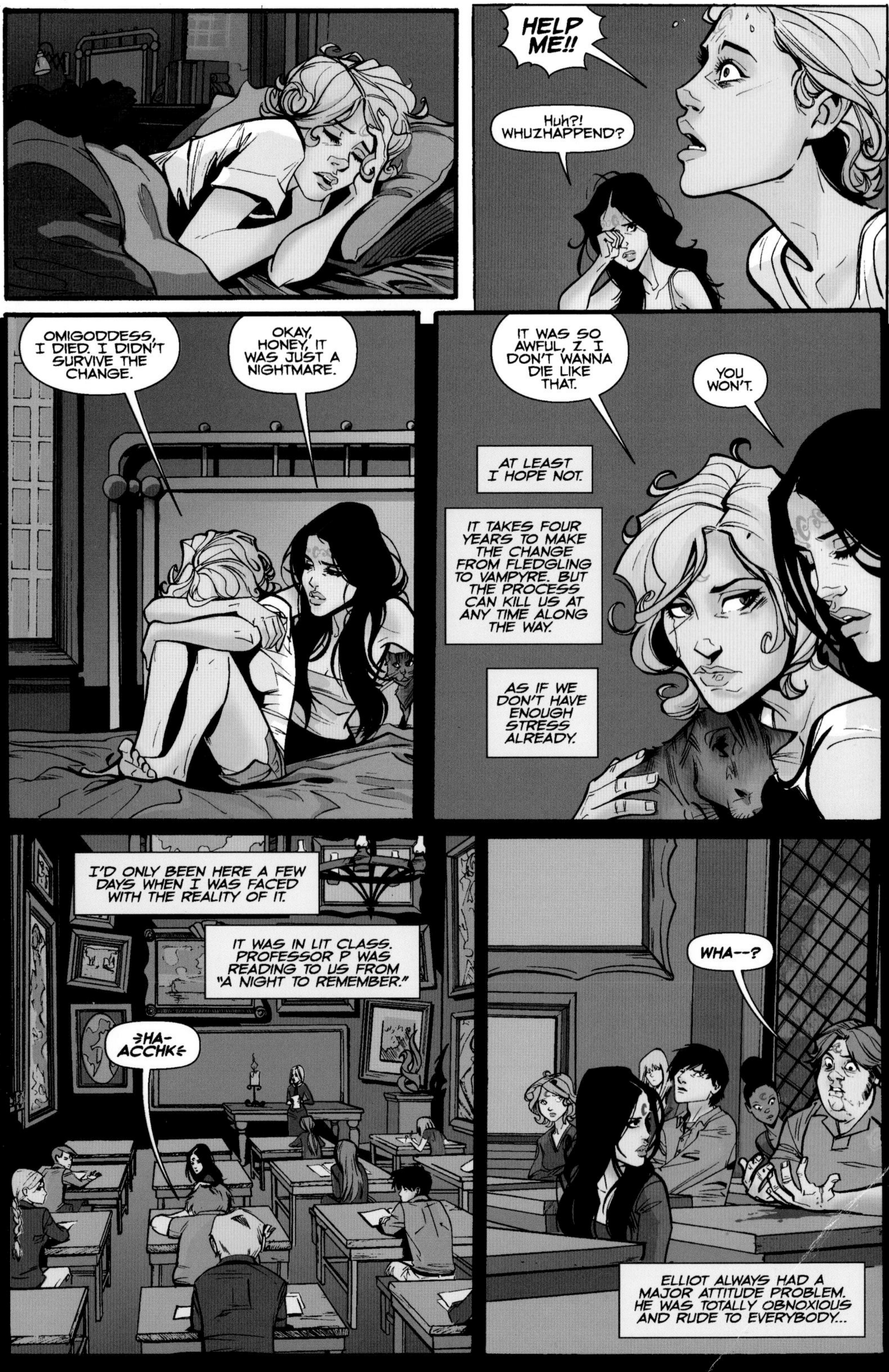
HELP ME!!
Huh?! WHUZHAPPEND?
OMIGODDESS, I DIED. I DIDN'T SURVIVE THE CHANGE.
OKAY, HONEY, IT WAS JUST A NIGHTMARE.
IT WAS SO AWFUL, Z. I DON'T WANNA DIE LIKE THAT.
YOU WON'T.
AT LEAST I HOPE NOT.
IT TAKES FOUR YEARS TO MAKE THE CHANGE FROM FLEDGLING TO VAMPYRE. BUT THE PROCESS CAN KILL US AT ANY TIME ALONG THE WAY.
AS IF WE DON'T HAVE ENOUGH STRESS ALREADY.
I'D ONLY BEEN HERE A FEW DAYS WHEN I WAS FACED WITH THE REALITY OF IT.
IT WAS IN LIT CLASS. PROFESSOR P WAS READING TO US FROM "A NIGHT TO REMEMBER."
HA-ACCHK
WHA--?
ELLIOT ALWAYS HAD A MAJOR ATTITUDE PROBLEM. HE WAS TOTALLY OBNOXIOUS AND RUDE TO EVERYBODY...

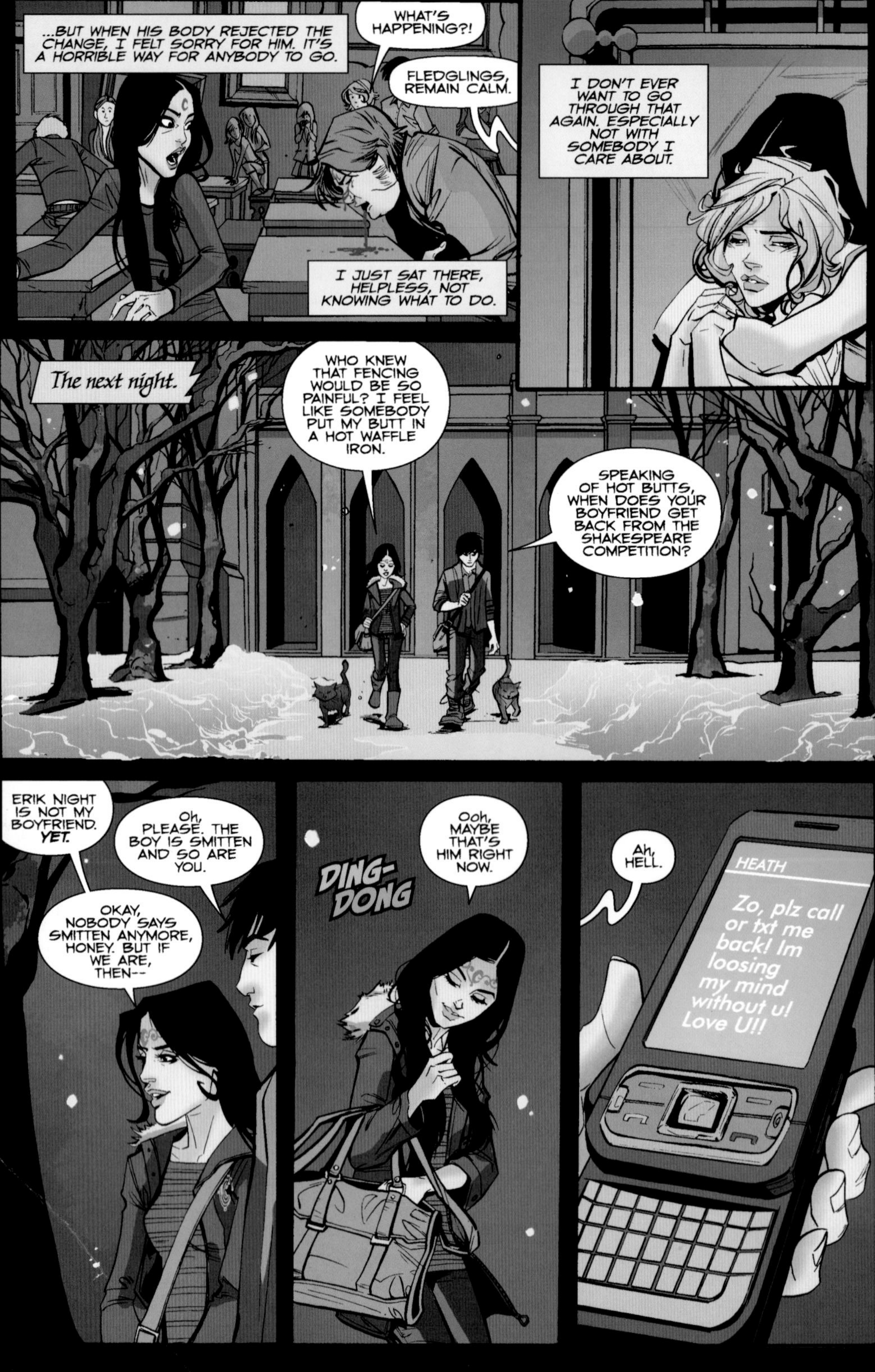
...BUT WHEN HIS BODY REJECTED THE CHANGE, I FELT SORRY FOR HIM. IT'S A HORRIBLE WAY FOR ANYBODY TO GO.
WHAT'S HAPPENING?!
FLEDGLINGS, REMAIN CALM.
I JUST SAT THERE, HELPLESS, NOT KNOWING WHAT TO DO.
I DON'T EVER WANT TO GO THROUGH THAT AGAIN. ESPECIALLY NOT WITH SOMEBODY I CARE ABOUT.
The next night.
WHO KNEW THAT FENCING WOULD BE SO PAINFUL? I FEEL LIKE SOMEBODY PUT MY BUTT IN A HOT WAFFLE IRON.
SPEAKING OF HOT BUTTS, WHEN DOES YOUR BOYFRIEND GET BACK FROM THE SHAKESPEARE COMPETITION?
ERIK NIGHT IS NOT MY BOYFRIEND. YET.
Oh, PLEASE. THE BOY IS SMITTEN AND SO ARE YOU.
OKAY, NOBODY SAYS SMITTEN ANYMORE, HONEY. BUT IF WE ARE, THEN--
DING-DONG
Ooh, MAYBE THAT'S HIM RIGHT NOW.
Ah, HELL.
HEATH
Zo, plz call or txt me back! Im loosing my mind without u! Love U!!

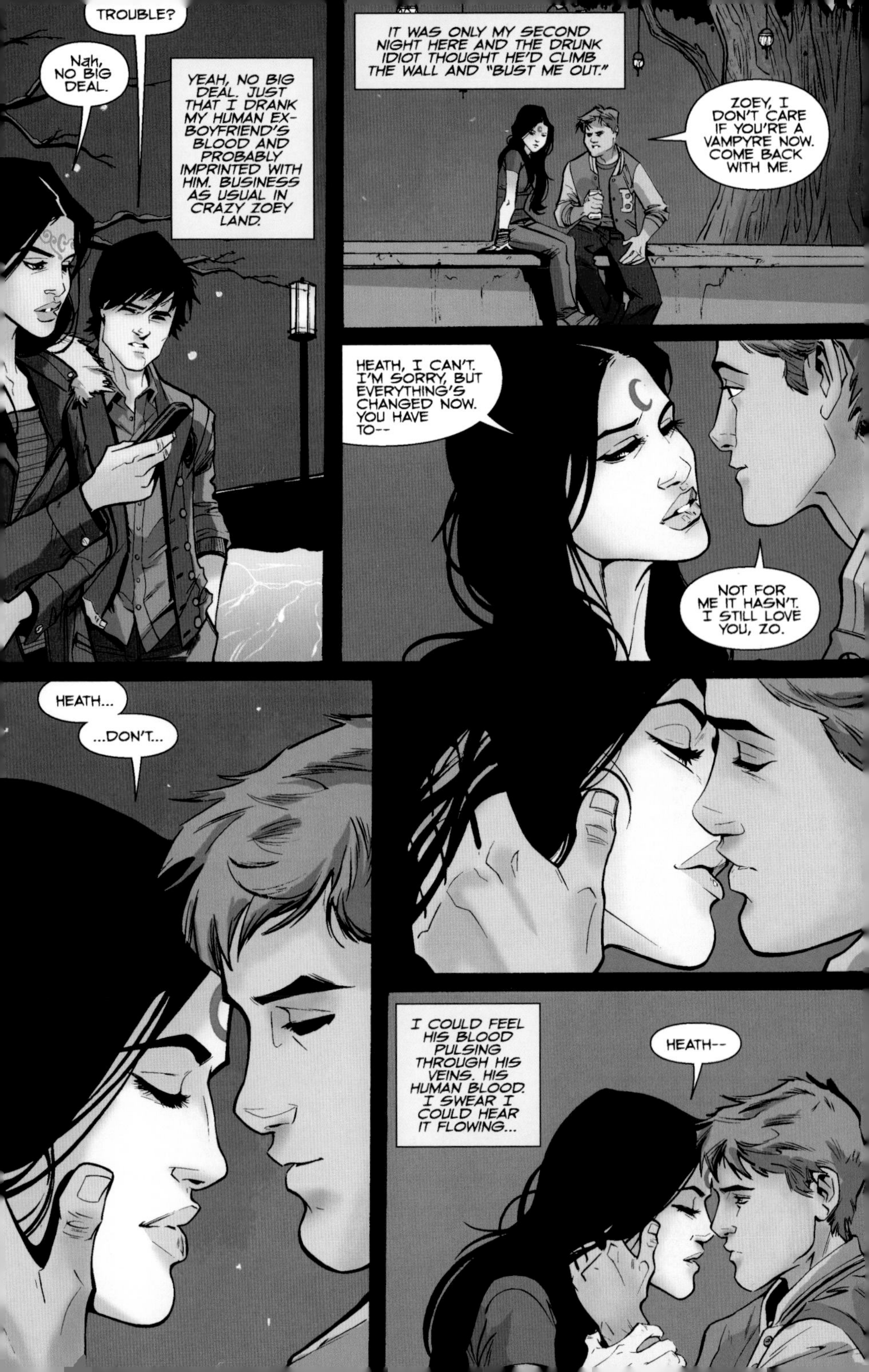
TROUBLE?
Nah, NO BIG DEAL.
YEAH, NO BIG DEAL. JUST THAT I DRANK MY HUMAN EX-BOYFRIEND'S BLOOD AND PROBABLY IMPRINTED WITH HIM. BUSINESS AS USUAL IN CRAZY ZOEY LAND.
IT WAS ONLY MY SECOND NIGHT HERE AND THE DRUNK IDIOT THOUGHT HE'D CLIMB THE WALL AND "BUST ME OUT."
ZOEY, I DON'T CARE IF YOU'RE A VAMPYRE NOW. COME BACK WITH ME.
HEATH, I CAN'T. I'M SORRY, BUT EVERYTHING'S CHANGED NOW. YOU HAVE TO--
NOT FOR ME IT HASN'T. I STILL LOVE YOU, ZO.
HEATH...
...DON'T...
I COULD FEEL HIS BLOOD PULSING THROUGH HIS VEINS. HIS HUMAN BLOOD. I SWEAR I COULD HEAR IT FLOWING...
HEATH--

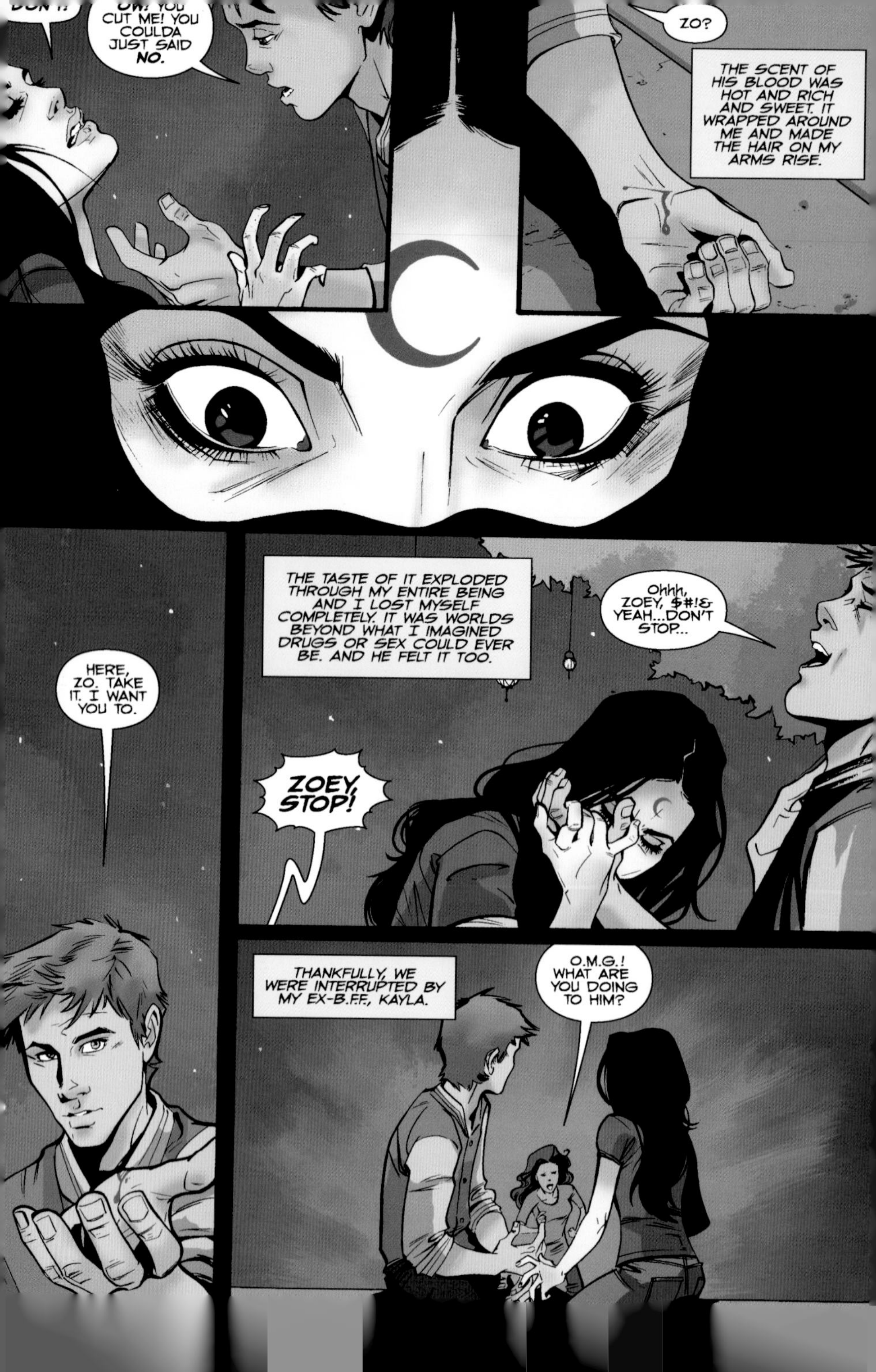
DON'T!
OW! YOU CUT ME! YOU COULDA JUST SAID NO.
ZO?
THE SCENT OF HIS BLOOD WAS HOT AND RICH AND SWEET. IT WRAPPED AROUND ME AND MADE THE HAIR ON MY ARMS RISE.
HERE, ZO. TAKE IT. I WANT YOU TO.
THE TASTE OF IT EXPLODED THROUGH MY ENTIRE BEING AND I LOST MYSELF COMPLETELY. IT WAS WORLDS BEYOND WHAT I IMAGINED DRUGS OR SEX COULD EVER BE. AND HE FELT IT TOO.
Ohhh, ZOEY, $#!& YEAH...DON'T STOP...
ZOEY, STOP!
THANKFULLY, WE WERE INTERRUPTED BY MY EX-B.F.F., KAYLA.
O.M.G.! WHAT ARE YOU DOING TO HIM?

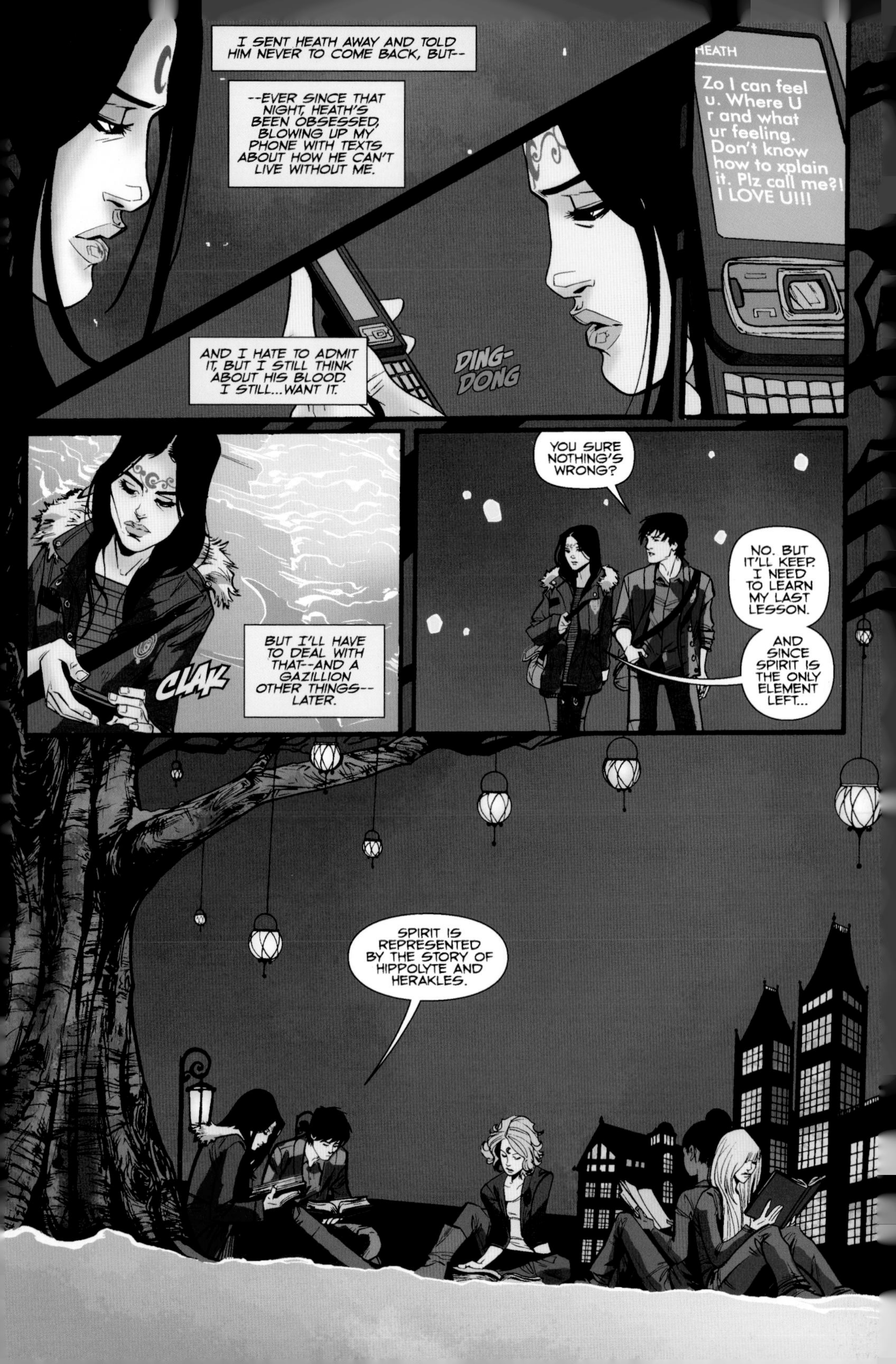
I SENT HEATH AWAY AND TOLD HIM NEVER TO COME BACK, BUT--
--EVER SINCE THAT NIGHT, HEATH'S BEEN OBSESSED, BLOWING UP MY PHONE WITH TEXTS ABOUT HOW HE CAN'T LIVE WITHOUT ME.
AND I HATE TO ADMIT IT, BUT I STILL THINK ABOUT HIS BLOOD. I STILL...WANT IT.
DING-DONG
HEATH
Zo I can feel u. Where U r and what ur feeling. Don't know how to xplain it. Plz call me?! I LOVE U!!!
CLAK
BUT I'LL HAVE TO DEAL WITH THAT--AND A GAZILLION OTHER THINGS--LATER.
YOU SURE NOTHING'S WRONG?
NO. BUT IT'LL KEEP. I NEED TO LEARN MY LAST LESSON.
AND SINCE SPIRIT IS THE ONLY ELEMENT LEFT...
SPIRIT IS REPRESENTED BY THE STORY OF HIPPOLYTE AND HERAKLES.

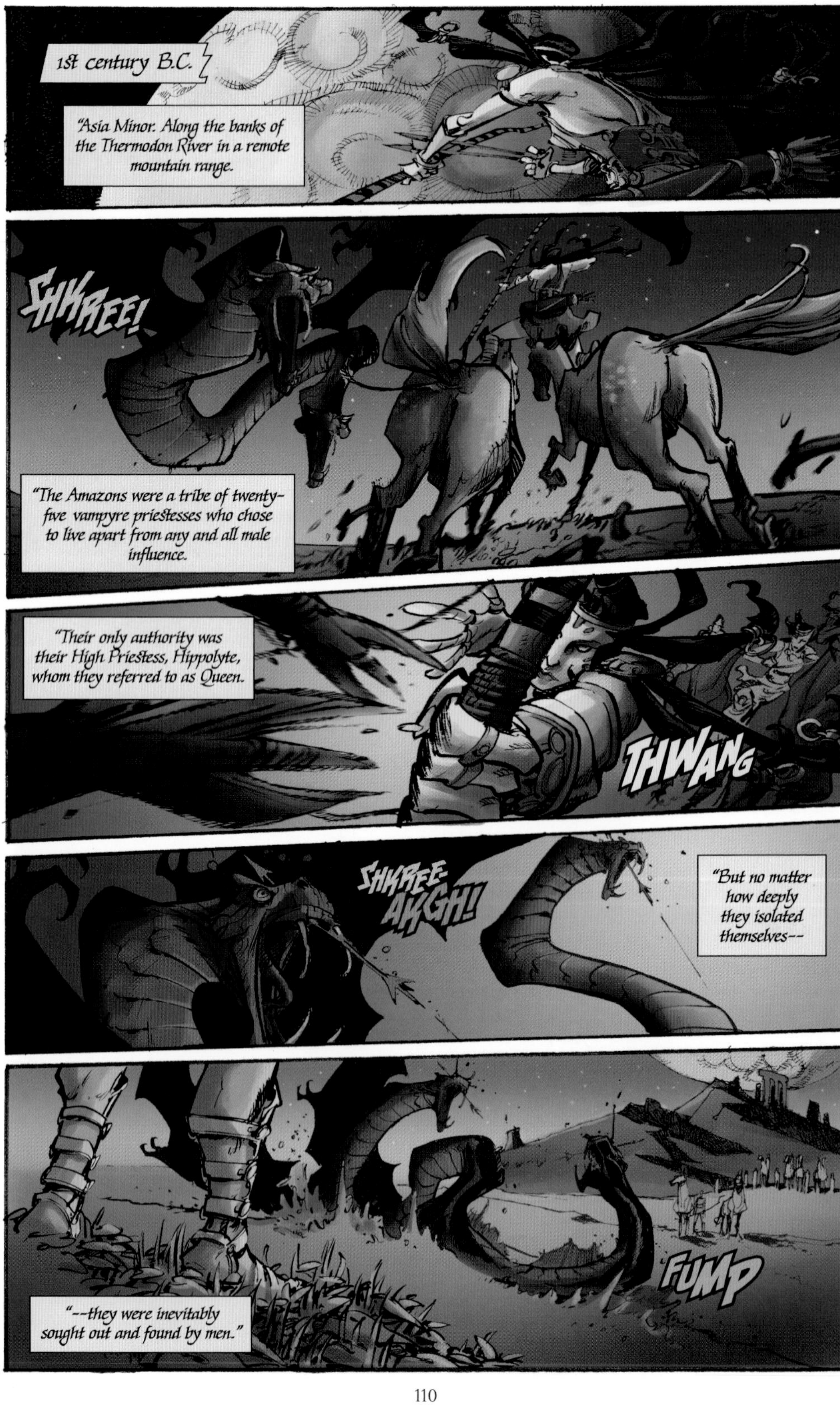
1st century B.C.
"Asia Minor. Along the banks of the Thermodon River in a remote mountain range.
SHKREE!
"The Amazons were a tribe of twenty-five vampyre priestesses who chose to live apart from any and all male influence.
"Their only authority was their High Priestess, Hippolyte, whom they referred to as Queen.
THWANG
SHKREE-AKGH!
"But no matter how deeply they isolated themselves--
FUMP
"--they were inevitably sought out and found by men."

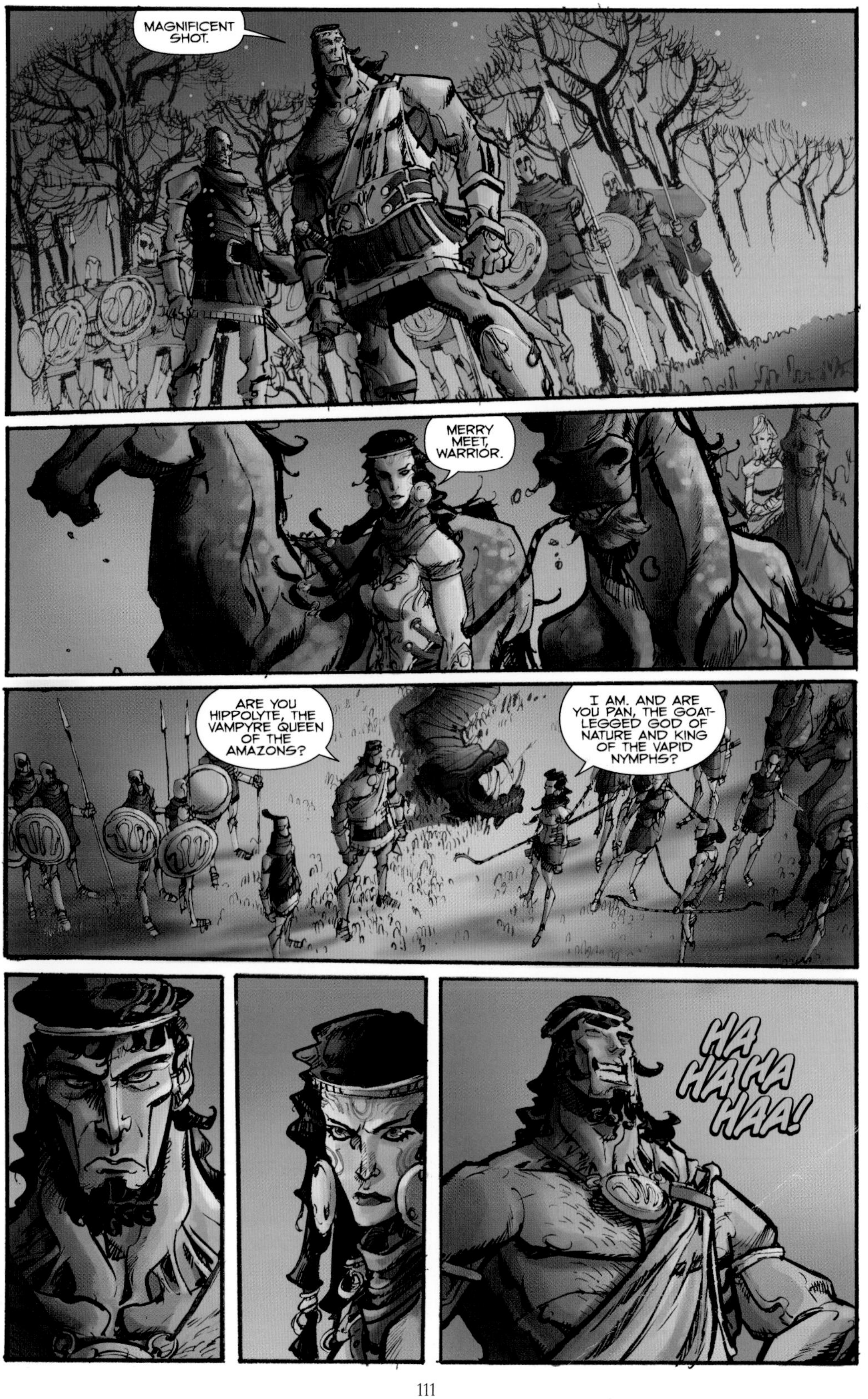
MAGNIFICENT SHOT.
MERRY MEET, WARRIOR.
ARE YOU HIPPOLYTE, THE VAMPYRE QUEEN OF THE AMAZONS?
I AM. AND ARE YOU PAN, THE GOAT-LEGGED GOD OF NATURE AND KING OF THE VAPID NYMPHS?
HA HA HA HAA!

I LIKE HER SHARP TONGUE.

HE IS THE MIGHTY HERAKLES, IMMORTAL HERO OF MYCENAE! AND HE HAS COME FOR YOUR GOLDEN BREASTPLATE!

WHICH GOLDEN BREASTPLATE IS THAT?

THAT ONE.

SNAP

AAHH!

I DON'T RECALL GRANTING YOU PERMISSION TO TOUCH ME.

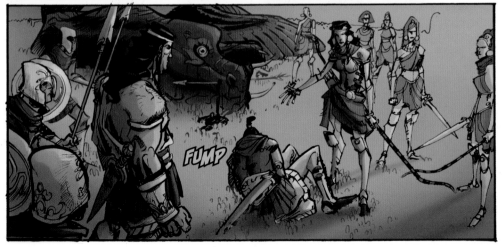

FUMP

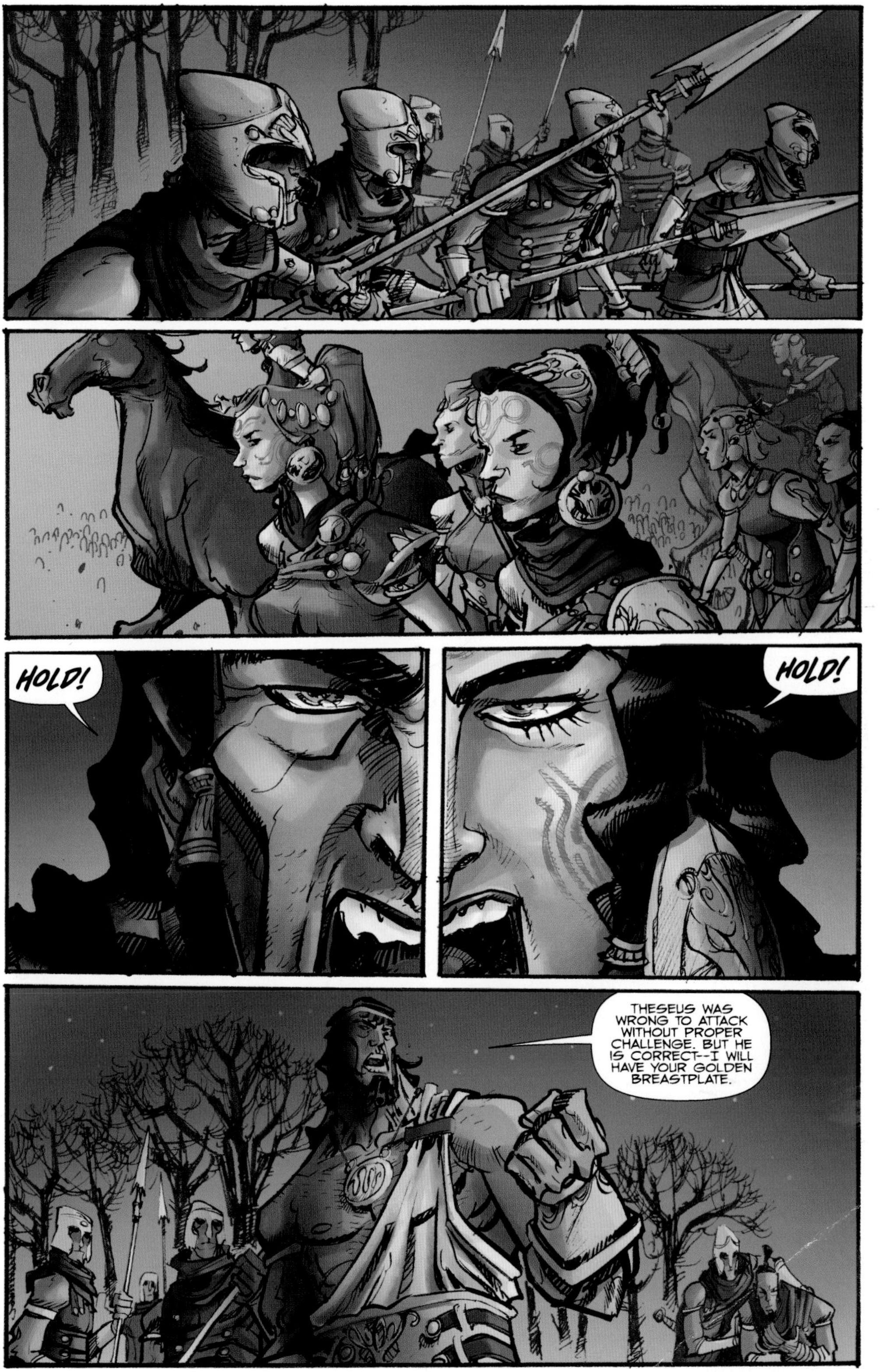
HOLD!
HOLD!
THESEUS WAS WRONG TO ATTACK WITHOUT PROPER CHALLENGE. BUT HE IS CORRECT--I WILL HAVE YOUR GOLDEN BREASTPLATE.

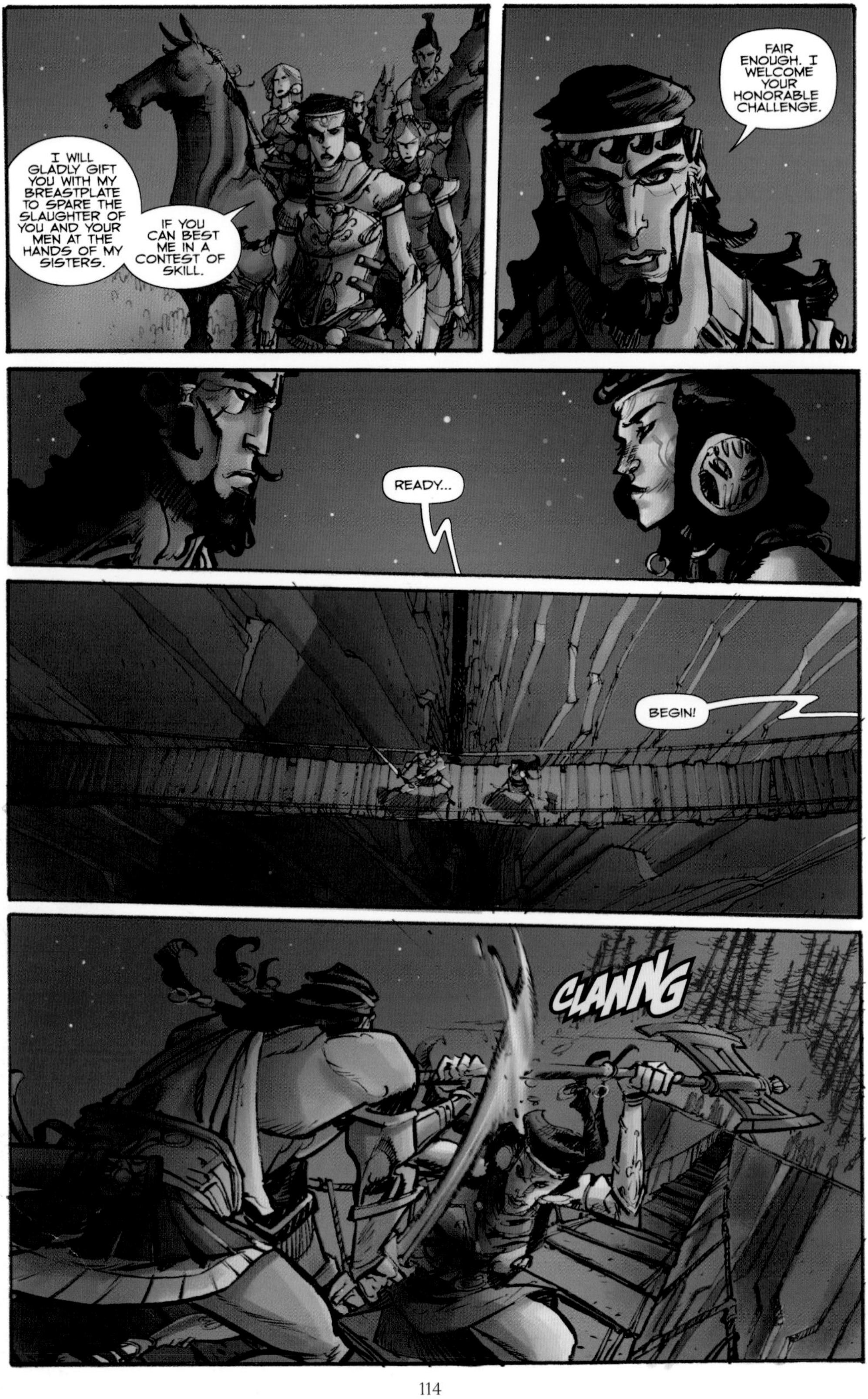
I WILL GLADLY GIFT YOU WITH MY BREASTPLATE TO SPARE THE SLAUGHTER OF YOU AND YOUR MEN AT THE HANDS OF MY SISTERS.
IF YOU CAN BEST ME IN A CONTEST OF SKILL.
FAIR ENOUGH. I WELCOME YOUR HONORABLE CHALLENGE.
READY...
BEGIN!
CLANNG

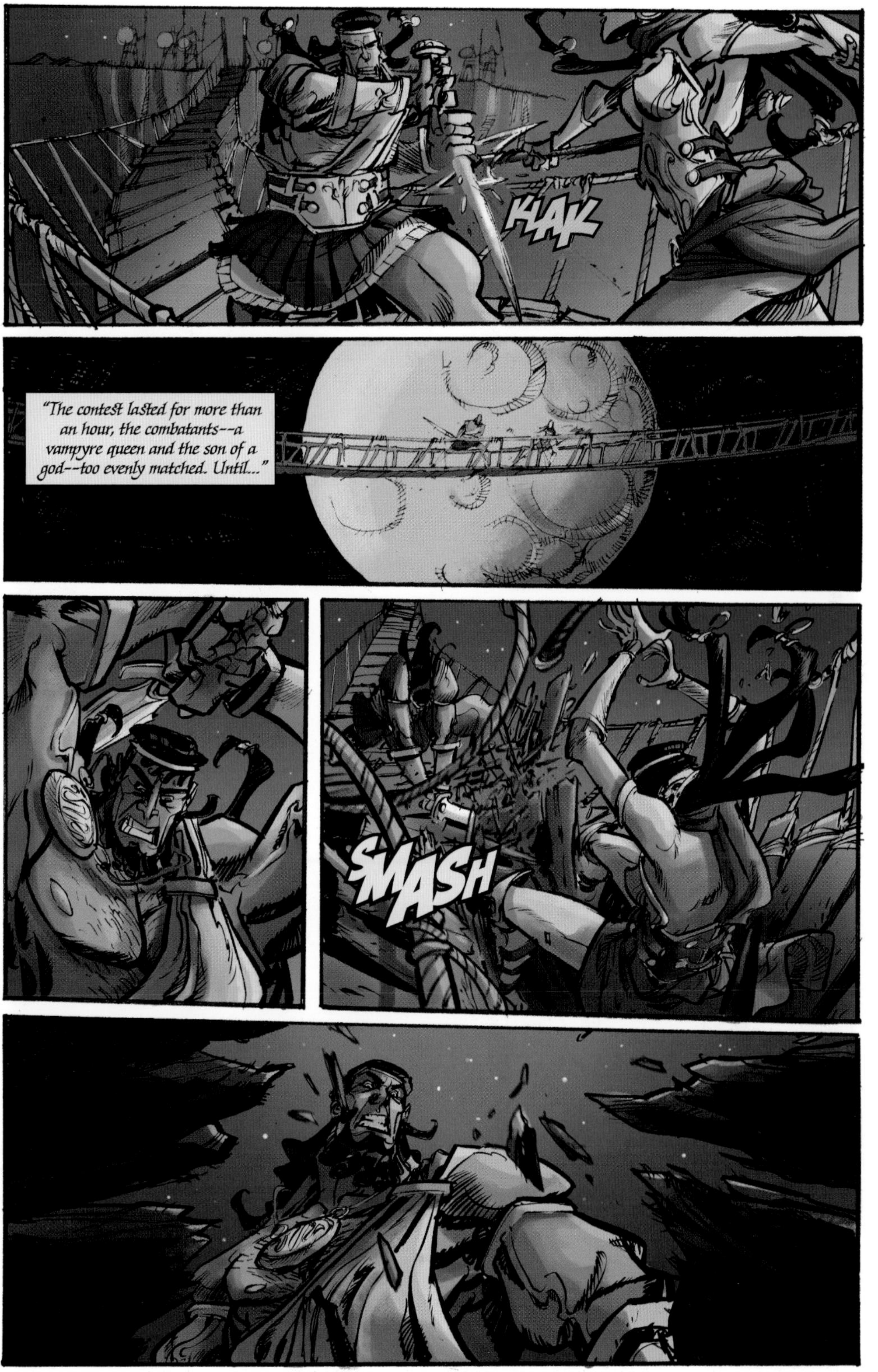
KLAK
"The contest lasted for more than an hour, the combatants--a vampyre queen and the son of a god--too evenly matched. Until..."
SMASH

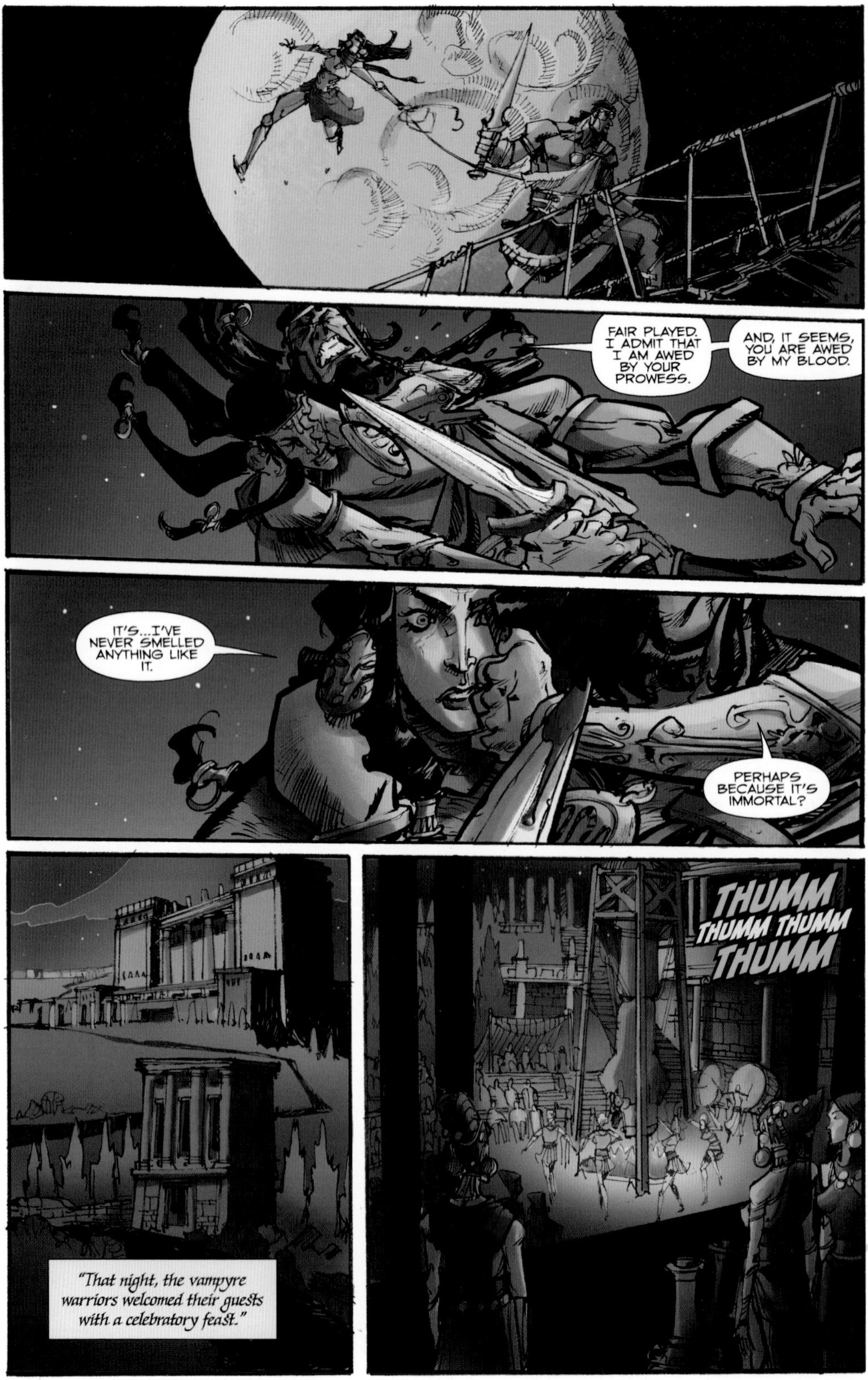

FAIR PLAYED. I ADMIT THAT I AM AWED BY YOUR PROWESS.
AND, IT SEEMS, YOU ARE AWED BY MY BLOOD.
IT'S...I'VE NEVER SMELLED ANYTHING LIKE IT.
PERHAPS BECAUSE IT'S IMMORTAL?
"That night, the vampyre warriors welcomed their guests with a celebratory feast."
THUMM THUMM THUMM THUMM

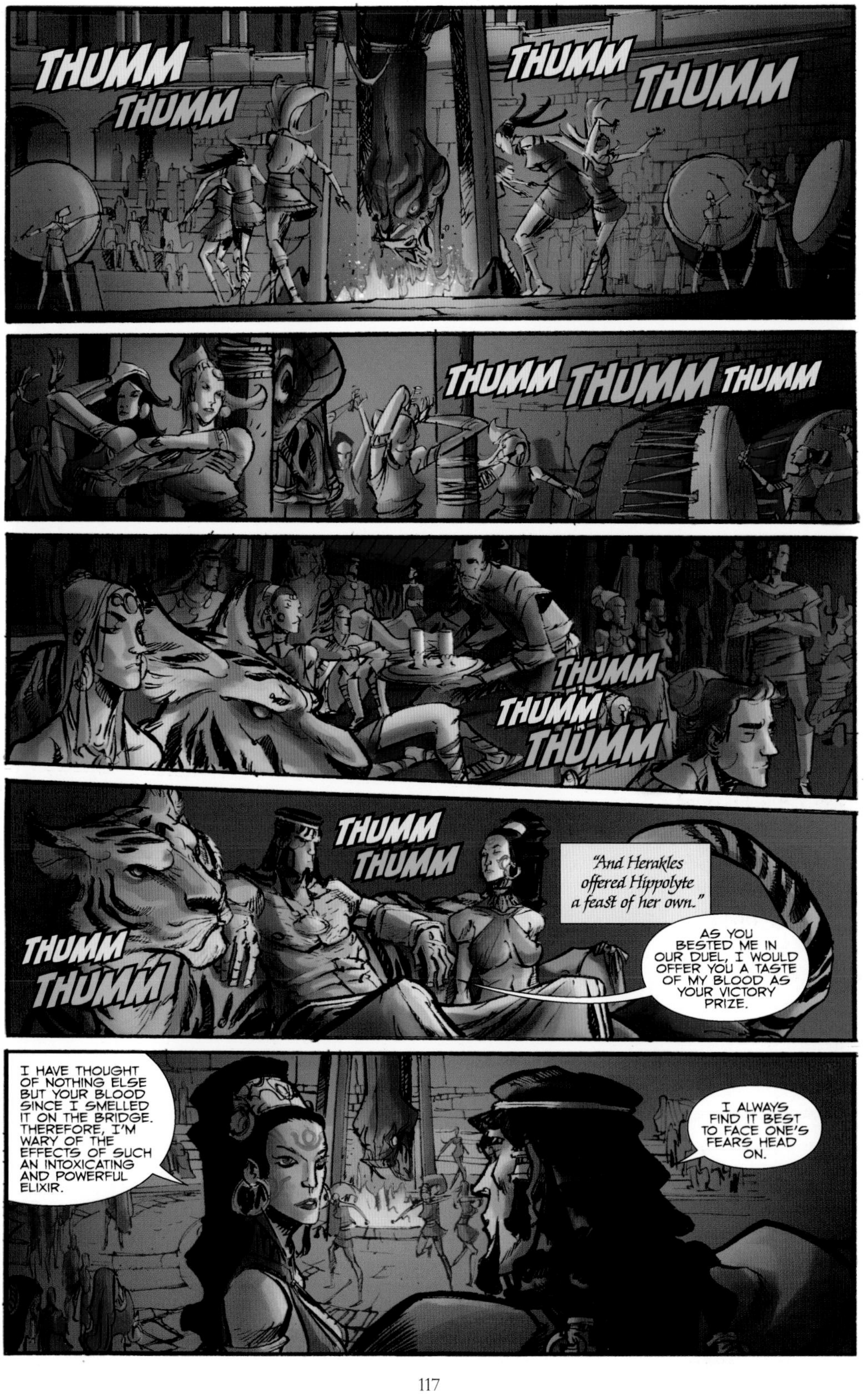
THUMM
THUMM
THUMM
THUMM
THUMM THUMM THUMM
THUMM
THUMM
THUMM
THUMM
THUMM
THUMM
THUMM
"And Herakles offered Hippolyte a feast of her own."
AS YOU BESTED ME IN OUR DUEL, I WOULD OFFER YOU A TASTE OF MY BLOOD AS YOUR VICTORY PRIZE.
I HAVE THOUGHT OF NOTHING ELSE BUT YOUR BLOOD SINCE I SMELLED IT ON THE BRIDGE. THEREFORE, I'M WARY OF THE EFFECTS OF SUCH AN INTOXICATING AND POWERFUL ELIXIR.
I ALWAYS FIND IT BEST TO FACE ONE'S FEARS HEAD ON.

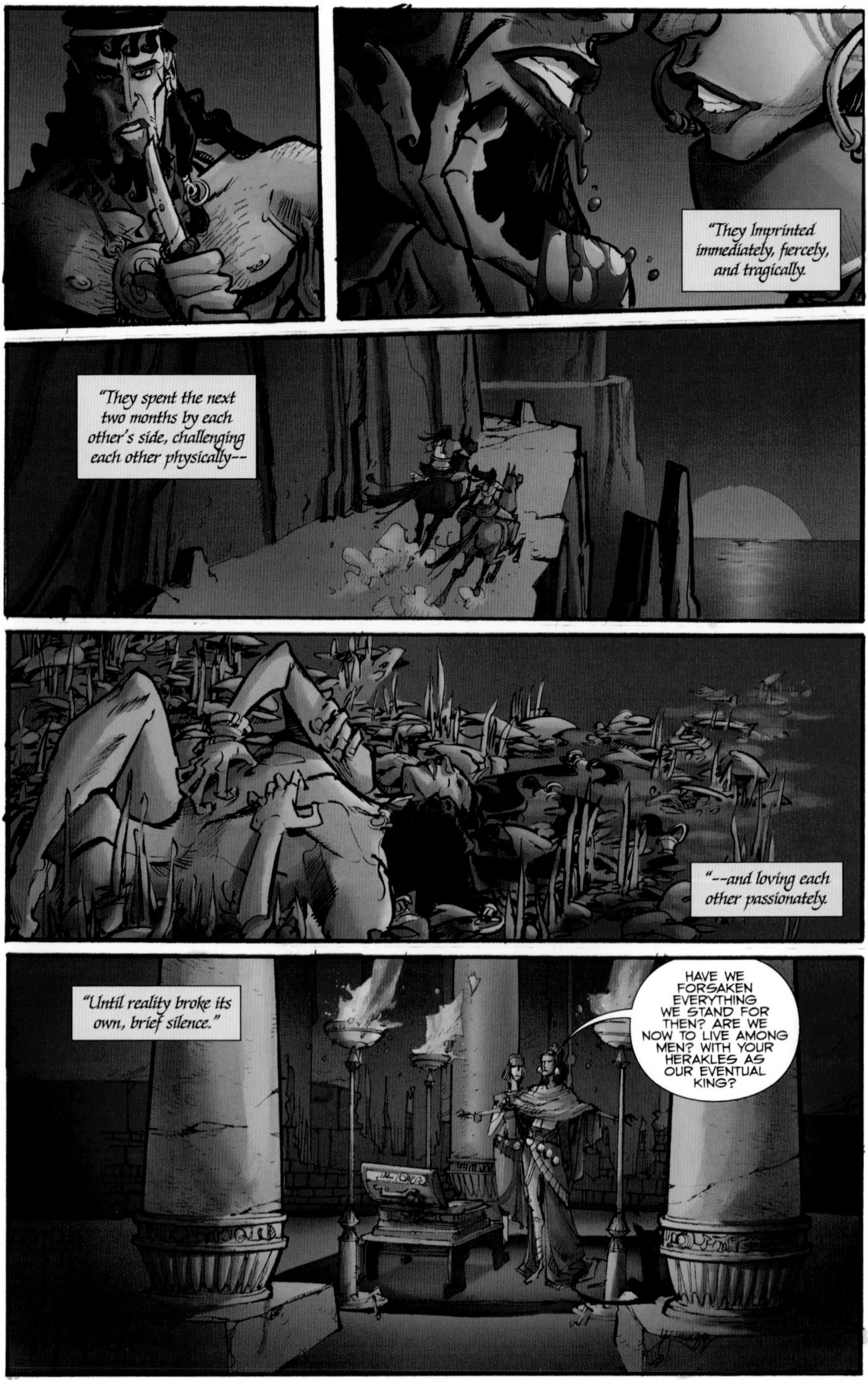
"They Imprinted immediately, fiercely, and tragically.
"They spent the next two months by each other's side, challenging each other physically--
"--and loving each other passionately.
"Until reality broke its own, brief silence."
HAVE WE FORSAKEN EVERYTHING WE STAND FOR THEN? ARE WE NOW TO LIVE AMONG MEN? WITH YOUR HERAKLES AS OUR EVENTUAL KING?

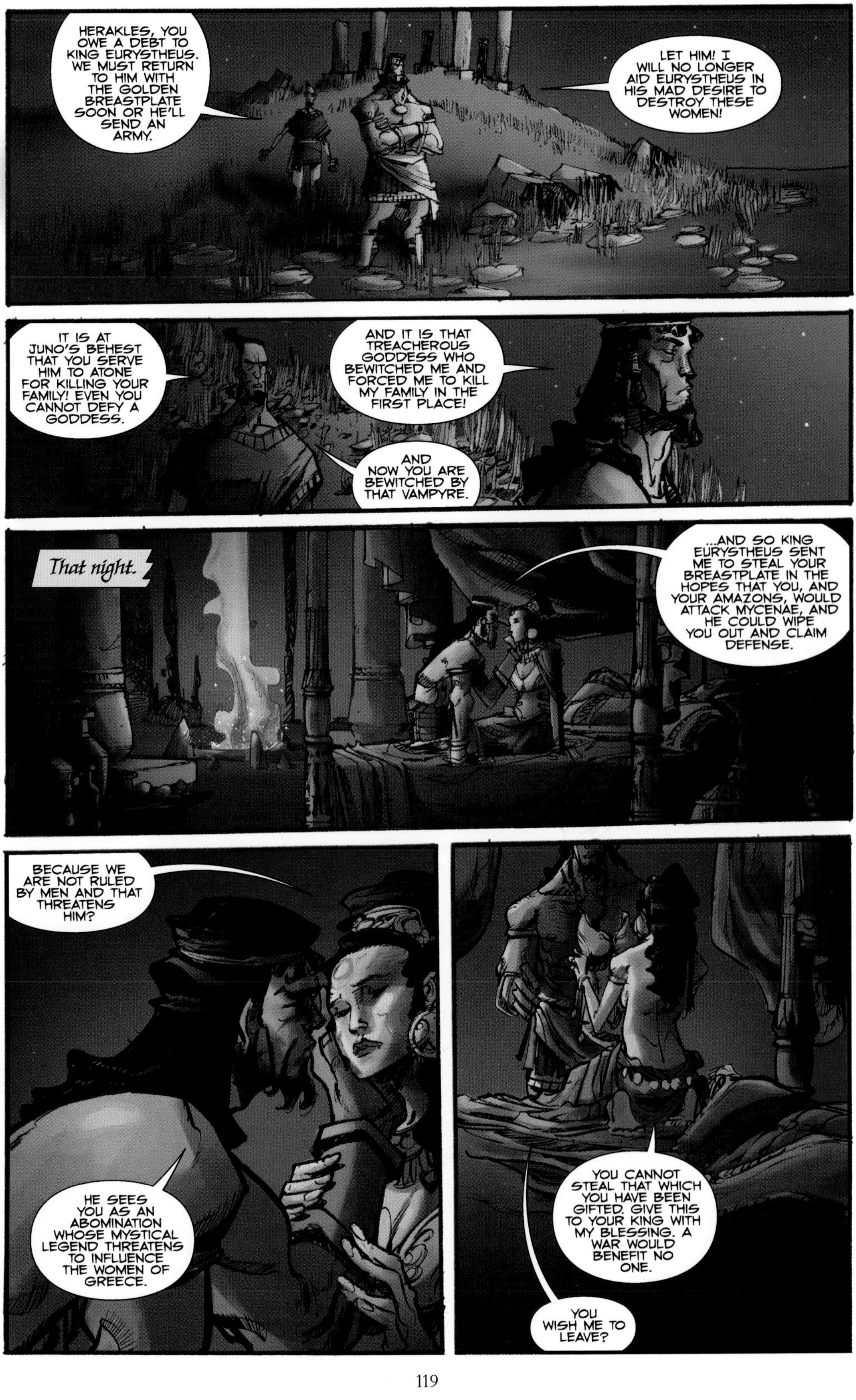
HERAKLES, YOU OWE A DEBT TO KING EURYSTHEUS. WE MUST RETURN TO HIM WITH THE GOLDEN BREASTPLATE SOON OR HE'LL SEND AN ARMY.
LET HIM! I WILL NO LONGER AID EURYSTHEUS IN HIS MAD DESIRE TO DESTROY THESE WOMEN!
IT IS AT JUNO'S BEHEST THAT YOU SERVE HIM TO ATONE FOR KILLING YOUR FAMILY! EVEN YOU CANNOT DEFY A GODDESS.
AND IT IS THAT TREACHEROUS GODDESS WHO BEWITCHED ME AND FORCED ME TO KILL MY FAMILY IN THE FIRST PLACE!
AND NOW YOU ARE BEWITCHED BY THAT VAMPYRE.
That night.
...AND SO KING EURYSTHEUS SENT ME TO STEAL YOUR BREASTPLATE IN THE HOPES THAT YOU, AND YOUR AMAZONS, WOULD ATTACK MYCENAE, AND HE COULD WIPE YOU OUT AND CLAIM DEFENSE.
BECAUSE WE ARE NOT RULED BY MEN AND THAT THREATENS HIM?
HE SEES YOU AS AN ABOMINATION WHOSE MYSTICAL LEGEND THREATENS TO INFLUENCE THE WOMEN OF GREECE.
YOU CANNOT STEAL THAT WHICH YOU HAVE BEEN GIFTED. GIVE THIS TO YOUR KING WITH MY BLESSING. A WAR WOULD BENEFIT NO ONE.
YOU WISH ME TO LEAVE?

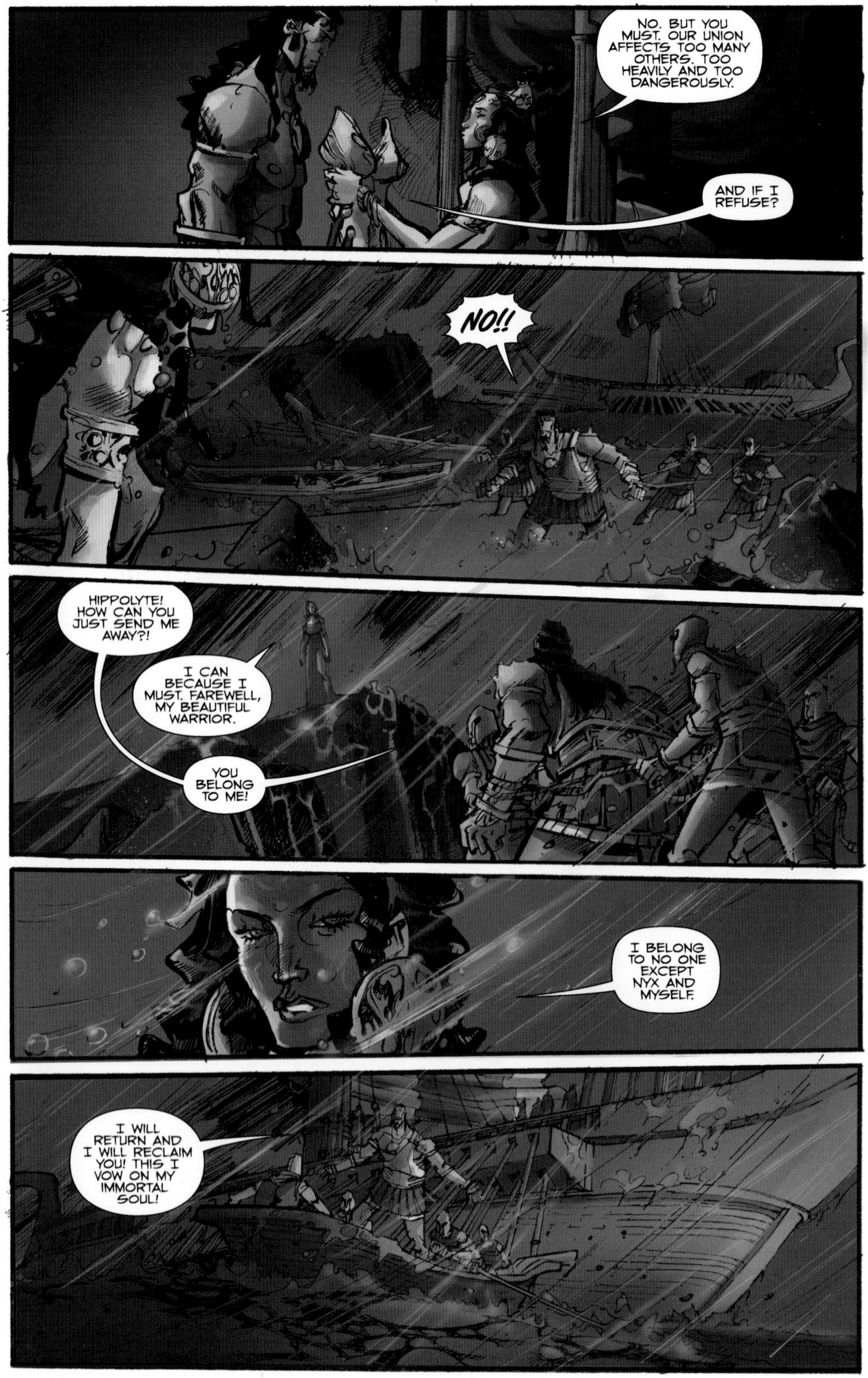
NO. BUT YOU MUST. OUR UNION AFFECTS TOO MANY OTHERS. TOO HEAVILY AND TOO DANGEROUSLY.
AND IF I REFUSE?
NO!!
HIPPOLYTE! HOW CAN YOU JUST SEND ME AWAY?!
I CAN BECAUSE I MUST. FAREWELL, MY BEAUTIFUL WARRIOR.
YOU BELONG TO ME!
I BELONG TO NO ONE EXCEPT NYX AND MYSELF.
I WILL RETURN AND I WILL RECLAIM YOU! THIS I VOW ON MY IMMORTAL SOUL!

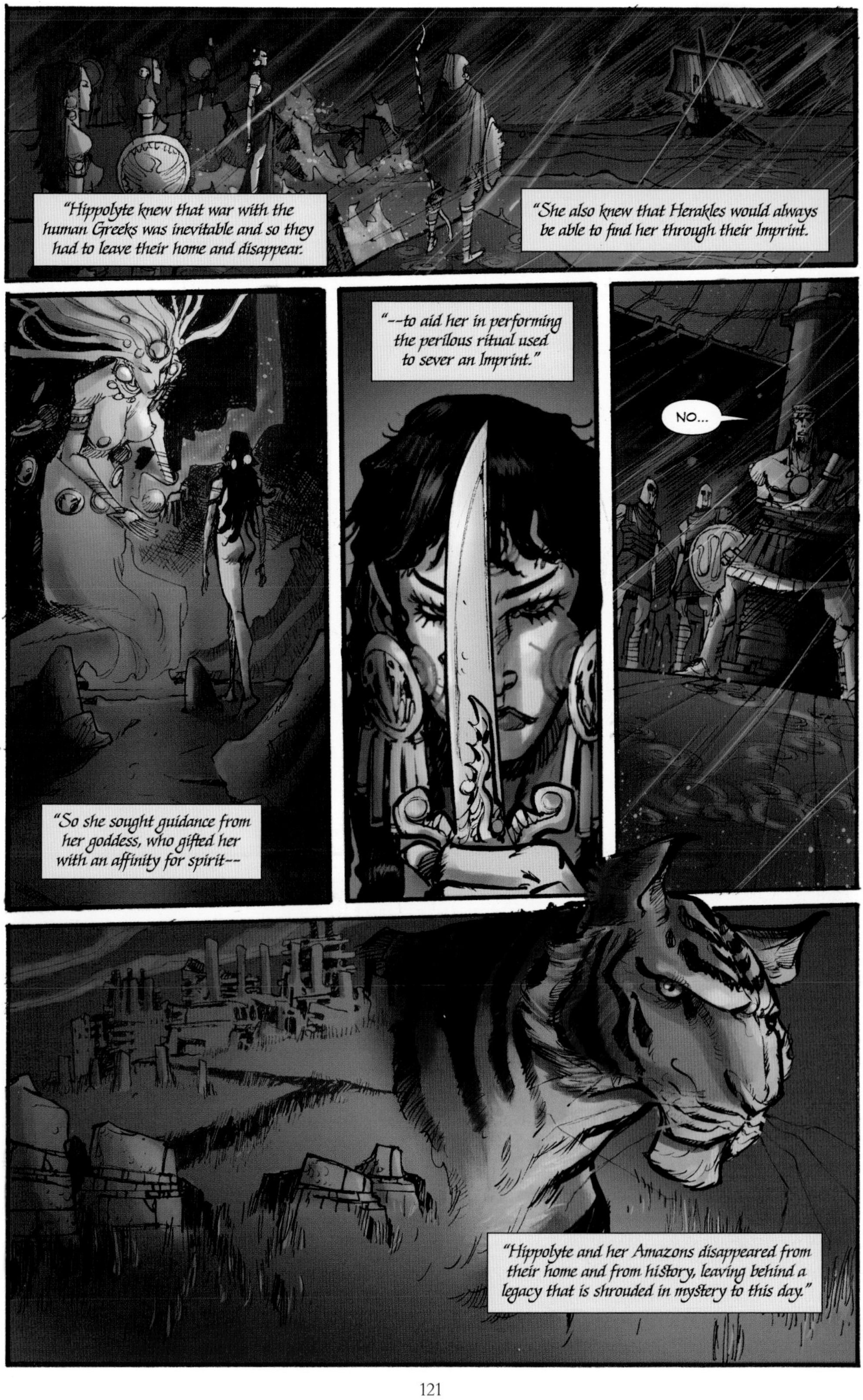
"Hippolyte knew that war with the human Greeks was inevitable and so they had to leave their home and disappear.
"She also knew that Herakles would always be able to find her through their Imprint.
"So she sought guidance from her goddess, who gifted her with an affinity for spirit--
"--to aid her in performing the perilous ritual used to sever an Imprint."
NO...
"Hippolyte and her Amazons disappeared from their home and from history, leaving behind a legacy that is shrouded in mystery to this day."

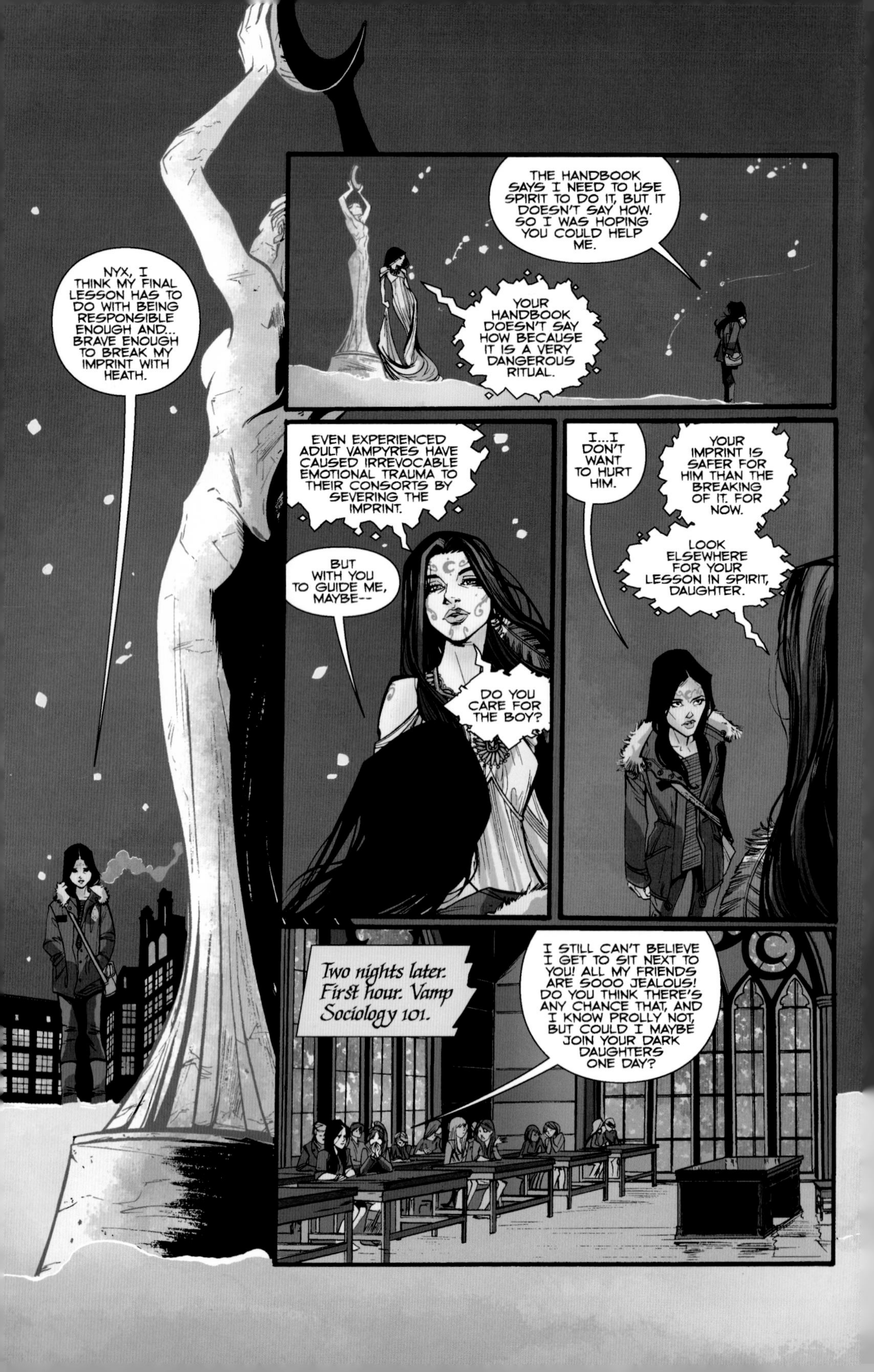
NYX, I THINK MY FINAL LESSON HAS TO DO WITH BEING RESPONSIBLE ENOUGH AND... BRAVE ENOUGH TO BREAK MY IMPRINT WITH HEATH.
THE HANDBOOK SAYS I NEED TO USE SPIRIT TO DO IT, BUT IT DOESN'T SAY HOW. SO I WAS HOPING YOU COULD HELP ME.
YOUR HANDBOOK DOESN'T SAY HOW BECAUSE IT IS A VERY DANGEROUS RITUAL.
EVEN EXPERIENCED ADULT VAMPYRES HAVE CAUSED IRREVOCABLE EMOTIONAL TRAUMA TO THEIR CONSORTS BY SEVERING THE IMPRINT.
BUT WITH YOU TO GUIDE ME, MAYBE--
DO YOU CARE FOR THE BOY?
I...I DON'T WANT TO HURT HIM.
YOUR IMPRINT IS SAFER FOR HIM THAN THE BREAKING OF IT. FOR NOW.
LOOK ELSEWHERE FOR YOUR LESSON IN SPIRIT, DAUGHTER.
Two nights later. First hour. Vamp Sociology 101.
I STILL CAN'T BELIEVE I GET TO SIT NEXT TO YOU! ALL MY FRIENDS ARE SOOO JEALOUS! DO YOU THINK THERE'S ANY CHANCE THAT, AND I KNOW PROLLY NOT, BUT COULD I MAYBE JOIN YOUR DARK DAUGHTERS ONE DAY?

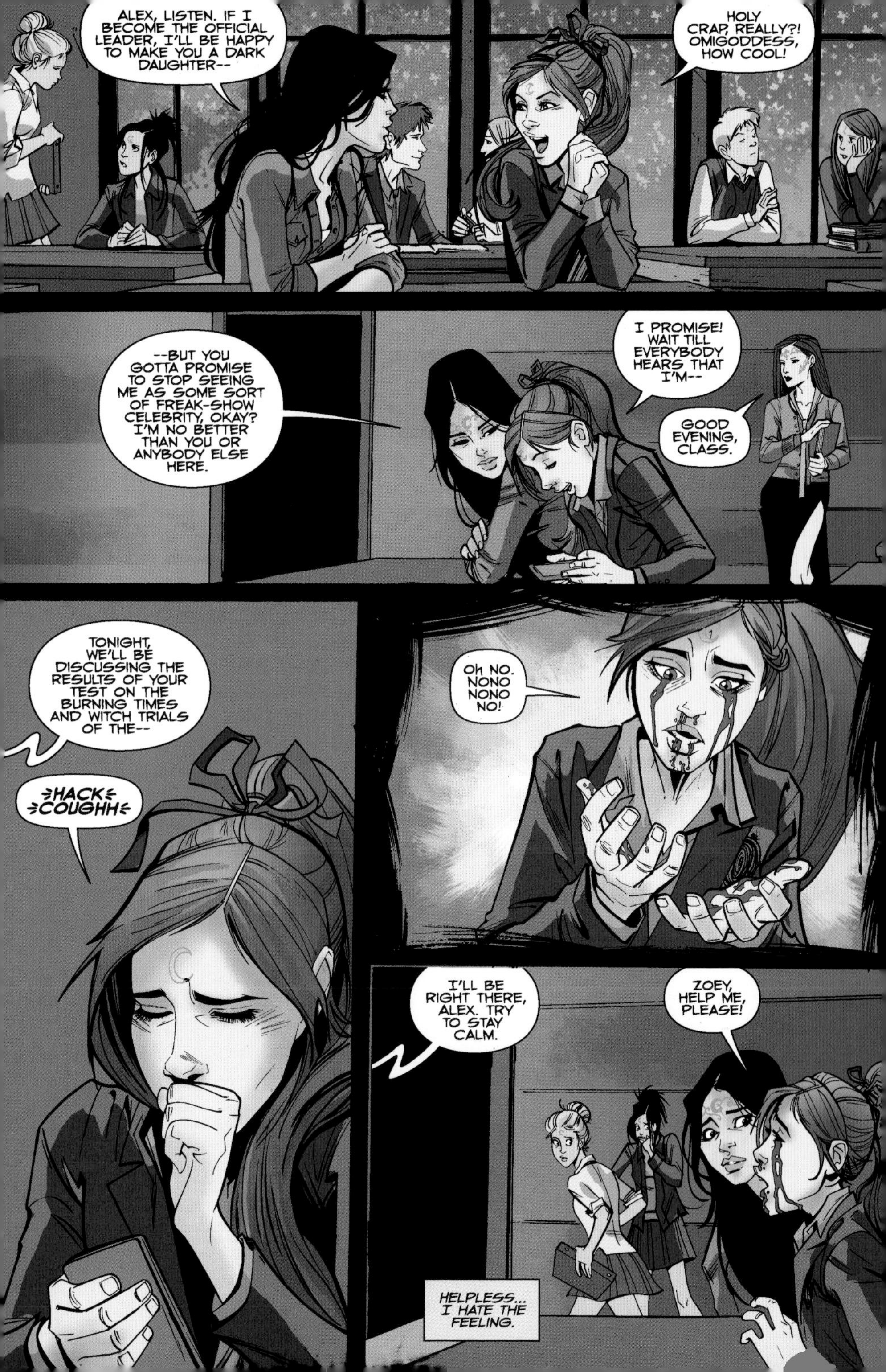
ALEX, LISTEN. IF I BECOME THE OFFICIAL LEADER, I'LL BE HAPPY TO MAKE YOU A DARK DAUGHTER--
HOLY CRAP, REALLY?! OMIGODDESS, HOW COOL!
--BUT YOU GOTTA PROMISE TO STOP SEEING ME AS SOME SORT OF FREAK-SHOW CELEBRITY, OKAY? I'M NO BETTER THAN YOU OR ANYBODY ELSE HERE.
I PROMISE! WAIT TILL EVERYBODY HEARS THAT I'M--
GOOD EVENING, CLASS.
TONIGHT, WE'LL BE DISCUSSING THE RESULTS OF YOUR TEST ON THE BURNING TIMES AND WITCH TRIALS OF THE--
HACK COUGHH
Oh NO. NONO NONO NO!
I'LL BE RIGHT THERE, ALEX. TRY TO STAY CALM.
ZOEY, HELP ME, PLEASE!
HELPLESS... I HATE THE FEELING.

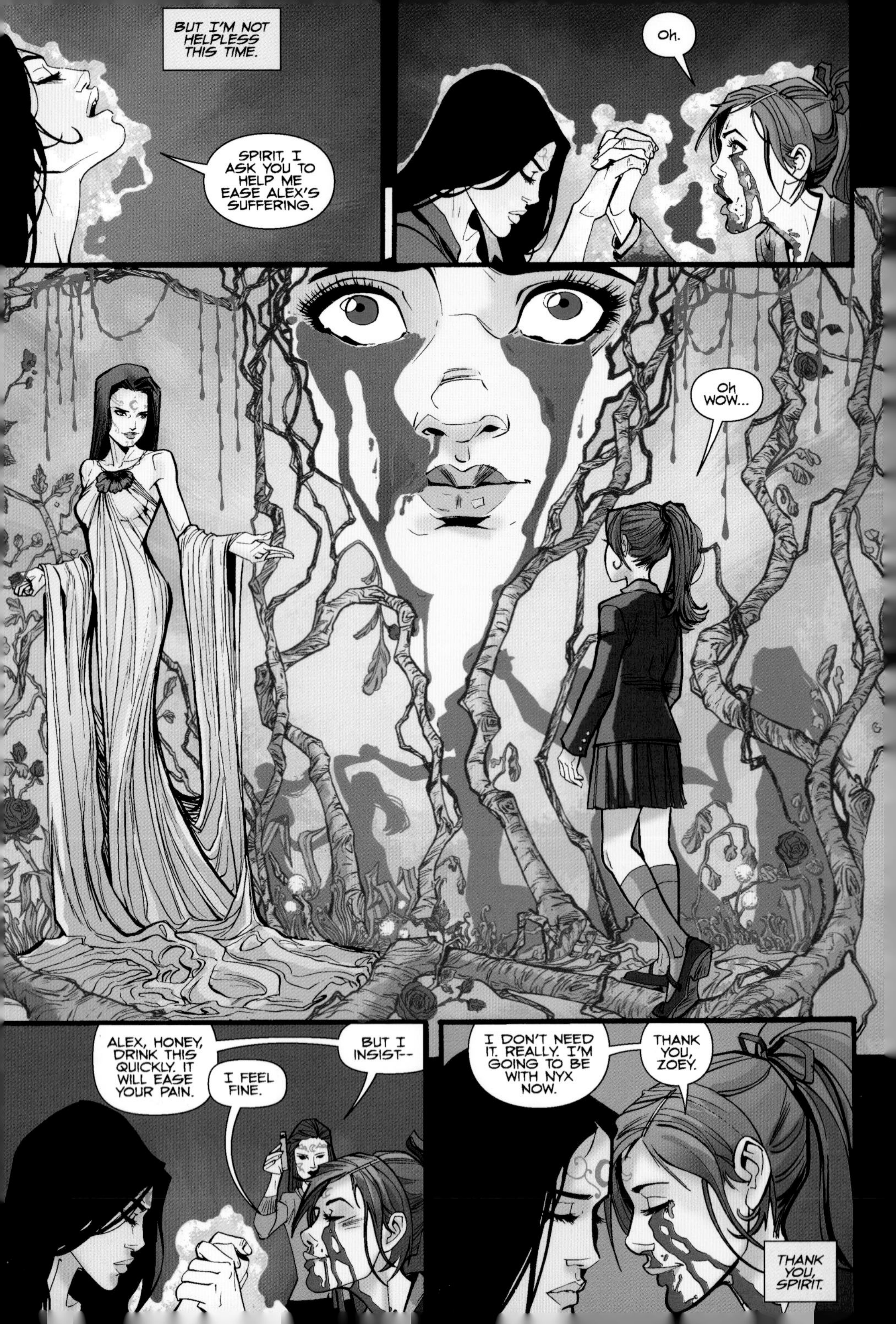
BUT I'M NOT HELPLESS THIS TIME.
SPIRIT, I ASK YOU TO HELP ME EASE ALEX'S SUFFERING.
Oh.
Oh WOW...
ALEX, HONEY, DRINK THIS QUICKLY. IT WILL EASE YOUR PAIN.
I FEEL FINE.
BUT I INSIST--
I DON'T NEED IT. REALLY. I'M GOING TO BE WITH NYX NOW.
THANK YOU, ZOEY.
THANK YOU, SPIRIT.

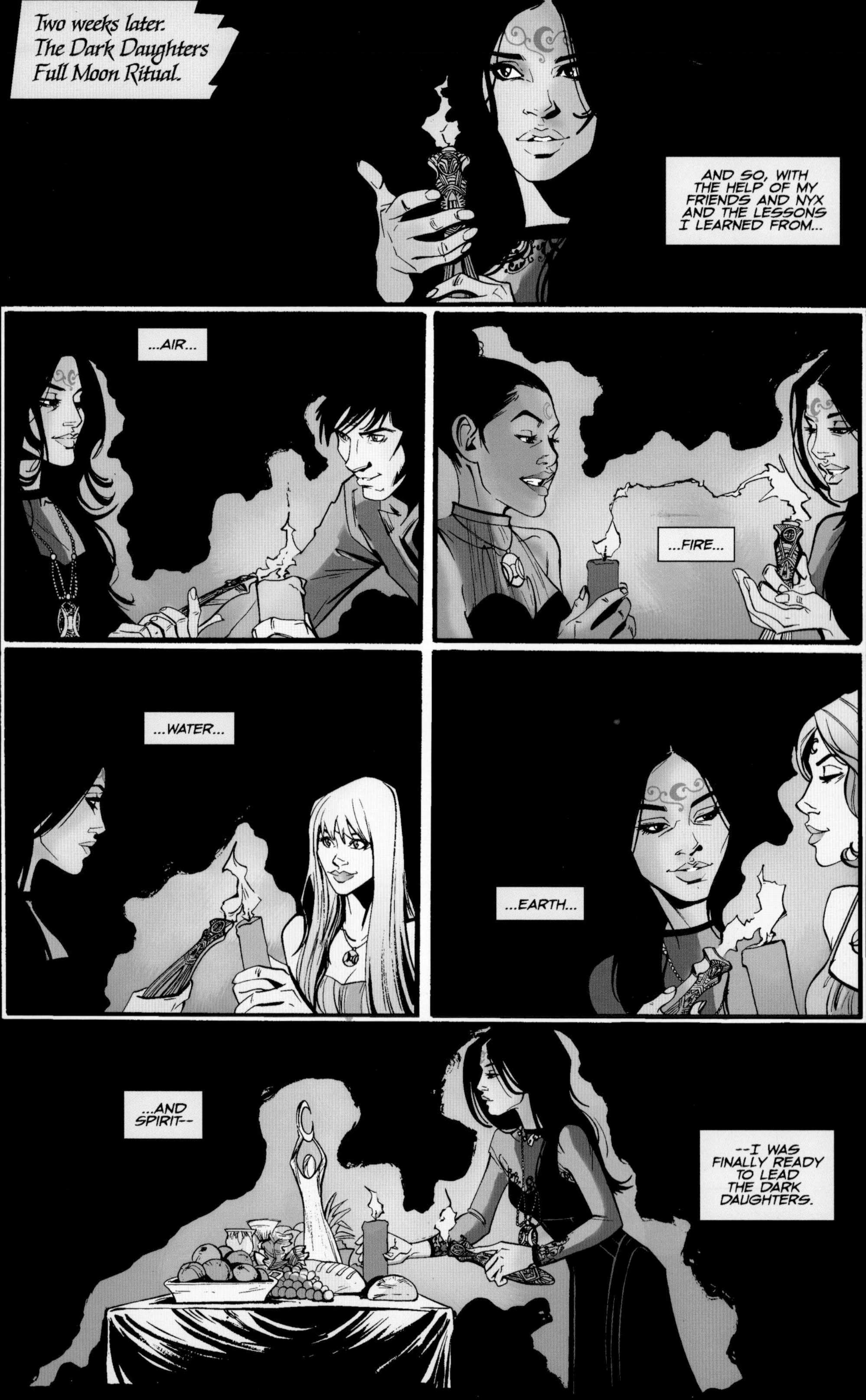
Two weeks later.
The Dark Daughters
Full Moon Ritual.
AND SO, WITH THE HELP OF MY FRIENDS AND NYX AND THE LESSONS I LEARNED FROM...
...AIR...
...FIRE...
...WATER...
...EARTH...
...AND SPIRIT--
--I WAS FINALLY READY TO LEAD THE DARK DAUGHTERS.

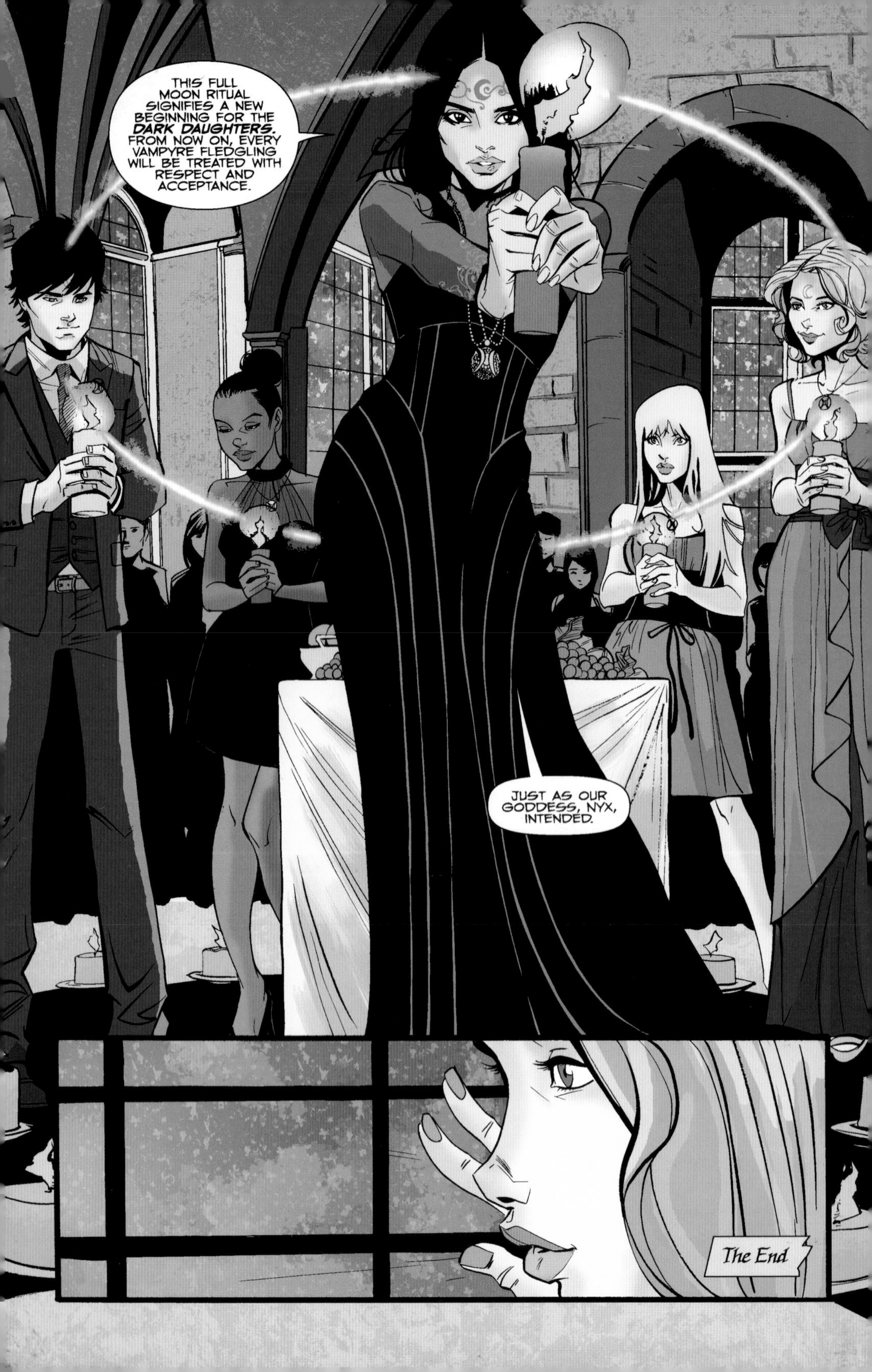
THIS FULL MOON RITUAL SIGNIFIES A NEW BEGINNING FOR THE DARK DAUGHTERS. FROM NOW ON, EVERY VAMPYRE FLEDGLING WILL BE TREATED WITH RESPECT AND ACCEPTANCE.
JUST AS OUR GODDESS, NYX, INTENDED.
The End

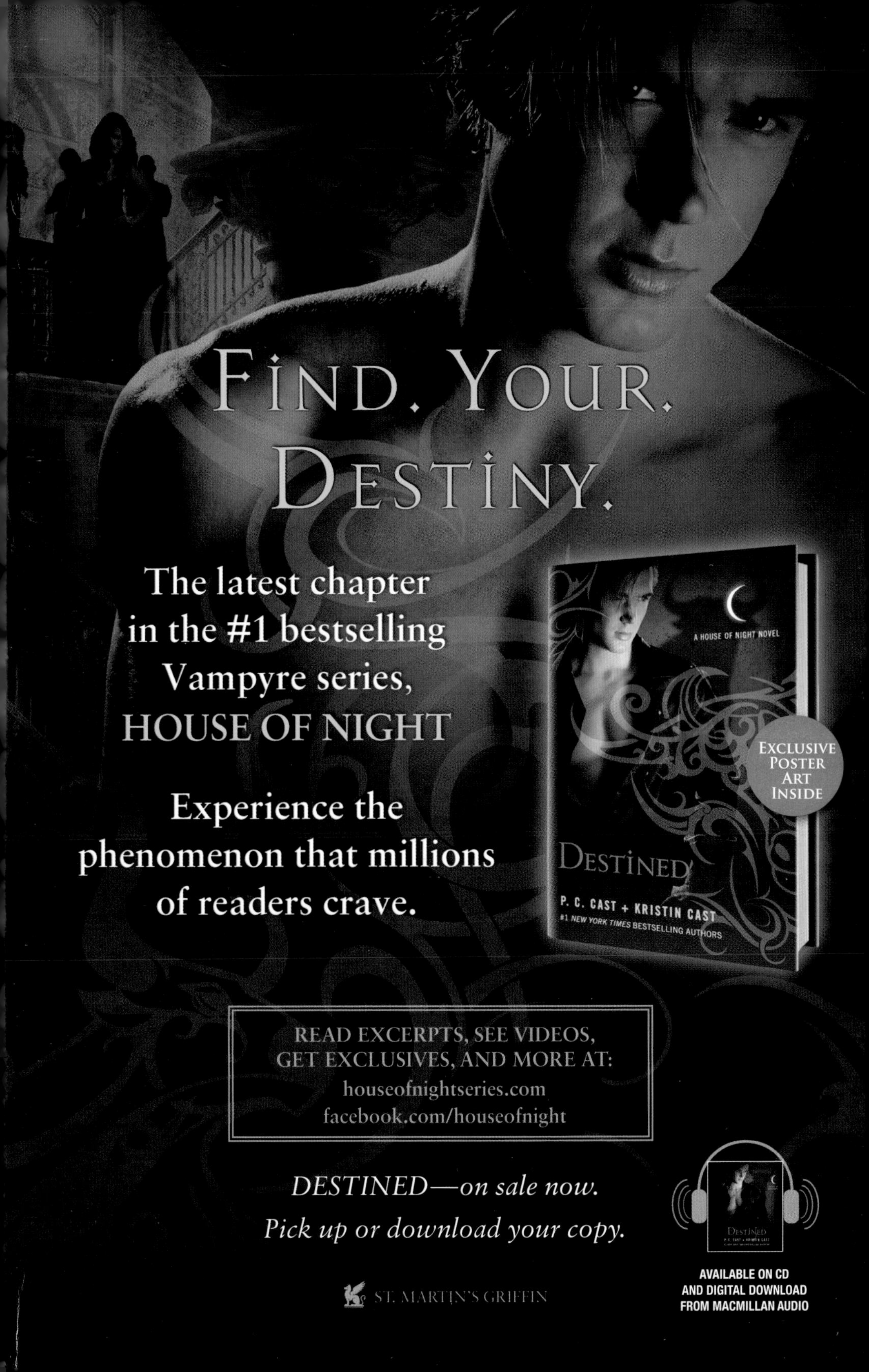
FIND. YOUR. DESTINY.
The latest chapter in the #1 bestselling Vampyre series, HOUSE OF NIGHT
Experience the phenomenon that millions of readers crave.
A HOUSE OF NIGHT NOVEL
DESTINED
P. C. CAST + KRISTIN CAST
#1 NEW YORK TIMES BESTSELLING AUTHORS
EXCLUSIVE POSTER ART INSIDE
READ EXCERPTS, SEE VIDEOS, GET EXCLUSIVES, AND MORE AT:
houseofnightseries.com
facebook.com/houseofnight
DESTINED—on sale now.
Pick up or download your copy.
ST. MARTIN'S GRIFFIN
AVAILABLE ON CD AND DIGITAL DOWNLOAD FROM MACMILLAN AUDIO

SPECIAL THANKS TO SCOTT ALLIE, MEREDITH BERNSTEIN,
AURA BUINEVICIUTE, ANTHONY AND RUTH BURDEN,
CINDY DEES, AND ANDY TRAPANI

President and Publisher MIKE RICHARDSON / Editor SIERRA HAHN
Assistant Editor JIM GIBBONS / Collection Designer TINA ALESSI

NEIL HANKERSON Executive Vice President TOM WEDDLE Chief Financial Officer RANDY STRADLEY Vice
President of Publishing MICHAEL MARTENS Vice President of Book Trade Sales ANITA NELSON Vice President
of Business Affairs DAVID SCROGGY Vice President of Product Development DALE LaFOUNTAIN Vice President of
Information Technology DARLENE VOGEL Senior Director of Print, Design, and Production KEN LIZZI General Counsel
MATT PARKINSON Senior Director of Marketing DAVEY ESTRADA Editorial Director SCOTT ALLIE Senior Managing
Editor CHRIS WARNER Senior Books Editor DIANA SCHUTZ Executive Editor CARY GRAZZINI Director of
Print and Development LIA RIBACCHI Art Director CARA NIECE Director of Scheduling

HOUSE OF NIGHT: LEGACY

This series takes place between scenes from Betrayed, *the second novel in the House of Night series.*
This volume reprints the comic-book series House of Night #1–#5 from Dark Horse Comics.

Published by Dark Horse Books, a division of Dark Horse Comics, Inc.
10956 SE Main Street, Milwaukie, OR 97222

DarkHorse.com

To find a comics shop in your area, call the Comic Shop Locator Service toll-free at (888) 266-4226.

First edition: July 2012
ISBN 978-1-59582-962-7

1 3 5 7 9 10 8 6 4 2
Printed at Midas Printing International, Ltd., Huizhou, China